In Search
of
My Homeland

In Search
of
My Homeland

A Memoir
of a Chinese Labor Camp

Er Tai Gao

TRANSLATED BY
Robert Dorsett and David Pollard

An Imprint of HarperCollins*Publishers*

HarperCollins books may be purchased for educational, business, or sales promotional use. For information, please write: Special Markets Department, HarperCollins Publishers, 10 East 53rd Street, New York, NY 10022.

FIRST EDITION

Designed by Suet Yee Chong

Library of Congress Cataloging-in-Publication Data
has been applied for.
ISBN: 978-0-06-088126-9

09 10 11 12 13 OV/RRD   10 9 8 7 6 5 4 3 2 1

Acknowledgments

The author and translators wish to thank the following organizations for their generous support: the International Institute of Modern Letters in Las Vegas, Nevada; the International Center for Writing and Translation at the University of California, Irvine; and Black Mountain Institute at the University of Nevada, Las Vegas.

Contents

Acomprehending young man, intelligent, insouciant in behavior, haphazard in study, dreamy, neglectful even, becomes a highly talented artist and, at the age of nineteen, writes an essay that grabs national interest—and so sets in motion one of those sagas in which, art, politics, and history intertwine to produce a lasting literary work.

Gao Ertai was born to an educated family in Gaochun, Jiangsu province, in 1935. During the time of the War of Resistance [1] against Japan, the family hid in a rural village, where Gao learned the unfamiliar, even mysterious, culture of the locals. After the War of Resistance concluded, not long after the family returned home, the Communist regime took power: Gao's father was deemed "a counter-revolutionary landlord" during the "campaign to suppress counter-revolutionaries." For his son's safety, his father sent Gao to school in Suzhou. Gao's family was consumed in the ensuing political turmoil, and Gao never saw his father again. All this is gist of Part One of the memoir.

In 1957, when Gao was in Lanzhou, Mao decided the time was right for China to be fully realized as a Communist state and initiated a period of relaxed censorship in order to elicit, allegedly, constructive criticism from intellectuals and artists. Although many commentators have reckoned this was a sincere attempt on Mao's part, Gao makes it clear that, from his later perspective at least, it was a cynical ploy to tempt dissidents into the open and to throttle opposition. It was at this crossroads between philosophy and history that "On Beauty" was written. For the regime, beauty was objective (in the Marxist sense) and collective, whereas Gao wrote not only that beauty was subjective, realized through an individual's response, but also that he would not even use dialectical materialism as a theoretical basis. To cap it off, he called for divergent opinions. The response was damning.

Elegantly, powerfully written, Gao's work teaches us that the most important political stand for an artist is to be free and to be able to choose to dissent from or assent to any ideological position. So the free expression of beauty is, in this deeper sense, political, and beauty (i.e., its creation and perception) is the symbol of freedom.

Gao asserts that artistic freedom must be absolute and unconditional. But in order for this to be true, the self—despite popular theories that deny selfhood, which, if taken seriously, would obviate individual resistance—must preserve its integrity against the encroaching disintegrating forces pressing from outside.

A large work in three parts (we have translated only the second part here), meticulously written under great risk, in a tiny script on easily hidden bits of scrap paper, Gao's memoir has an epic scope reaching from the depth of work ditches in the Gobi Desert to the heights of the Buddhist heavens depicted on the Dunhuang cave ceilings. The chapter "Facing Walls" is a prose poem, an act of defiance, which, if discovered, could well have cost Gao his life. And this defiant beauty lies not only in the style of the language but also in the descriptions.

Gao emphasizes not only the environment but also the men and women inhabiting it. Gao refuses to blame. He patiently and empathetically shares a drink with a broken old man who had once denounced him. Not a word is said. But we understand the psychology of oppression: how readily and too obligingly otherwise humane and thoughtful people surrender that humanity and become willing victims of or turn viciously against others.

It is of the utmost importance to Gao that he tells the facts, that he reports events and people—but the artist is always at work revealing structure and symbol. Gao's memoir demands attention, insight, and interpretation by the reader.

A clarification of a few terms may be helpful. A "cadre" is roughly the equivalent of a "Party member with executive functions." If not a "cadre" or a "Party member," anyone still in good standing would be part of the "revolutionary masses"—a single person would be called "one of the revolutionary masses," while two or more "the revolutionary masses." The "cowshed" is an invention of the Cultural Revolution. In concrete terms, a cowshed would be any structure without a roof, with no furniture, and where the temperature is the same as the ambient temperature, but in abstract, psychosocial terms, it is a condition of banishment and exile from the human world.

Each chapter was translated independently by either David Pollard or myself. The Gao family wishes to acknowledge, with gratitude, the close friendship and support they have been given by Eric Olsen since they have come to the United States. I would like to add my own thanks to Eric for his invaluable help.

At this point, before the writing of "On Beauty," our story begins. . . .

Robert Dorsett
August 2008

Fragments
in
the Sand

ONE

No Choice

I n the summer of 1955, more than a hundred college graduates were "gathered to be assigned" in the Northwest to "support the border." We were put up in a tiny hostel on a small street in Lanzhou, where we waited for almost a month for further assignment, left with nothing to do.

In the ancient city of Lanzhou, the Islamic-style houses were mostly adobes. Viewed from Gaolan Mountain on the outskirts of town, apart from a few newly constructed ash-colored buildings they were all the same dirty greenish yellow. From a distance, they resembled the houses in a small Middle Eastern village or one of the Santa Fe Indian settlements in the southwestern United States.

Day and night, the surging Yellow River roared around the city, transmitting its vast and restless sounds into every corner. Along the riverbanks, many gigantic waterwheels revolved sluggishly, irrigating orchards that stretched for more than ten miles. In spring, their flowers wove a luxuriant tapestry; in summer, their dense foliage cast layers of shade; in autumn, manifold trees sagged with fruit, and in winter, snow accumulated over several months, leaving a sheath of silver-white. After the river froze, horse carts and automobiles traveled back and forth across it. With the coming year, the melting ice bumped and jostled with a crackling sound until April and May, when the ice vanished silently and without a trace.

The majority population was Han, with many minorities from bordering areas mixed in. The minority people frequently assembled to sell their wild game, fruit and melons, furs and hides, spices and balms, lamb shish kebabs, and a diversity of exquisite handicrafts. On the bumpy, unpaved, potholed streets, dogs, goats, chickens, and pigs refused to give way. Between scattered piles of construction materials and building-site trash, closely packed street vendors laid out on the ground their dazzling arrays of merchandise. Local specialty wares and light industrial products from outside the province were jumbled together. People in automobiles and on foot, in horse and donkey carts, on bicycles, or pulling handcarts shouted at and dodged each other, while horse tenders, camel drivers, and raftsmen shoved and pushed, stopped and moved on. Hui, Tibetans, Yugurs, Dongxiang, Uigurs, Kazaks, as well as Han, who had come from all over the country to "support the borders," wearing brilliantly varied costumes and accessories, bought and sold in a confusion of languages, accents, and gestures. On clear days yellow dust whirled; on rainy days mud splattered; but despite the hectic turmoil a sense of freshness and vitality shone through.

The development of oil resources in the Northwest turned Lanzhou into a continually evolving, burgeoning industrial center. In the late '70s, when I returned, the chimneys stood thick as trees in a forest. This modern city with its population of over two million had replaced the old dilapidated town that was once redolent with rural atmosphere and historic charm. Seen from Gaolan Mountain, smoke and dust gripped the city; the ash-colored haze, like a sea of clouds, sometimes obscured the roofs of the tall buildings. The Yellow River no longer froze over and, even on the coldest days, flowed with spume of oil and grease. The slowly turning waterwheels, unable to keep up with the new pace of life, had vanished. But in 1955, we didn't foresee any of this. Those days, we halfheartedly took in the many novelties, but because of the morass of filth and inconveniences, we never really wanted to go anywhere. We stayed in the hostel all day, playing poker, chess, or lying around reading, even though there were no good books. Each day seemed a year.

One day we were informed that the director of the Gansu Department of Education, Liao Haisheng, wanted to "receive" us. I had no idea what it might mean to be "received." Soon after, we climbed onto a truck and bumped along to some official auditorium, where several hundred people were seated. They were all recent graduates from institutions of higher learning throughout the country, assigned here and waiting to be reassigned within the educational system. On the dais several people sat behind a long table. One, it was said, was the director, Liao Haisheng, an expressionless, thin man with loose skin who leaned back on his chair as if he, like the rest of us, was very much bored and each day seemed to him a year.

First, a man sitting alongside him stood up and welcomed everyone. He introduced us to the conditions in Gansu and its glorious outlook for development. The director then gave his welcome: he praised us for unselfishly harkening the call of the motherland; he hoped we would put down roots and fervently sacrifice our youth to this grand enterprise. His eyes flashed fire; he was a changed man. After he finished, he sat and leaned back on his chair. His eyelids drooped, and his old appearance returned.

Student representatives mounted the platform to thank the director for his concern and encouragement. They said we would not fail to live up to the Party's expectations. One among them had an impressive, unique style, and even today I remember that intonation: "I represent [pause] the entire student body [pause] to say to [pause] the senior cadre officers [pause] we resolutely guarantee to completely [pause] unconditionally [pause] obey the directive . . ."

My classmate in art school, Wang Xizeng, another student representative, said he was a Party member and was answering the trailblazing call to one of the country's harshest areas. A painter, he'd brought along mostly ochre and earth-yellow oil pigments, but once here, he said, he found he couldn't use them—he needed more greens. The greens at Gansu, he announced, did not take second place to those in the south of the Yangtse River; no, he went on, the greens here were *better*. He had never seen so many large fruits and vegetables and had never eaten such flavorful steamed lamb dumplings or beef pulled noodles. An ox couldn't drag him from such a wonderful place. He could grow old and die here without complaint or regret. Everyone laughed and applauded; even the blank-faced director raised an eyelid and glanced at him.

After the class representatives finished, assignments were announced: everyone was to teach at various middle schools in Lanzhou. I, along with eleven others from Sichuan, Guizhou, Guangdong, Guangxi, Nanjing, and Shanghai, including my eloquent classmate, was assigned to Number Ten Middle School on the north bank of the Yellow River. When we returned to the hostel, representatives from each school were already waiting in the front hall to receive the new teachers.

TWO

Wild Goose Tracks in Mud and Snow[1]

anzhou Number Ten Middle School was located on the north bank
of the Yellow River on a foothill called Saltfield-Town-Temple-Dune,
well outside the city. Not only was the name grating, the landscape
was ugly. The newly built three-story school, resembling a gray matchbox,
stood solitary above innumerable low and broken-down adobe houses,
which, like rows of fish scales, extended downward to the river, where
green orchards lined the banks. Beyond the grounds irrigated by the
waterwheels, not a blade of grass grew. From the river's edge, a narrow
dirt path twisted up for about ten li to our school.[2] Continuing farther,
the houses became fewer and fewer, until there was only the dirt-covered,
adobe-colored mountain—barren, without trees, grass or stones—and
behind it, more indistinguishable mountains. Looking from the highest
peak, thousands upon thousands of mountains formed a greenish yellow expanse, and yet in that hard-featured monotony there was a fierce,
untamed ruggedness.

The small gray patch on the yellow slope near the foot of the mountain was our school's roof. The school held sixteen classes and almost
a thousand students of different ages, all starting middle school. I was
nineteen; many students were older. The teachers were mostly local, but
some veteran teachers had been transferred from other middle and pri-

mary schools, while others were recent high-school graduates. Everyone's curriculum was packed full. The ten or so of us who were assigned from the outside were immediately thrown into work with heavy responsibilities. I taught art for the entire school. Every week I taught sixteen classes, and every week I repeated the same lectures and critiqued about a thousand papers. Besides eating and sleeping, all I did was work; I became a machine.

The lecture and research rooms, along with the teachers' dormitory, were on the third floor. Each dorm room housed two people, and by chance, my roommate was the person who spoke so impressively at the reception. Xun Xuewen was a native of Shanghai and a graduate in history from Hua Dong Normal College. He was five years older than me. I found the gold-rimmed glasses perched upon his high-bridged nose, the perfect fit of his clothes, and his sonorous voice very imposing. Every evening he folded his pants neatly and placed them under his pillow in order to ensure they'd be pressed with a pencil-straight crease the next day. Beneath the bed he kept a row of brightly polished leather shoes.

At the morning bell Xun jumped out of bed, placed a dance record on his phonograph, and hummed the melody, then quickly dressed, folded his quilt, combed his hair, washed and polished his shoes to the beat of the music, twirled several times, turned off the phonograph, grabbed his bowl and chopsticks, and turned to leave. When he reached the door, he'd shout, "Hurry up, food's ready!" Then followed the crisp, sharp sound of his leather shoes quickly going down the concrete staircase, *tap, tap, tap, tap.*

Xun had many good books, which he allowed me to borrow. The volumes on world history filled three wooden crates. He had read them assiduously, densely underlining them in red and adding insightful margin notes. Speaking with him was illuminating. He said Hugo and Dickens didn't understand the French Revolution, and as for Germany, the culprit wasn't Hitler but Bismarck, and that sort of thing. It was unusual for someone to have his own opinions, whether right or wrong. His dissertation was on the Foreign Affairs Movement.[3] He could only scratch the surface of this intriguing subject, he said, and thought if he had time he'd examine it more deeply and write a book.

One time I brought up his speech at the reception and asked how, without authorization, he could take it upon himself to represent all students. He told me the Provisional Party Branch had arranged it, and that although he wasn't a Party member, he had already submitted several applications and they wanted to nurture him. His father was a functionary in the old society and a Christian, and even though his father had passed away, these factors still hindered Xun's application, and he had to make strict demands on himself. Long a nonbeliever, he was now an atheist and a thorough materialist. Feuerbach's "Lectures on the Essence of Religion" first convinced him, he said.[4] I didn't doubt it.

During the "Anti-Rightist Campaign" of '57, Xun informed on me and I lost a journal and many manuscripts. After I was labeled a rightist and discharged into re-education through labor, he was also labeled a rightist, and shortly thereafter jumped to his death from the school's third story. When I heard of this twenty-one years after it happened, it was hard to believe. His vital, candid, and optimistic character and his ability to lead an interesting life amid these monotonous, mechanistic, and anxiety-producing surroundings had impressed me.

We ten or so outsiders, who for a time couldn't blend in with local society, formed a loose social circle. Those within the circle, except for me, were members of the Communist Youth League, and one, the twenty-five-year-old Xie Shurong, was a Party member. We called her Big Sister Xie. She was from Sichuan and a graduate of the biology department of Sichuan University. She taught biology and concurrently held the position of branch secretary of the Communist Youth League Teachers. She took ideology seriously, and when she spoke, because of her sincere, burning idealism and the purity and sacredness that flashed in her eyes, people were moved. I was, too, though I didn't believe a word she said.

Once, the Party general branch secretary and school principal, Lei

Xuhua, asked her in for a talk.[5] He wanted to introduce her to a "companion." This "companion," he explained, was a "senior cadre," and if she agreed to the match, why, she could start spending his money right away! Stunned and unable to speak for a long while, Xie Shurong sputtered, "Principle Lei . . . you . . . this isn't appropriate for someone in your position." When she reached the door, she turned and snapped, "Shameful!" The more she thought about it, the more incensed she became. Pale and trembling, she came to our dormitory to talk. Now it was our turn to teach ideology. Everyone told her this wasn't a bad offer. She was chosen because Principal Lei thought highly of her. If she didn't agree, that's fine, but she shouldn't be angry. But she was angry and struggled unsuccessfully for a long time to get a transfer. After the "Anti-Rightist Campaign," there was the "Struggle Against Right Deviation," and she was labeled a "right deviation opportunist" and sent into hard labor. When I returned to Lanzhou in the late '70s, a friend showed me a letter mailed by her from Tibet. Xie Shurong wrote that her life was meaningless. She was exhausted and had nothing to live for.

My classmate from art school, Wang Xihui, was assigned to the Northwest Middle School in the south of the city. Our schools were far apart and we were both busy, so it was hard to get together. The day he did come to see me he shouted excitedly, his eyes gleaming: "The railroad between Lanzhou and Xinjiang has been connected. Did you know?" It turned out the Northwest Middle School was near the railway, and he'd lie awake late each night listening to the westbound locomotive's *choo, choo, choo, choo* . . . (he imitated the sound exactly). Elated, he felt our great motherland was advancing toward victory, and as he spoke, he gestured wildly, stamped his feet, and smiled broadly. He was that kind of person—sincere. In the '50s many people were like him. After I was labeled a rightist, we lost contact. Later I heard he was at one time the director in charge of student behavior at the Northwest Middle School, but was seized during the Cultural Revolution and developed schizophrenia. I don't know what happened to him after that.

THREE

The Failure of "On Beauty"

I was busy and tired; my life in Lanzhou was dull and unhappy. I could not comprehend why my fate should be in the hands of people who had no concern for me and weren't as intelligent or as well disposed as I thought I was. How was it possible they could control me, while I couldn't resist? Over time, my hatred of authority grew.

Looking at the rapid changes and increasing expansion in Lanzhou, I believed the national economy was taking off, but I knew that for the economy to take off, innumerable people had to pay with their freedom and were going to have to pay again and again. I couldn't accept that it was just to use one generation as fertilizer so the next generation could be nurtured (as they put it), and I couldn't accept that an invisible hand, forcibly assigning roles and tasks, represented the sole truth.[1]

No one else seemed to feel the same. I felt I was alone. Five days each week, after supper at the canteen, I rode a bicycle for two hours into the city to study Russian at the Russian Language Evening School run by the Sino-Soviet Friendship Association. As soon as I returned to the school late at night, I pulled the blankets over my head and fell asleep. I felt frustrated. I had many thoughts I needed to express and wanted to find someone I could talk to. I had read three of Romain Rolland's biographies and his novel *Jean-Christophe*, which moved me.[2] In his writing I found a soul mate, so I wrote a long letter to his translator, Fu Lei, telling him my distress, and mailed it to the Ping Ming Publishing House to be forwarded. It was a shot in the dark.

I didn't know that Ping Ming had been incorporated into the New Literature and Art Publishing House.[3] Incredibly, the letter was forwarded to Mr. Fu Lei, who replied that dialectical materialism and historical materialism have already answered all the questions I'd brought up. For example, spirit versus matter, the relationship between the economic base and the superstructure, which includes morality, art, ideology, sociology, etc., etc., have been explained very clearly and haven't been questioned for a long time. "Why do you still need to ask?" he wrote. "You repeatedly said you're searching for truth, when the truth is before your eyes; you just won't see it. Do you think this is intelligent?"

It was as if a Party branch secretary was straightening me out, and the more I thought about it, the more rebuked, oppressed, and rebellious I felt. With nowhere to vent, I could only let out my thoughts on paper as if talking to myself. At first it was a trickle, a jumble, which touched on cultural values, the pros and cons of Daoism, Buddhism, and Confucianism, and then extended to issues of time and space, being and nonbeing, and so forth. After a while, the thoughts consolidated and became systematized, just as in an essay. I had little knowledge, no professional discipline, and was ignorant beyond belief, but I wrote down whatever came to my mind, and I felt exhilaration and discovered a meaning in life.

I used the little free time I had available for this. By the next year, 1956, I had completed "On Beauty." At that time, all thinking in our country was derived from Marxism and Leninism, and aesthetics, not an exception, was seen as entirely objective and reflective, deduced from materialist principles.[4] It was emphasized that beauty has an objective existence unaffected by human subjectivity. I didn't buy it. I believed beauty couldn't be separated from its perception and was contingent upon people, things, time, and space, and therefore was subjective and expressive. After I came to this conclusion, I wrote confidently and was more eager to challenge authority. I no longer studied Russian. I worked carelessly, ate and drank absentmindedly, and spoke without thinking. Objects before me were like illusions, and the illusions became real. I looked at the scenery outside the window and thought of the withered grass in bleak weather all over the world and it broke my heart.

I was pleased with my essay and meticulously transcribed two copies onto draft paper. I mailed one copy to the Beijing monthly *New Construction*. I wanted to find several knowledgeable people and show them the other copy. The chairman of the Chinese department at Lanzhou University, Mr. Shu Lianjing, was the first to read the essay. He said the subject was too broad: If I wrote about the beauty of a single painting, one poem, one scene, one objet d'art, it would be easier for me to delve deeper and to expand, and it would be more substantive and convincing. A broad subject wasted effort without yielding results. I nodded. I thought, if a prominent professor felt this, whom else could I turn to? I felt alone in a vast universe.

Later, I heard that the president of Northwest Normal College, Xu Hefu, formerly a professor in the philosophy department at the University of Moscow, was highly thought of. I liked the name Hefu, which seemed both cultured and demotic.[5] I thought this man would understand my paper, so I took a draft and looked him up. The Normal College was located far in the upper reaches of the Yellow River at a town called Ten Mile Shop. There was a sandstorm in the afternoon when my bus arrived, so I was covered head to foot with dust and my clothes were disheveled when I knocked on the door of the dean's office. The man who opened the door blocked my way.

He said, "Professor Xu's very busy. Please take up any problems with the department chair."

I said, "I'm from outside the school."

"Outside the school!" He slammed the door.

I knocked again. He opened the door and slammed it. I knocked again. A short, slightly bent old man, balding but with some white hair, came out.

"I am Xu Hefu. What do you want with me?"

I said, "Would you please read my paper?"

Without waiting for his reply, I held out the manuscript. He hesitated, took the manuscript, looked at the title, looked again at me, and said, "All right, I'll read it. Come back on Friday in two weeks."

In two weeks I returned. The same person opened the door. I assumed a combative stance, but he smiled and invited me in. The old man was in a good mood. He asked me where I was from, what my parents did, and praised my talent and writing ability, but said my viewpoint was wrong. He said it was "typical Machism," which had long been disproved by Lenin.[6] He asked me if I had read Lenin's "Materialism and Empiro-Criticism," and told me to read it thoroughly. He shoved a pile of papers across the desk and said he had written down specific comments and I should return home and look at them, and if I had any questions we could discuss it further.

This commentary of more than eight thousand characters was written superbly.[7] I admired it for its strong belief, its persuasive logic, and its erudite knowledge of the history of philosophy and art. Although it had a Marxist-Leninist premise like all other writing at the time, it didn't feel coercive. I admired it, appreciated it, but couldn't accept it. I wrote a letter telling him I needed to think further. Later, Mr. Hong Yiran, a professor at Northwest Normal College and a friend who was introduced to me by Mr. Xu, told me my refusal of help hurt Professor Xu. At that time I didn't foresee that Xu would be deposed from his position and denounced as an anti-Party, anti-socialist rightist. When I visited him again in 1960, he was a chronically ill, ordinary citizen. Not long after, he was dead.

In February 1957, "On Beauty" was published in Beijing by *New Construction*. The editor added a commentary expressing his disagreement with my premise. He said he published my paper only in accordance with the party's "Double Hundred Policy," in order to "open up debate."[8] He also announced that readers should take note that the next issue would contain criticisms of my essay. A personal letter from Mr. Zhu Guangquin was forwarded to me.[9]

Zhu said my viewpoint was idealistic and that I should review Lenin's criticism of Mach. Subsequently, in March of the same year, the same magazine published Mr. Zong Baihua's "Some Questions after Reading 'On Beauty'" and Mr. Hou Muze's "The Aesthetics of Subjective Idealism, a Criticism of 'On Beauty.'" Following this, *Literature and Art*, *Philosophical Studies*, *Scholastic Enquiry*, *Scholastic Monthly*, and other magazines, one after another, published criticism, unanimously calling me an idealist. First it was said that the beauty of the five-star red flag came from the great achievements of the New China and therefore had to be objective. Then it was said that Marxism and Leninism developed out of the struggle against idealism, and from that, the struggle between materialism and idealism became the struggle between revolution and counter-revolution.

Those debates on aesthetics of the '50s had one defining characteristic: each opposing side (except for me) emphasized that its viewpoint was Marxist-Leninist while the other side's was not. Not all these intellectuals were opportunistic; many were honest and had integrity and deeply believed in Marx and Lenin, but I thought it was strange all of them were so completely in agreement.

Mr. Hong Yiran said, "No doubt you think everyone is wrong and you alone are right?"

I replied, "Truth's not determined by ballot. It needs proof."

Hong said, "It's already been proven and so everyone believes it. Open your eyes and catch up with the times."

This repeated what Fu Lei had said.

In my isolation I sometimes doubted myself. I thought about the many things I didn't know concerning the universe, life, history, science, religion, and the current human condition. My knowledge was shallow. How could I be so confident? But on further thought, I realized that because I was ignorant, I needed to study, and I wasn't going to throw myself at the foot of some ultimate truth, nor was I about to relinquish my right to free inquiry or my freedom to believe what I choose, especially when in the name of this ultimate truth we have been stripped of everything.

Of course, to question and debate opponents are forms of study, but because of the conditions that developed, these were impossible. Very quickly academic debate became political criticism with many hidden traps; a single reply and you fell. For instance, when someone said societal standards, which everyone shares, wouldn't cease to exist because you didn't accept or recognize them, I answered that standards have no relation to beauty and standards are not absolute. And with that, I fell into a trap. My answer was interpreted to mean that I wanted bourgeois standards to replace proletarian standards. When someone said existence determined state of mind and so the exquisite life in New China determined our happiness, I replied that people who love the sea live by the sea, people who love the city live in the city, both happily, but if you switch their positions, even though the sea and the city remain the same, the happiness of the people is lost. Again I fell into a trap. This answer was later interpreted to mean that I didn't think New China was happy.

My defense, "On the Absolute Nature of the Perception of Beauty," was published in the July issue of *New Construction*. My main point was that a material object is not the same as experience, and experience is not the same as society; therefore society cannot be objective. Experience evolves while a material object is concrete and, correspondingly, fixed and permanent. A material object elicits many different experiences, each one individual, and it's these individual experiences that belong to society. Mixing up these concepts and tagging them as materialist or idealist proves nothing. When this was published, the Anti-Rightist Campaign had begun. No one paid any attention to my arguments; they just politicized their criticism.

Some criticisms of my ideas were relatively mild, such as "Opposing Mao's Thoughts On Art." But the author of a criticism published in *Flow-*

ers of Long wrote, "The enemy sharpens his blade.[10] The phantom of Hu Feng is resurrected in Gao Ertai."[11]

At this point, what could I say? I had no choice but to quietly face the encircling enemy. I felt as if I were watching a play.

Later, when I reread "On Beauty," I discovered many problems. I didn't differentiate the "one" from the "many." The word *ren* in the text sometimes refers to "one person" and sometimes to "people," and that ambiguity disarranged the logic (the subjectivity of people could be objective to a person). Although all my critics missed this point, I was upset and regretted that I hadn't put the article aside and looked at it again before I sent it out. On the other hand, if I hadn't been hasty, the paper would never have been published and, like my other papers of the time, would have been confiscated during the Anti-Rightist Campaign and lost without a trace.

Now, rereading "On Beauty," I feel it revealed both my immaturity and a lack of cogency. But it also raised a political question even my most merciless critics didn't catch: To emphasize the subjectivity of beauty is to emphasize human subjectivity. The right to be free and to call forth the plurality of the human spirit is the same as challenging authority. It wasn't intentional; everyone overlooked it, but that didn't help me in the least, because the name of the crime they fabricated and imputed to me was more serious by far: "To plan, step-by-step, an attack on the Party." This was a set sentence applied to rightists, which the newspapers used daily. I knew there was no escape, and yet I wasn't afraid, because I didn't understand the seriousness of the situation and I had nothing to lose. I was fed up with the kind of existence others had arranged for me. I didn't mind a change.

I didn't write any more. Whenever I had time, I'd take a stroll. The scenery wasn't worth seeing; I was merely passing time before the coming storm. There was a level, open square not far from the back of the school, where soldiers broke horses. Often I sat on the side and watched for a long time.

They tied seven or eight ropes, each rope gripped by one man, around one of those obstinate, fierce horses. When a horse refused to be mounted, the men jerked the ropes, sending the horse sprawling. If it still refused, they yanked the ropes again and again until it was subdued. One especially wild and stubborn horse kicked to its feet continually, then bucked furiously, unwilling to give in, its mane flying like a black flame. Whenever it threw a rider, it reared high, shuddering and whinnying. I looked at the horse and thought, There are men everywhere—how can you escape? If you don't want to be ridden, they'll skin you and eat your flesh, and that would be worse. I asked myself, if I were that horse, what would I do?

I didn't know.

FOUR

Gongs and Drums in a Movie

At twenty-one, I was still teaching at my small, secluded school in the remote Northwest region, unaware that there was an "early spring for the intellectuals." I read the newspapers, of course, but that jubilant drum roll for "speaking out freely and airing views fully" and the subsequent "indignant condemnation" was to me like gongs and drums in a movie.

The writing and publishing of "On Beauty" was accomplished entirely by blind luck. Since it came out in Beijing in a so-called central publication and had been criticized nationwide, our principal, Xiao Ying, thought it was significant and hurried to the Lanzhou Party Committee to report this "serious situation." She was received by a young bureaucrat, Xie Changyu (afterward chairman of the Provincial Artists and Writers Association), who, after listening to her report, said it was part of a healthy academic debate, not a political matter, and she shouldn't worry.

The Gansu Provincial Party Committee convened a meeting to which I was issued an invitation. I didn't care, I didn't respond, and I didn't go. Xiao Ying sought me out for a talk. She said this conference was very important, yet I took it upon myself not to go. It was "breaking away from politics," it "was liberalism" and "a pure technocrat's attitude."[1] She advised me to concern myself with politics and showed me a printed document, one of Mao's speeches "passed down" at the conference.[2] I wasn't allowed to take it away but had to read it and return it. I looked it over. Primarily it asked everyone to "speak out freely" and help the Party "rectify itself": "Let a hundred flowers bloom, let a hundred schools of thought contend," "the speaker can't be blamed, the listener is duly warned," and so on, and so on.

Mr. Hong Yiran came for a visit. After attending the provincial three-day conference, he was elated. He asked why I didn't go and said Zhang Zhongliang (the First Provincial Party Secretary of Gansu) sent me his greetings. Mr. Hong said the conference went very well. People spoke very fervently from their hearts. Someone said this; someone else said that; each time more and more acutely. Zhang Zhongliang also said everyone spoke well. Their free and straightforward speech proved they trusted the Communist Party. The Party and the people must unite and show the deepest mutual sincerity before they can progress together.

I asked, "Haven't you read the latest editorials in *The People's Daily*, *Why*, and *The Workers Speak*, which urge counterattacks? Those people in Beijing are suffering reprisals for 'speaking freely.'"

Hong answered, "Zhang Zhongliang told us this was aimed at rightists. If you're not a rightist, you've no reason to fear. Chairman Mao himself published the guarantee 'the speaker can't be blamed.' And still you don't trust!"

Soon after, the newspaper reported Mao's speech, but it wasn't the same one "passed down" at the conference. Basically it was about the "six political criteria" for "distinguishing fragrant flowers from poisonous weeds" and said the two most important criteria were the leadership of the Party and the institution of socialism. Not only Beijing periodicals but also regional periodicals initiated attacks on rightists; for many successive days the *Gansu Daily* ran the large banner headline "Resolutely Smash the Bourgeois, Rightist Vile Offensive." Edition after edition reported the reactionary speeches that surfaced at the Provincial Committee conference. The Provincial Consulting Congress chairman, Shui Zi; the editor of the

Gansu Daily, Wang Jingchao; the dean of Northwest Normal College, Xu Jiefu; and the dean of Lanzhou University, Chen Shiwei, were named. "The mass of workers and peasants" vehemently denounced these anti-Party, anti-socialist rightists as the evil enemies of the proletariat.

Immediately, the Lanzhou Party Committee convened another three-day conference, to which I was invited. This time they dispatched a sedan and I had to go.[3] Our new principal, Lei Xuhua, accompanied the man they sent to fetch me; both smiled broadly as they urged me into the car.[4] This was my first time in a sedan and the first time any automobile had passed through these mazelike narrow alleys that twisted and turned between the adobe houses. Wedged within these alleys, the car crawled along, suddenly leaning left or right, bumping up and down. Frequently we came upon a place that was too narrow and had to back up and look for a new passage. The driver was impatient. Many times he violently lunged the sedan forward, sending chickens flying, dogs running, while children, who had plastered themselves flat against walls, sucking on their blackened fingers, their dirty bellies protruding, screamed and scattered. In contrast the person who came for me smiled steadily, amicably, in the rearview mirror.

Listening to the opening ceremony was like listening to a report. A hundred or so people sat below, with about ten on the platform. Again they "passed down" Mao Zedong's words: "Let a hundred flowers bloom, let a hundred schools of thought contend," "the speaker can't be blamed, the listener is duly warned." Afterward, Zhang Zhongliang, as Provincial Party Secretary, guaranteed everyone's safety. This person I had met before. The previous year he transferred me to the Industrial Agricultural Exhibition to paint political posters. His review of my portfolio was discriminating and quite knowledgeable, and he liked my paintings. This time he said the Party had the faults of subjectivism, sectarianism, bureaucratism, dogmatism, and so forth. He asked everyone to give their opinion and help rectify the Party. "By all means 'say all you know and say it without reserve.' If you say something wrong, it's not important; we know your intentions are good. We 'correct our mistakes if any and keep our good record if none has been committed.'" In the middle of this he asked, "Is Mr. Gao Ertai here?"[5] Someone said yes. "You're here—welcome, welcome. The last time we invited you, you didn't come. It was regrettable. You had your opinions but nowhere to express them, so you published them in Beijing, which shows our work has already lost its connection with the masses. Come on, let it out; there's nothing to prevent you." And on and on like this. When he finished, he left. We continued our meeting. The Party Committee Secretary (I forget his name) spoke and encouraged everyone to speak out freely and to dispel misgivings.

The discussion was enthusiastic; everyone spoke eagerly, but from start to finish I didn't open my mouth. After dinner the conference broke up, leaving ten or so people, including me, in a small room for another meeting. Peony brand cigarettes, Longjing tea, olives, and preserved plums were provided. Every Party committee member came; some acted benevolent and sincere, others straightforward and frank. A vague haze of cigarette smoke made the ambience cordial. The secretary sat alongside me; our knees touched; he stroked my back, hot as a brazier fire, and asked me to give the Party my valuable opinions. I insisted I didn't have any. He said, "Wasn't your opinion published in Beijing any good!"

"It wasn't an opinion," I said. "It was a discussion of aesthetics."

"Not at all, not at all. You're too polite. We're one family now. Say anything you want. Don't stand on ceremony."

I couldn't come up with an answer but could only repeat, "No, no, no, I don't have an opinion," like an idiot.

During the summer break, the "re-education through labor stipulations" endorsed by Zhou Enlai were made public, and the Anti-Rightist Campaign reached its peak. The Lanzhou Municipal Education Bureau notified all middle and primary school teachers to "speak out freely" and ordered us to pack our bags and gather at several middle and primary schools in the center of the city for a meeting. This was not an invitation but an order. There was the same rhetoric: "Pass down" the words of Mao, the secretary pledges safety to everyone, the bureau chief urges everyone "to speak out freely," and more of the same—"Help the party rectify," "a wholehearted welcome," "the speaker can't be blamed," "the listener is duly warned." However, it wasn't a three-day meeting, it was a monthlong meeting with a preset daily agenda: first "speak freely" then "oppose the rightists." "Take the lid off class struggle during the school break; let denunciation and criticism continue throughout the year."

I thought people weren't that stupid. Under these conditions, who'd dance when they played the flute? But strangely it was as animated as before. Everyone looked at what had happened but couldn't see. We lived ten to twenty in a classroom. During the day the desks were arranged as meeting tables and at night they were first separated, then pushed together as beds. For half the day we held meetings to "speak freely" and during the other half we wrote big-character posters. The Bureau of Education supplied all the pens, paper, and ink we needed. Everyone wrote happily, pasting the walls completely over with narratives, commentaries, doggerels, comic dialogues, and even cartoons. I remember that Xu Zhiben of the Women's Normal College wrote many poems. After posting them, she walked up and down in front listening, very self-satisfied, to everyone's praise. I remember only two poems entirely. One was about hunger in a village:

> a grain of rice makes ten bowls of gruel
> the east wind blows gentle waves upon the gruel's surface
> one ladle scooped from the mirror of the West Lake
> reflects an entire family swimming.

Another poem was about the tensions of city living:

> two families live in one room
> every weekend they're busy changing shifts
> open or close the door and an argument ensues
> a child returns and calls to the wrong mother.

It was like being in a cartoon, but I didn't say so. Whatever big-character poster I looked at, I expressed no opinion. Someone had a lengthy script and, seeing I had nothing to do, asked me to help make a few copies. I refused. Someone pasted up a petition, which many signed, and wanted me to add my name. I refused. I didn't want to get my hands dirty. During the entire process of "speak freely," from beginning to end, I didn't say or write a word.

I didn't expect I'd be the first to be exposed as a rightist.

Our school had a woman teacher, over forty, named Yang Chuntai, whose husband was the director of the department of geology at Northwest Normal College. They lived at the college. One morning, when I met her in the courtyard, I asked her how the college dealt with rightists, and she told me the college hadn't done anything yet. That afternoon a big-character poster appeared on the wall, entitled "A Challenge to Gao Ertai." It read, "If you're not a rightist, why did you sneak around asking how rightists are dealt with at the school? If you're not a rightist, why did you remain silent and reveal nothing during the 'speak freely' sessions?" The signatures below this, many of which I saw for the first time, took up several times the space as the actual text.

A few days later, all the big-character posters on the auditorium's eastern wall were replaced. A slogan was written in black ink across a horizontal line of newspaper pages, one word to each page—twenty characters—more than ten yards long: "Drag out before the public the anti-Party, anti-socialist bourgeois rightist Gao Ertai." It was like a newspaper's banner headline. The big-character posters below it were denunciations, which, except for political criticism of "On Beauty" quoted from newspapers and periodicals, were compiled from material taken from the rectification movement that happened two years earlier, including a letter I had written to my good friend Liu Han. I was still in college then and had to go through "struggle and criticism" but wasn't disciplined. It seemed all this material had been kept, but how did these people find out? Who gave it to them? Where were so many big-character posters written? How did they paste them up without me knowing? It was baffling.

One big-character poster had newly fabricated charges. It said that during a dream late one night, I had cried out, "Kill, kill, kill!" The man who had written this was a geology teacher at our school named Zheng Jun, from Min Jin County in Gansu. The deep wrinkles in his bronze-colored face resembled those of an old farmer. A quiet man, he kept to himself. There had been no animosity between us.

After school started, I was named an extreme rightist during the "struggle and denunciation" sessions and was sent west for "re-education through labor."

Twenty-one years later, after the "reverse verdict," I returned to Lanzhou University to teach at the Philosophy Department.[6] I had many of the same painful memories as the "former Gentleman Liu."[7] I had gone away and now I returned to revisit old places. At Number Ten Middle School the people and surroundings had completely changed, except for an old acquaintance, the teacher Zheng Jun, who was now an old, feeble man with sparse white hair and weak legs. Extremely happy to see me, he grasped my hand tightly for a long time and insisted I go with him to his third-floor quarters for a drink, obviously very moved at meeting someone from the past.

After twenty-one years, the Lanzhou cityscape had undergone great changes. But Gaolan Mountain and the Yellow River remained the same; when I looked from the third-floor window, the heavy evening mist and city smog congealed into a purple haze and the scenery resembled that of old times. As the elderly man spoke about the past, his countenance darkened. That year his wife had starved to death, and his son had gone to labor at a hydraulic project along the Tao River and also died. After Mr. Zheng retired, he had nowhere to go and had to remain dependent upon the school. He didn't have a single person with whom he could talk.

Not knowing how to be of comfort, I sat with him and drank silently.

Alongside the setting sun, winter crows scattered into thousands of dots; flowing water encircled the lonely city.

FIVE

God Casts the Dice

In 1956, I was twenty. When I first went out into the world, I was naïve. I had no idea of the conflicts between people or of personal responsibility. I was a bookworm; my mind was elsewhere. I didn't know what the future held, but since I had no control over what happened to me, I didn't really have a future; so I went along with those who manipulated me, figuring there'd be less trouble, and left everything to chance. That year, disengaged though I was, I did two things that changed my life.

One was writing "On Beauty." I paid no attention to anything concrete around me but thought long and hard about time and space, the universe, the meaning of life, the value of existence, and other far-reaching questions. I shut my door and deliberated late each night until I produced that inopportune treatise. It was exactly at the time of "entice the snakes from their holes," so it was published and subjected to nationwide criticism. One moment of fame turned into twenty years of misfortune. Twenty years after it was published, the "Reform and Open Door Policy" began, and scientific and technological information from America, Europe, and elsewhere entered the country. Some of the new ideas were compatible with mine. It was serendipitous, of course, but again I had a bit of fame and became a scholar and professor. Even the National Science Committee allowed the title of "National Expert with Outstanding Contribution" to be conferred upon me. Gain, loss, ups, downs; all came and went as in a children's play, and this play started with "On Beauty."

The other thing I did was to visit Mr. Lu Sibai. My work was monotonous, and I had nowhere to go after I finished; when I wasn't reading or writing in my spare time, I was painting. I painted oils in a classical, realistic style and wanted someone to instruct me. I heard that the renowned oil painter, Lu Sibai, was director of the department of fine arts at the Northwest Normal College in Lanzhou, so I rolled up a few paintings, knocked on his door, and asked for guidance. Mr. Lu looked them over and told me to bring back to him everything I painted from then on. I was inexperienced and didn't realize that it was very rare for a famous painter to treat a nameless young person like this; I just assumed he should have done so. From then on I visited him often, and my technique improved immensely.

Mr. Lu said if I wanted to be a painter, I needed to take part in fine-arts activities, let more people see my paintings, and gain acceptance from my peers before doors could open. He wrote a letter introducing me to two leaders of the Gansu provincial fine-arts community, Mr. Chen Boxi and Mr. Mi Ying, and asked them to look after me. Because of this, I received traveling funds to sketch from nature during that year's summer break. I went to the foot of the Qilian Mountains, where several minority groups lived, saw the great steppes, expansive forests, and various lifestyles and people. I learned how to ride a horse, wrestle, and eat half-cooked meat. When I returned, the principal asked me in for a talk. He told me the provincial authorities had decided to transfer me to work at the Agricultural and Industrial Exhibition. A replacement teacher had already been found; he exhorted me to go and do well but to tidy up. If I were rumpled like a beggar, it would reflect poorly on everyone.

From the time I had left for school and had to take care of myself I was sloppy; I carelessly let it become a habit that was hard to change. Those who knew me said I didn't care about small things; those who didn't know me dismissed me as lazy. Each week, I taught sixteen classes and corrected more than a thousand homework assignments, and after work, I only wanted to do what I enjoyed, nothing else. The day I went to the Fine Arts Section Meeting at the Exhibition, my hair was uncombed, my face dirty, and my clothes tattered. The unit's gate attendant wouldn't let me in and still wasn't satisfied after he saw my identification papers. He led me to the conference room and wouldn't leave until he handed me over to the person in charge.

The room held an immaculately laundered white tablecloth and bright green carpet. About twenty people sat scattered around the conference table or on a sofa pushed against the wall. I had just arrived in Lanzhou and didn't recognize any of them. Looking at their woolen suits and leather shoes, snow-white shirts, pitch-black hair, the light reflecting from their eyeglasses while they elegantly drank tea and smoked cigarettes, I felt self-conscious. I limped over to an empty upholstered chair in the corner of the room and sat down. Everyone lowered their eyes to the faint trail of yellow footprints on the carpet that led from the doorway to my feet. To conceal my embarrassment, I leaned back and crossed my legs. Unexpectedly, sand poured from a hole in the heel of my cloth shoe, while from the shoe's torn front my toes were exposed like a row of teeth in a grin. Everyone stared. Annoyed, I put down my foot and glared at one of the starers. He averted his eyes. I sighed in relief.

Assignments were distributed at the meeting. Following a designed plan, a requirement to paint the prescribed pictures fell to each person. When the meeting was over, all the assignments had been given out and I didn't have any—no doubt because I looked like a tramp and they wouldn't trust me. So in the following days I walked around watching them paint. Sometimes the other painters told me to sweep the floor or empty the dirty water used for cleaning brushes, which I didn't like but figured I might as well do. Sometimes I'd wander around the New China Book Store, stroll through streets and back alleyways, returning only to eat. They worked until one or two o'clock in the morning and then had a hearty meal; I'd get up from sleep, eat, then go back to sleep. After two months, the preparatory work was mostly completed. The Provincial Committee Secretary, Zhang Zhongliang, led a group for inspection. Some explanatory notes needed rewriting, some pieces needed rearranging, and none of the paintings passed. Everyone went back to work, more anxious than ever.

Two weeks later, at the second inspection, two large oil paintings still didn't pass. This time Zhang Zhongliang brought along Mr. Lu Sibai. Lu called me out of the group and asked me to do additional work on the two oil paintings. Zhang, beside him, said the subjects weren't exciting; I needed to improve them before they could be used. Lu said I should use a style that would please the masses, and I said I understood. After they left, I worked day and night, devoting my energy and time to creating something to please the masses. And to render those paintings exquisite with as much verisimilitude, delicacy, and vigor as possible, I differentiated the flesh tones of men from women, the texture of burlap from other cloths, the sun's reflections on a copper brazier from the luminosity of its fire reflected from within, and depicted such items as earrings, buckles, or other jewelry so realistically that they appeared like actual objects that could be taken off and put back on again. The paintings went on preliminary display ten days later and were well received.

Because of this, Zhang Zhongliang remembered my name, and in '59, when the "Ten Years of Accomplishment in Design Exhibition" was being planned, he asked for me. I was in the Jiabiangou Collective Farm in the Gobi Desert then, undergoing re-education through labor. I was extremely weak from hunger and exhaustion, and while people around me were dying, unexpectedly two policemen brought me to Lanzhou to paint and I was able to escape from death into life. Whether I lived or died was capricious, and I owe my survival to a morning three years earlier when dust filled the air and I washed my face, wedged a roll of paintings under my arm, and paid a visit to an artist I had never met before.

SIX

The Gate of Hell

D uring the 1957 Anti-Rightist Movement, we teachers who had been denounced, so-called Rightist Elements, labored under supervision in the school grounds, waiting to be dealt with. Being without previous experience, we did not know what there was to fear, and in our rest periods we laughed and joked. Someone had brought along a copy of *Selected Poems of Li Bai*, and we used it to divine our future. The idea was that you closed your eyes, opened the book, and pointed at random, and the couplet you pointed to would predict what was in store for you. I didn't believe in that stuff, but I played along. The couplet I pointed to was:

> *Since in this wide world he can find no kindred spirits,*
> *Better to float off like the clouds to that fair land in the*
> *West.*

Soon afterward I was dismissed from public employment and sentenced to re-education through labor in the district of Jiuquan on the far western end of the Gansu Corridor, the old frontier region. A short, fat, florid-faced political cadre belonging to the school's Party branch office, Zhang Zhengtai by name, escorted me there. He carried a bulging briefcase. I guessed it contained my dossier, but I didn't know what was written in it. Must be a hell of a lot, I thought. I was twenty-one that year, as daft as they come. I bought my own ticket and boarded the westbound train with him. On the journey I pictured myself as Chernyshevsky heading for Siberia, a martyr to truth.[1]

On the morning of the third day we alighted at Jiuquan station, got in a car, and after a bumpy ride of more than half an hour, arrived in Jiuquan town. It was Gobi Desert all the way until the outskirts of the town, where the stony wastes gave way to fields dressed in the depressing clothes of late autumn. The town streets were narrow and deeply rutted by cart wheels. Lining the roads were large numbers of towering old trees that emphasized the lowness of the houses. The houses were uniformly gray-yellow—"Few footfalls on the road, wind soughing in the poplars"— the bleakness of a frontier town. We ate a meal of dumplings in mutton broth in a small shop, after which Zhang Zhengtai commented, "First class—much more like the real thing than what you get in Lanzhou." Those were the only words he spoke to me on our journey.

Round the corner was a newly built dark gray building of three stories, the highest structure in town. On the gate to the compound there was a sign that read, "Gansu Management Bureau for Labor Reform: Jiuquan Department." Two lines of people snaked along the walls of the big compound. One line of a hundred or so was all male, the other line of twenty to thirty was all female. Everyone was sitting on their belongings. No one spoke. Some policemen were walking back and forth across the empty middle space. Zhang handed me over to one of them, then went into the building with the briefcase under his arm. The policeman told me to tag onto the men's line. I put my luggage on the ground and sat on it like the others.

A big dust-laden truck pulled into the compound. The police ordered the men at the head of the line to stand up, fall in, number off, and climb onto the truck. They were taken away. We moved forward in turn. New people arrived in dribs and drabs and filled in behind me. Before the dust stirred up by the truck had completely settled, the line had regained its original length. Zhang emerged at that point, his briefcase now flat, and walked straight out through the gate. Suddenly he turned back and walked up to me. He said: "Your train ticket—it's no use to you. Give it to me. I can get a refund." He was off like a shot when I handed it over.

Before long another truck loaded us up and jolted out of town. We passed through deserted fields and a few widely separated hamlets, and headed into the vast Great Gobi. The yellow clouds of dust the truck churned up stretched far behind in an unbroken trail. Every trace of human habitation was rapidly lost to sight. The landform of the Gobi Desert is an unvaried gravel plain: you drive for hundreds of miles, and it is all the same. It deadens you, makes you lose the concept of time and space. After we had driven for ages, the Gobi changed to saline and alkaline land. In this wilderness, a few light coffee-colored bogs showed up, and white salt drifts, and gray-green reeds. From time to time we came across one or two desert jujube trees, dreary gray, very much like the reeds in color. The masculinity of the imposing and measureless Great Gobi was gone, and in its place a dead-and-alive limpness.

Eventually some bare plowed fields came into view, and at the same time we could see in the distance a square earth-built fortress with watchtowers situated on the high ground, standing all by itself in the boundless wastes. Lit by the setting sun of late autumn, it looked just like a medieval castle.

The truck stopped before the fortress. Some middle-aged men came through the iron gate and yelled at us to get off the truck, fall in, and number off. Their tone was very fierce. The truck left when we had numbered off. Then one by one they inspected our luggage and searched us, again with particular roughness. Cash, papers, watches, knives and scissors, matches, belts and shoelaces, plus the ropes we used to tie our baggage, all came in for confiscation. Holding up their trousers with one hand and carrying their hastily thrown-together things with the other, those who had been searched went aside to repack. I hadn't foreseen that I would run into this kind of thing and was caught completely unprepared. Besides books, notes, and such things, I lost a diary that I had kept hidden all through the Anti-Rightist Movement.

The sun had long since gone down, and it was getting dark. The farm workforce dribbled back listlessly. Their contingents moved very slowly and in absolute silence. They did not enter the iron gate of the fortress. Two of our number were called inside, came out again carrying a wooden tub, and doled out a scoopful of the contents to everybody. For containers we used the bowls, pots, lunch tins or tea mugs we had brought with us; those without used their washbasins. We gulped down a supper—of what, we could not tell in the dark. Afterward someone returned our ropes to us, ordered us to tie up our luggage, put it on our shoulders, form ranks, and set off.

There was a path across the wasteland. It gleamed white under the moon. Our luggage on our backs, one hand holding up our trousers, we walked a long, long time. We got to our destination in the middle of the night. It consisted of rows of low mud-brick buildings. There were no frames in their window openings, no doors in their doorways. A cold, bare, and miserable place. Someone with a lantern led us into one of the buildings. We caught a whiff of rank body odor: There were men in there, sleeping on the ground. The one with the lantern shouted to them to get up and shift their bedding closer, so as to make room for us. After that he took back our ropes, retrieved his lantern, and left. Groping around in the dark, I found there was straw on the ground. I spread my bedding any old how. Hands cupping my head, I lay awake a long time.

By and by the moonlight coming through the window shifted around to my bed space. It was very bright. Outside the window, the rows of dark, forbidding mud huts were edged a bluish silver. I remembered the ballad from my childhood that began "The moon so bright / Makes our village light," and felt that this hideous night still had some tender coloring. The voices of my mother, father, sisters, even my grandmother who had passed on, mixed with many scenes of my boyhood, swept uncontrollably into my mind, like a clamorous tide. But then I remembered that my diary had been taken when I was searched, and I felt a sudden tremor of terror. I thought of escaping. I thought of the impossibility of getting away in a wilderness like this. I thought of finding no refuge even if I did manage to get out of the wilderness. I thought of things I had read in books, the line Dante wrote over the Gate of Hell: "Abandon hope, all ye who enter here," and Lu Xun's words, "The vainness of despair is no different from the vainness of hope." I thought of the prisoners in Siberia who learned to make leather boots for themselves, and wondered if I might be able to learn some handicraft here. Listening to the waves of snores rolling around me, I realized there was no sound of autumn crickets. Feeling thirsty, I thought of my aluminum flask, whose lid I had lost on my way: I'd have to make another one, but of what? If I could find a branch of the same diameter as the mouth of the flask, that would do, but I hadn't seen a tree since getting off the truck . . .

I learned only later that this place was called "Jiabiangou State Farm Under Local Administration." Such a sign had indeed been hung beside the iron gate of the fortress where we had been searched, but I was so disoriented that I had not noticed it. That was the camp headquarters. The place where we were now was a new extension, called "Xintiandun Work Station of Jiabiangou Farm."

Jiabiangou Farm was originally a prison farm for "reform through labor," founded in 1954. The fields had been brought under cultivation by the prisoners of those years. In 1957 the "reform through labor farm" was renamed "re-education through labor farm." It was a center for the incarceration of Rightist Elements and Bad Elements who had not been sentenced by the courts but sent directly by the Party organization of their place of work, and hence had no fixed term of imprisonment. It was still controlled by the Management Bureau for Labor Reform of the Gansu Province Security Department. It did not employ the armed police; it was managed by civilian policemen, called disciplinary cadres. The original prison installations were no longer used, but still stood. With its four-square, massive high walls, its watchtowers thrusting skyward on the four corners, the camp stood isolated and marooned in the back of beyond. Because it could not contain the dramatic increase in prisoners, they set up this sub-farm eight kilometers to the northwest of the farm, the Xintiandun Work Station.

SEVEN

Desert Jujubes

1.

Xintiandun Workstation was situated on the wide barren plain between the Badanjilu Desert and the Great Gobi. Apart from patches of desert sand and Gobi gravel, the greater part of this wasteland was saline-alkali soil, which to the distant view presented an unbroken whitish landscape. It was not the pure, sparkling whiteness of a snow plain but a sickly whiteness, due to the constant deposition of dust blown from the desert. To the near view the surface was mottled, and under the burning sun it gave off the pungent, acrid smell of caustic soda.

Our task was to dig ditches to drain the salts from the terrain, the ditches spaced about a third of a mile apart. The idea was to let the salty water drain away underground, not letting it rise to the surface, so you could cultivate the upper stratum. The breadth of the ditch opening was invariable, roughly sixteen feet. The width of the bottom of the ditch was also invariable, roughly one foot. The depth and slope of the ditch depended on the topography: the depth could vary between seven and sixteen feet, the limit being when you dug down to water. The excavated earth was piled on both sides of the ditch. Four brigades, numbering over a thousand men in all, were responsible for completing the lengths assigned to them, and moved on to a new site when the intersection points were reached. We concentrated our manpower on finishing one ditch, then moved on to open a fresh one. What was meant by "finish"? How long was a ditch? How many should be dug? We had no idea. We simply dug where we were told to dig. We dug all day; we dug all the year round.

Sometimes a completed ditch would be blocked by windblown sand and had to be promptly cleared. If action was not prompt, the passing of sandstorms could level whole sections. The objection had been voiced that this was fruitless labor. At our regular "political study" evening meetings, each team concentrated its fire for a time on this "fruitless labor" view. All agreed that our labor was not solely intended to remake nature; in fact its primary purpose was to remold man. You could not do the economic accounts alone; first and foremost you did the political accounts. Someone said that if our thoughts had not been remolded after a day's work, *that* would be fruitless labor. Someone else said, no, that would not be fruitless labor; that would be a case of *resisting* remolding.

The evening meetings were normally small-team meetings. A small team consisted of eight or nine men, maybe a dozen. They shared the same billet, shared the same platform bed; each man sat on his own space on the bed for the meeting. A kerosene lamp made out of an ink bottle was lit, its tiny flame like a glowworm. In this half-light we spoke in turn. We analyzed ourselves, informed on others. Who wasn't pulling his weight, going off from the work site and stooping down pretending to have a crap; who was discontented, kicking over a wooden peg on the boundary line marked in lime; who was a wimp, dawdling about afraid of getting his feet wet when the water froze over . . . and so on and so forth. When the whistle went, the talking stopped, the lamp was put out, and we lay down to sleep.

In this way we labored in the daytime, studied in the evening, every day alike. Countless days came and went, and all the days put together seemed the very same day.

2.

Apart from the few months when the days were long and the nights short, we left for work before daybreak and did not knock off until nightfall. Except for when the wind came up, we had our breakfast by starlight and our supper by moonlight.

Breakfast and supper were the same: boiled cabbage, turnips or such, with corn flour or some other flour stirred in, and that was it. We called it "goo." It was very thin. If a bit thicker, it would have been good for pig food. Every team collected half a tubful from the cookhouse and divided it up themselves. The team leader gave each man a scoopful of this watery goo, roughly two pints. If any was left over, it was shared out again. The noonday meal was dry rations, usually corn-flour buns or sorghum pancakes, sometimes wheat-flour steamed buns, as big as your fist. Those were handed out at breakfast time, one per person, to be taken and eaten at the work site.

But no one took them to the work site—they were wolfed on the spot, and washed down with the goo. Having licked our bowls dry, we scraped the empty tub, polishing off the thin layer that adhered to its sides. At first we fought to scrape the tub; later on we agreed to take turns. The disciplinary cadres let us get on with it. The tub was made of wood, about the size of a washtub, only narrower and deeper. I used to tilt it on its side and swivel it around to scrape it with an aluminum spoon, eating as I scraped. The soup scraped out contained wood fibers, the tang of wood and aluminum, and at the bottom there was coal slack and grit, too. It all went down the same way. When I had finished I was still hungry; it was as if I hadn't eaten at all. All I had left was to look forward ten hours to the evening meal.

If the work site was not too far away, we had water to drink at noon. A whistle was blown as soon as the water carriers sent by the companies came back. We put down our shoulder poles, baskets, pickaxes, and shovels, and crowded around the water buckets. In the absence of food, a drink of water can still be sustaining. Sometimes the drainage ditches stretched for miles, and it took two hours to walk to where we had to dig and two hours back, so then we had to go without noonday water for perhaps a fortnight. At noon the whistle for the rest period sounded in the far distance, its shrills like the despairing cries of a lost wild bird carried on the wind. The men put down their tools, dragged themselves out of their ditch, and lay down where they were. From then until work resumed, no one spoke, no one stirred.

I was twenty-two that year, and was not long out of college. I had been keen on athletics and represented the college in track events, breaking a Jiangsu Province record and equaling a national one. Despite that, I had no desire to stir when I lay down now. To get up I had to clamber slowly to my feet, because it took time to get my back and legs straight. Many times I thought I couldn't go on like that. Once by an act of will I saved my noonday dry ration until noon, but hardly had I taken it out before I heard the sound of eyes pivoting around with one accord, from far and near, looks as boring as bradawls, scorching as braziers, unbending as nails. I swallowed my bun in a couple of hasty mouthfuls and never repeated the experiment.

3.

One day, taking a midday break at a new work site, I was propped up against a basket, gazing into the distance. I saw a lone tree, and suddenly my eyes shone. It was far away, and I could not see it clearly, but I was convinced it was an oleaster, or desert jujube.

The desert jujube is a perennial plant, quite common in the Northwest. It blooms in late spring, its white flowers giving off a heady fragrance. The jujube fruits ripen in late autumn, their size that of an almond, their color golden yellow. Their skin is thick and their pit large. The flesh is starchy, slightly sour, slightly sweet, puckery if you eat a lot. Previously I had seen village girls hawking them from wicker baskets in Lanzhou, ten cents for a bowl of thirty to forty. No other trees grow in the Gobi or on the salt flats, only those, and they are few and far between. It was now late autumn; the jujubes would be ripe. I spent the whole afternoon turning over in my mind how I could get my hands on them.

The sun was already sinking when we stopped work. I hung around a bit and joined the end of the column. Making sure no one was watching, I dived into a hollow and lay doggo. When the column had distanced itself, I got up and, bending double, ran toward that fuzzy speck, black against the sunset clouds. Though I was bent double, if anyone in the distant column turned his head he might have discovered me. Luckily no one turned.

The alkali drifts were spongy, each step making a hole; progress was like wading. Though I was buoyed up, I hadn't the strength to run fast, and dusk had closed in by the time I reached my goal. It was indeed a desert jujube. The tree was small, the fruits not plentiful but more than enough for my needs. As I picked them I ate some and stuffed others in my clothes, working very fast. By stuffing them through holes in my padded jacket I was able to load up a lot. When well loaded I hurried back, eating as I went.

By then the sunset clouds were breaking up and the first stars appeared. The darkness thickened and soon I couldn't see my earlier footprints, so could only make a rough guess as to my direction. As I trudged on and on the ground got harder, and more and more came the crackling sound of dry crust under my feet. To my bafflement I found myself in the middle of sand dunes. That stopped me in my tracks.

The sand dunes were less than a man's height, their slope gradual on one side, steep on the other. Their rows receded into the darkness like waves. The layer of sand between two rows of dunes was very thin, the ground underneath firm. This then should be Gobi, not sand desert. Where the last red glow died in the sky should be the west, in which case the dunes were ranged on an east-west axis, and if I went straight ahead I should be able to get through. I had thought in fact I was heading east, and if I carried on it should be right. Yet that was obviously wrong, because I hadn't seen any dunes on our way to work.

I climbed a dune, but still could see no farther. There was no glimmer of light, other than the stars in the sky. There was not the faintest sound, other than my own breathing. I was the only living creature, up against this primeval universe. A wave of terror swept over me. I sat down and stood up again, got down from the dune and clambered up another dune from the steep side. There was absolutely no point in that, as every dune was the same.

Soon the moon came out, dark red. Though big, it shed no light; it just made the wasteland seem darker, the surroundings more implacable and inhospitable. I thought of stories of people who had lost their way and met their death in the Gobi Desert. I thought about the fragility of life and the power of the inorganic world. I thought of home and family. None of which gave me a lift. Yet I calmed down, said to myself, "Don't panic—let's think of a way." I reckoned I could not have strayed very far, because I hadn't been walking long. But since I had no bearings, "not far" was no guide. My sweat-soaked clothes stuck to my body, icy cold. Luckily there was no wind.

As the moon rose higher, growing whiter, smaller, and brighter, the features of the landscape became clearer. Straining my eyes, I made out a slender, dark silhouette, as if someone had lightly penciled a line with a ruler on silver-blue paper. It could only be the earth from the drainage ditch, thrown up all along its way.

I knew I was saved.

The path that men had trodden out alongside the ditch showed up white in the moonlight. I walked very quickly, eating my jujubes as I went. The column always moved very slowly, so I reckoned I could catch up with it. If by some mischance I couldn't catch up, I'd be in big trouble. I became anxious and broke into a run again.

Desert jujubes contain soda; too many of them make your lips burn and your tongue dry. I had been thirsty enough to start with, and now this was piling on the agony. Of course there was water in the ditch, but it was brackish, undrinkable. I just had to stick it out, walking and running in stretches. In my weak condition normally any movement took an effort, but now I could actually run, and ran so much. It was the strangest thing.

In the newly dug drainage ditch a thread of water reflected the light from the sky, now dim, now bright, like a trembling zither string, wiry yet pliant. As I followed its course I could picture myself as a lone wolf. Having no will of my own in the collective, I had lost my self. Unexpectedly I could now take control of myself, and was suddenly moved: I felt a flicker of wonderment, a glimmer of happiness. Like notes struck from a zither string—*ding ding thrum thrum*, then lost without a trace.

To own oneself was to own the world. This oneness with the world, was it not the freedom I had long dreamed of?

> *The moon chills the border desert*
> *Stars hang over the barren wastes.*
> *A free man was in hot pursuit of prison.*

4.

I caught up with the column at last as it neared the farm buildings. I intended to say something to the men I fell in with, to show I was there, but I couldn't get a word out. I suddenly keeled over, and could not get up for the life of me. I was propped up on both sides, dragged into the billet, and thrown onto the bed platform.

It was as if all the bones in my body had been dislocated. I couldn't move a single joint. Memories from far away and long forgotten resurfaced, fleeting yet crystal-clear: a saying of my mother's, a corner of my boyhood garden.... In contrast, everything that was presently happening was a blank. I momentarily suspected I had died, only my brain staying briefly alive. But I heard the whistle for the doling out of supper, and smelled the scent of goo.

As always, it was the enticement of food that reactivated the potential for life. I climbed gingerly to my feet, went out of the hut with my mess bowl, and collected my scoopful. When I got back with it, the others were crawling over my bed space, scrabbling about in a frenzy. Their agitation fanned the tiny flame of the kerosene lamp, making it gutter. The cause of all this was that lots of jujubes had spilled out onto my bedding, and they were fighting over them.

In the aftermath, the first thing to be done was to search me, which they did so thoroughly that my padded jacket got fresh holes in it. The company leader asked me, "If you had the balls to escape, how come you came back again?" Then he added, "Everybody has responsibility for the bad eggs in the team getting out of hand. You haven't exercised mutual supervision, which shows you haven't remolded yourselves . . ."

He broke off in midstream and bellowed: "You're all still eating! There'll be bugger all evidence left! Hand over your jujubes, everybody!"

So there was a big hustle to hand over jujubes. In fact there were very few left: some had only one or two, the largest number being no more than a handful. The team leader felt everybody's pockets, went around collecting the jujubes in a hat, and placed the hat on the stand by the door of the hut, in preparation for handing the jujubes over to the disciplinary cadre first thing the next day.

When I woke up the next day, the hat was empty.

EIGHT

The Escapee

The prisoners in Jiabiangou Farm were overseen by civilian Public Security officers, not guarded by armed police. When I first got there I thought of escaping, but not for long. You were surrounded by salt flats, Gobi scrubland, and desert, which you could not get across on foot, especially if you didn't know your way.

There was a certain Li Husheng, only nineteen years old, who had come from Shanghai to the Northwest to "support the construction of the border areas." He said there were many hundreds in his batch, and they all felt very let down when they got here. He ganged up with some others to sneak off back to Shanghai. Once he was home, though, everybody got at him: the local police, the district officers, the residents committee, even the old ladies with bound feet in the back alleys got at him. With endless cross-questioning, with "educating and inspiring," they badgered him to go back and would give him no peace. He said to them, "It's not as if I'm a Bad Element."

They answered, "You wouldn't want to *become* a Bad Element, would you?"

So in the end, he and his companions went back, one and all. When he returned, the leadership said he was the ringleader and sentenced him to re-education through labor. He accepted his punishment without protest.

"Never mind not being able to get away," he said. "Even if you do get away, there's nowhere to go; forget it!"

Actually everyone knew that without being told. Therefore people didn't try to escape, generally speaking. Yet there *was* one person. I don't know his name and never saw his face. When the whole camp assembled that day after the evening meal to hold the struggle meeting against him, he was already unable to stand up. He had been trussed hand and foot, dragged prostrate onto the platform, and dumped there like a heap of rags. I was sitting a long way off, and in the darkness I couldn't see the way he lay on the ground clearly. Not until I heard the speeches made by designated representatives of the various units to which he belonged did I learn he was an "escape criminal"—that is to say, not a criminal who has escaped, but one who has committed the crime of escaping.

He hadn't been given a label. He was not a Rightist, not a Historical Counter-Revolutionary, not a Current Counter-Revolutionary, nor yet a Bad Element. It was because he was lackadaisical in his work, would not go where he was directed, and contradicted his superiors that his organization passed him on to the farm to have him straightened out. He was not the only one on the farm to arrive in such circumstances, but he could not reconcile himself to this treatment, and was very bolshie. He was always going on about what a monstrous humiliation it was and what maltreatment to endure drudgery along with us social dregs. He wanted that injustice put right. No one paid any attention, so he decided to escape. Once he did a runner, *then* he really was guilty of a crime. The speech makers were unanimous that by so doing he had "alienated himself from the people" and he could take the consequences.

He was not recaptured; no one pursued him. He came back himself. He did not come back because he recognized he was in the wrong; it was because he walked for two days without getting out of the salt flats and Gobi scrubland. So he followed his own footprints back. He had fallen senseless somewhere nearby, had been discovered and tied up and delivered to the camp HQ. Camp Commander Liu did not lose his temper.

He just said, "You don't know how lucky you were, you little runt. If a wind had blown up in those two days, your footprints would have gone, you'd have been written off, and I'd have been saved some trouble." He ordered his ropes untied and told him to go back to his unit. He would be sentenced later.

Camp Commander Liu was famous for his wit. At the end of the struggle session he summed up, saying: "If you want to run, then run. We won't stand in your way. In fact, best if you tip me off beforehand, and I'll give you water and dry rations, as much as you can carry, on condition that you don't come back. If you do come back, you'd better watch out. This one here on the ground will show you what you'll get. I meant to have him tell us what he went through after he made a run for it, but since he prefers to play dead, we'll have to do without. You can work it out for yourselves. I've heard some very fine speeches, but when you've criticized others you need to go on to take a good look at yourselves. If you buggers can't even make a go of mutual supervision, you can bloody well kiss goodbye to being reformed!"

Camp Commander Liu's address was the sole topic at the following evening meetings. We were in complete agreement that we must step up mutual supervision.

NINE

Storm

In the winter of 1958 I was "reforming through labor" in Jiuquan. The days were short, the nights long. When we marched out in the morning, the day was just dawning. Normally it got lighter as we marched, but one day it got darker. A native northwesterner in our company said it was going to blow, and not a small wind by the looks of it. Yet it wasn't the season for strong winds, and we couldn't figure out why it should get darker and darker. The opaque gray-yellow sky above was the same in color to the Gobi sand under our feet. It pressed down heavily on us, getting ever lower till it finally merged with the land. Distance was blotted out; spatial dimensions ceased to exist. It was like being wrapped in a thick, suffocating blanket—a very uncomfortable feeling. When the first gust of wind came, everyone breathed a sigh of relief.

The wind blew from behind us, its gusts stepping up in frequency. Its roar mingled with a high-pitched note as if countless airplanes were sweeping low overhead. The wind carried stones as well as dust and salt. The small stones were like sorghum grains, the big ones like soya beans. They pelted the bare back of your neck, quite painfully. They pelted your padded clothes, stiff from the encrustation of salt, making a rattling sound like a deluge of rain.

I leaned back as far as I could, in the same way as you lean back when pulling a cart down a slope, digging my heels in at every step, letting the wind blow me along. Coming across a sand dune, I squatted down on its leeward side in order to shelter from the wind's full blast. What I hadn't reckoned on was an eddy that swirled around the dune, skimming the ground. Carrying even more grit with it, it brazenly attacked head-on. In an instant it filled ears, nostrils, and crevices between the teeth, poured into my collar, sleeves, tears and rents, and leveled all creases in my clothes. It threatened to turn me instantly into another sand dune. I scrambled up hurriedly and the grit rapidly flew away.

Struggling to stay on my feet, progressing inch by inch, I followed the newly dug drainage ditch. At the end of the ditch there materialized baskets, shoulder poles, pickaxes, and shovels half buried in sand, and some blurred human figures. I had arrived at the work site. I pulled a shovel free, and like the others planted it in front of me; turning my back to the wind, I leaned propped against it, forming a sort of inverted Y. I pulled in my head, closed my eyes, and let the wind do its worst, were it to bring down darkness on the face of the Earth and make spirits to weep and wolves to howl. Meanwhile my padded coat, no proof against the wind's cold force, stuck to my back like a lump of ice.

After some time, somebody bellowed in my ear to tell me to pack it in. I did my best to pass the message on to the man in front, for him to relay onward. Then I abandoned my shovel and turned back. The return journey was heading into the wind, and I made hardly any progress. By dint of tumbling and crawling and devious maneuvering, we eventually managed to get back to base. It was pitch dark in the billet; you had to feel your way at first, things only gradually becoming visible. People sat on their bed spaces, mute and lifeless, each one clay-yellow from head to foot. Eyebrows and mouths were indistinct, only the closed eyes under the clay-yellow eyebrows presented any relief, in the form of two slits of moist redness. Glimpsing them in the dimness was like seeing a row of clay statues. It gave me a creepy feeling to think that inside those statues there were living men's blood and hearts.

We sat and sat and sat, not knowing how much time passed. Outside the wind howled, shaking the tightly closed door and windows. There were plenty of gaps between the windows and the roof. Despite all the racket, one could still hear the grit blown in from all angles falling on shoulders with a susurrating sound. We were cold, hungry, and exhausted. We felt as if a layer of glue had been pasted on our skin, dried there, and stuck tight. Ears, nose, and spaces between the teeth were both dry and swollen from being bunged up with dust. Because lice don't like the cold, they all decamped from our ice-cold clothes to crawl over our parched skin, making us scratch all over with a terrible itch. In order to impede the activity of the lice we had to make our clothes rub against our skin, and to do that we had to squirm about. Finding myself amid a host of writhing clay statues sent tremors of horror through me.

Sitting, sitting, and more sitting drained my brain of thought. For the first time in my life I discovered the solidity of time. Time changed from a vital element in my life, if you will, an expression of my life, into my antithesis, like a big stone wall that pitted its cold, clammy, slippery weight against the tip of my nose, my forehead, and my chest.

For a long time after the storm passed, this feeling stayed with me.

TEN

An Zhaojun

1.

On October 1, 1958, the entire body of the inmates belonging to the four brigades of our Xintiandun sub-farm got up before daybreak, ate their breakfast in the dark, and taking with them their bowls and chopsticks, shuffled along the newly made cart road for two to three hours to the camp headquarters in Jiabiangou, where they were to take part in the National Day celebrations.

When we arrived, a sea of people were already seated on the ground in front of the temporary rostrum outside the HQ walls—an expanse of muddy gray, like a field of rags laid out to dry by a scavenger. The disciplinary cadres in their dark blue police uniforms with thin red edging (normally they did not wear them) were patrolling back and forth. Five-star red flags fluttered on the high walls under a dull sky. A portrait of Mao Zedong hung on the command rostrum under the walls, with the Party flag on one side of it and the national flag on the other, Mao smiling in the middle.

Scarcely had we sat down than the meeting commenced. A man

went up to lead us in the national anthem, so we all stood up again. That person's clothes were all patches, so he was evidently an inmate, but they were clean and neat, really quite smart. He was about forty, tall, pallid and thin, with a scraggy neck and prominent Adam's apple, broad forehead, and strong chin. From his long and bony face hung a full beard. His expression was stern as he faced the crowd. He stood motionless for some moments before opening his arms and starting to sing. His slightly hoarse voice had a totally unexpected depth and robustness.

> *Arise—arise—*
> *You who would not be slaves*

These were the words of the national anthem, their source being the "March of the Volunteer Army," composed in the war against Japan. To hear them then and there was redolent of absurdity. He raised his hands above his head and the whole assembly joined in. His gestures ranged wide as he conducted, his whole body moved, his eyes lit up. His long hair tossed as he threw himself into his performance. Below him the assembly of over three thousand men, weak and hungry, sang listlessly, each in his own way and at his own tempo. It both looked and sounded bizarre.

Next, Camp Commander Liu lectured us. "In the just one year you've been inside," he said, "on the outside they've realized the Great Leap Forward and entered the Communist Era. The food is free in the people's communes, the drive to break down selfishness and build public spirit is forging ahead nationwide at all levels, the whole population is smelting iron, every citizen a soldier, all working twelve to twenty hours a day, creating the miracle of one plot of land producing mountains of grain and twenty years' production achieved in one day. . . ."

All of which was totally new to me. When I looked around me, some people were catching lice, some sewing buttons, some had eyes closed in repose. The scene conjured up the lines:

Last night a great storm raged
I never heard a sound.[1]

Camp Commander Liu continued on about how great things were on our farm, giving percentages of those who resisted remolding, those who were recalcitrant, those who were willing to be reborn and to make new men of themselves, those who loved the farm like their home and wanted to settle here, and so on and so forth. Gradually I began to nod off.

All of a sudden, some words of his pierced my ears like a gimlet: "Certain individuals have had the barefaced audacity to keep a secret diary. . . . If I haven't punished you right away, it's to give you an opportunity to come clean on your own initiative. . . . If you don't come clean, we'll sit back and watch what kind of a show you put on."

Something went *boom* in my head like a sudden outburst of cicada drumming, and I snapped wide awake.

2.

The expression "re-education through labor," and the matters it referred to, was a manifestation of a new society. It originated in 1957, and was without historical precedent (previously there was only "reform through labor"). Before coming in, nobody knew what the "labor re-ed" farms were like. People drafted in from all corners of the land brought with them things that in retrospect were patently ridiculous: two-stringed lutes, accordions, violins, chess sets, ice skates, dumbbells, chest expanders . . . and so on and such like. A painter actually went as far as to bring paint box, easel, and a big roll of canvas, a load too heavy to carry. Some things (like cameras, binoculars, books, and picture albums) were confiscated on entry. Possessions not confiscated were an encumbrance to their holders while they lived, and after their death merely fuel to warm those who were later to follow them to the grave.

I myself brought a pile of books, and part of a diary that I had not handed over during the Anti-Rightist Movement. Its contents were the little passing thoughts of a lover of freedom, still green, still groping his way. For example, "The degree of individual freedom in a society marks the degree of progress of that society," or "My world is so big, a limitless panorama. My world is yet so small, a thousand miles squeezed into a small frame: hard to move a single step"—that kind of thing. There was absolutely no intention to translate these thoughts into action, and in themselves they were beneath notice. But if they fell into other hands, the consequences could be extremely serious. I had no one I could entrust the diary to in that period when rightists were pursued with hue and cry like rats crossing the street; neither was I resigned to burning it, so I kept it on me and ended up bringing it to the farm.

I liked the sound of "farm" for its suggestion of pastoral songs, and thought I would be safe here. I never imagined they would comb through my luggage, and do a body search besides, as soon as I arrived. That fatal diary had fallen into the hands of the disciplinary cadres, along with my cash, drawing tablets, belt, sneaker laces, watch, and problematic books. I suffered nightmares ever after. Every time I saw somebody trussed up and thrown on the ground for some misdemeanor, left there to lie as an awful warning, with black-red blood seeping from where the rope cut into the flesh, I thought my turn would come when one day the business of the diary blew up. Because of the seriousness of the case I would be tied up even tighter and left even longer. Very likely the rope would cut through my muscles, crippling me for life.

When nothing happened for a long time, I worried that an even more horrible fate was being prepared for me behind the scenes. At the evening team meetings, the routine of "declaring your stance" had to be gotten through, and when I declared my support of the Party, support of social-ism, I was always worried that if these declarations were matched against my diary they would constitute the crime of duplicity, and that would be added to my final reckoning.

However, almost a year had passed and nothing out of the ordinary had happened. I could not guess the reason, and was kept wondering. Only now did the penny drop. The explanation was that they were sitting back and watching what kind of a show I put on. I supposed that was the way a cat played with a mouse: the longer the play went on, the more relish it had. Fear is a living thing; it can grow in the fragile and isolated soul and manifest itself in different forms. Momentarily I felt the ground sink beneath my feet. Let alone what was happening outside the camp, even those people around me, busy catching lice, sewing buttons, and dozing, were like phantoms of another world. The voices and smiling visages of my father, mother, and sisters flooded into my mind. I feared I would never see them again.

The midday break started without my noticing the time. There was a buzz of voices; everywhere people were getting up to relieve themselves. The space between the brigades became a thoroughfare; the dust kicked up mingled with the smoke from homemade cigarettes to create a murky haze. The meal was a "taste of better life." The sweet steamed buns and millet gruel reached gastronomic heights previously unheard of on the farm. Despite being famished, I could not relish the food.

3.

Someone called my name. I started and jerked my head around. It was our brigade foreman, Chen Zhibang. Standing beside him was the man who had sung the national anthem. He nodded to Chen and said to me, "Come with me."

I followed him through the crowd and entered the compound behind the big walls and iron gate. Inside the compound there were rows of billets with their doors open, all quite empty. On the end wall at the head of each row were stuck each company's wall posters celebrating National Day and lauding the New China; gaudy and garish, they competed in floridity. He led me quickly past these and entered a billet in the center. Like the other billets it was about 130 square feet in area, most of which was taken up by an earthen sleeping platform, or *kang*. But in other billets the *kang* was packed with a dozen or more sleeping spaces, while on this there was only one set of bedding. Old newspapers were pasted over the other empty bed spaces, making the mud-baked surface very clean. On the inner half of the *kang* were placed bowl and chopsticks, washbasin, thermos, a bundle of clothing, and other such personal items, and in addition a foot-high stack of the *Work Site Express* that we rightist inmates compiled. The stack was exactly squared and securely bound. We received this news sheet at Xintiandun too, one copy a day distributed to each team. Since it was used to roll cigarettes and serve as toilet paper, all issues except the latest one had disappeared.

The rest of the *kang* functioned as a table. On it were some writing utensils, an alarm clock, some paper bags, and a sheet of glass, all set out in orderly fashion. Under the glass were some forms and a four-inch photograph. The photograph was of the singer's wife and two sons. He told me his wife's name was Liu Rong, and that she was the school doctor for Number Four Junior Middle School in Lanzhou. The older boy was called An Tai, aged five; the younger boy was An Shi, now two. He offered me a drink of water, and had me sit on the edge of the *kang* (the table side). He kept his voice low, but at the same time left the door wide open.

His name was An Zhaojun. He had been a historian, researching the history of Xinjiang at the Ethnology Institute. He was in the first batch of rightists interned after Jiabiangou Prison changed to a labor-ed farm, and was appointed foreman of the First Agricultural Brigade. It was very common in the labor reform and labor re-education brigades for inmates to manage inmates. The foremen of our four construction brigades were all undergoing re-education through labor, for example. But they did not serve for very long. I once witnessed the foreman of the Third Brigade, Shangguan Jinwen, being stripped of office on the spot by a disciplinary cadre because he had said the wrong thing. He was hogtied and thrown on the ground.

An Zhaojun, though, had held on to his job. When the disciplinary cadres had too much on their plate, they passed the odd job on to him. One of those jobs was to register under various headings the items that were confiscated. This was supposed to be done by the disciplinary cadres who carried out the searches. Previously their prisoners had been sentenced by the courts, and only one or two came in at a time, so the searching and registering were no sweat. But now they came in droves, and long lines formed day after day, so the cadres had time only to put each person's things in a paper sack with his name on it and leave the registering until later, a task that fell to An. After reading my diary, he did not register it. While helping in the cookhouse one day, he dropped it into the stove and burned it. "I got a lot of pleasure from reading it," he told me, "but there was nowhere safe I could keep it. The only thing was to burn it. Don't fret over it—safety first, don't you agree? People are more valuable than things; if there are people, things will follow, don't you agree?"

"Camp Commander Liu's speech just now frightened the wits out of me," I said.

"Now you can relax," An said. "That was psychological warfare. You have to be on the lookout for it. Once you get rattled, you're lost. Sometimes I've been worried that one day you might get in a funk, lose your grip, and go and confess on your own initiative, own up to the wrong of hiding your diary during the movement. Then I'd be in big trouble. Whenever Chen Zhibang came for a meeting I'd try to find out if the wind was blowing from that direction, but in time I stopped worrying."

"What has he said about me?"

"He's never mentioned you, and that told me all I needed to know. Chen Zhibang is not a bad sort. He was a career policeman, and he knows that gaining merit points does *not* get your sins forgiven, so there is nothing in it for him if other people get to suffer. What you have to look out for is the people who do have the idea that you can wash your slate clean by informing on people. That lot strike up conversations but say nothing for themselves, just want to listen to you. You need to be wary of them."

I said yes to that.

"Well, then," An said, "you reckon you can stick it out?"

"I guess so."

"Reading your diary I found rather too much reliance on ideas and sense perceptions, too little knowledge of real life. Of course, you're still a bit of a kid, aren't you?"

"I'm twenty-two," I said.

"There you are, then. I'm twice your age. I really am concerned about your endurance, you know. The more hopeless the situation, the less the will to resist. Particularly in our case. We're all on our own—no group support, no public opinion to back us up, no sympathy from society. People like us are the most liable to lose heart. I'll tell you some of the things that happen here: a famous actor steals someone's bread roll, a great musician shamelessly pesters you for a scrap of food, a scholar who has picked up two doctorates abroad fights hammer and tongs to scrape the food tub. Such things happen so often that they come to seem normal. As for slapping your own face, ratting on others, never washing your face or combing your hair or mending your clothes, that kind of thing is even more common. They're all evidence of nervous breakdown. The death rate is on the rise, and I reckon nervous breakdown and collapse of will is one cause, along with hunger and exhaustion. You're still young. You have to steel yourself, and steel yourself again, learn to stand rough treatment. Nobody can help you in that—it's all up to you."

He glanced at the alarm clock as he spoke, then stood up and said: "When you go back, you're on your own. Remember, it's not just a matter of staying alive; it's a matter of finding a purpose in staying alive."

I said yes to that, and stood up too. He pointed to that bundle of *Work Site Express* on the corner of the *kang* and said: "You see those sheets all the time. Don't dismiss them as so much waste paper; one day they'll be firsthand historical material, a real treasure. I've kept them carefully; there's not a sheet missing. If you can look to the future, the present takes on meaning, do you see? You step out on a journey, and a path is made where there was none before, do you see? All right, we've no time to talk more today. I'm sorry I haven't been able to hear your views. We have to go back—the speeches will be beginning."

He put out his hand and shook hands with me. His grip was exceptionally strong, exceptionally tight, exceptionally long. It carried a slight tremor. I felt a current of intense heat course from that hand through my whole body.

He relaxed his grip without releasing my hand. "If Chen Zhibang asks you what you've been doing," he said, "say I wanted you to identify a watch, but it wasn't yours. If he doesn't ask you, don't say anything."

"If he asks me why it took so long, what should I say?"

"He won't ask, but if he does, just say no, it didn't take all that long. That will do. Let's go."

I didn't move. "You should think about your own safety. To come across like you have done to a total stranger is too trusting. I'm afraid you run too big a risk."

He put his hand on my shoulder, as if to reassure me and also to hurry me up. "Don't let that concern you. I'm extremely cautious."

As we left, An Zhaojun added, "Don't forget, I've read your diary."

4.

After the National Day celebrations, the sub-farm sent our No. 4 Construction Brigade to help the agricultural brigades get in the autumn harvest. Our small teams were allocated to different strips. After harvesting one strip, we carried the sheaves of millet to the trackside to await collection by the horse carts of the agricultural brigade, and then moved on to our next strip. The track was made for the occasion. A gap was opened in the banks of earth separating the fields, and the ditches were filled in where the carts would cross, so the fields became tracks. After the sheaves were carted away, the banks and ditches were restored and track reverted to field. The soil was loose, the harvest scanty, so the job was easily done, much lighter than the usual digging of drainage ditches. Still, getting up before dawn and being short of food left us very tired. At the sound of the whistle for midday rest, people sat down where they were and napped.

One day while taking my nap, I heard singing. It was the *"Internationale."* The voice was deep and robust, its sound spreading out slowly but stubbornly, like a hot wind hugging the earth's surface:

> *The blood that fills our chests*
> *Has boiled over . . .*

I knew at once that was An Zhaojun singing. I rolled over and sat up. A horse cart was parked on a distant slope, and a bunch of men were scattered about it, either lying or sitting. They had come for the water the cart brought, and were taking their rest then and there. I went over and saw he had his back to the crowd and was lying on his side on a slope, propped up on his elbow. As I neared I saw from the side that tears filled his eyes and glistened on his beard. Fortunately it was a revolutionary song he was singing, so no one smelled a rat; they simply turned a deaf ear.

On seeing me he put a finger to his lips to indicate I shouldn't speak. He patted the ground for me to sit beside him, and put one hand on top of mine. We sat there in silence for a while, not moving. No breath of wind, no speck of green, no whisper of sound under that big sky, on that broad earth. The slanting autumn sun shone on those motionless human beings strewn around as if shining on lifeless rags scattered by the wind. The pale gray horizon was long and straight. For an instant I had the sense of being buried alive, and I too wanted to sing, but did not.

He had come to haul the grain. Once lifted, the grain would blow away if it was not carted away in good time. His partner, sleeping on the cart, yawned, got down, and squatted beside us. He dug a tobacco pouch and two slips of paper from his pocket and began to roll a cigarette, saying all the while, "I hear we're having buckwheat goo this evening, with some spuds."

On the farm, what we were to eat was the main news of the day—the listeners always excited, the teller always proud. An's partner, too, was pleased with himself. When he had finished rolling one cigarette, he nudged An's shoulder with the back of his hand and said, "Here you are, brigade foreman." Without turning his head, An took the roll-up from over his shoulder and started smoking. The man rolled another one, stuck it in his own mouth, and blew perfect smoke rings, one after another, as he looked at the sky through squinted eyes.

That sky was a vast blank.

The whistle to restart work sounded. An shook hands with me, with the same tightness, the same strength, and the same slight tremor as before. Once more that hand sent a wave of intense heat coursing through me.

That was the last time I saw him.

5.

At the beginning of March 1959, I was led away from Jiabiangou by two policemen from the Provincial Public Security Bureau in order to paint for the "Exhibition of Achievements of the First Decade of the People's Republic" in Lanzhou. After that job was finished, I was to be returned to Jiabiangou, but in that intervening year the Jiabiangou Farm was closed because the manpower was depleted by so many deaths there. Left without a "home" to go back to, I was sent to another farm, the Jiahetan labor-reform farm in Jingyuan.

In the summer of 1961 the Gansu Labor Reform Bureau transferred a group of men from the Hongshangen brick kilns to help us with the summer harvest. One of them was a lucky survivor from Jiabiangou, named Liu Wenhan. He had been a soldier, had fought and been wounded in the Korean War, got a commendation, and was afterward assigned to the police force. In '57 he responded to the Party's call to air views without fear or favor, and criticized the Elimination of Counterrevolutionaries Movement for "using a whip meant for tigers to flay sheep." Therefore he was classed as a rightist and sent to Jiabiangou to reform through labor. I learned from him that An Zhaojun was dead.

"God knows why," he said, "just when people were dying every day, the leadership decided to set up another sub-farm. They dispatched over a thousand men to Mingshui district in Gaotai county to open up virgin land. Jiabiangou was left with less than half its workforce. Our work load doubled, our rations cut by nearly half. Originally the rations were set at twelve measures a day; now it dropped to seven, and in reality we got to eat even less than that amount. What work could we do on that, I ask you! The cadres more or less gave up, too. They let us lie on our *kang* until the autumn crop had to be reaped. Every day the burial party was out pulling its flatbed cart around the compound. The people who had died in any billet were dumped outside, and they picked them up. Later on the flatbed cart was not up to the job, and they switched to the big horse cart."

I asked him where An Zhaojun had been: Mingshui or Jiabiangou?

"The latter. If he had been at Mingshui he would have died sooner. An was a funny old devil. He wouldn't face up to reality. Things had already got past the point of no return, but he still had to wash his face and comb his hair every day. He managed to wash by dabbing on a drop of boiled water from his cup. When food was doled out it disappeared down everybody's throat as soon as they got it, but he would find somewhere to sit down and eat. No matter what kind of slop it was, he spooned it up like a proper gent. Unlike the rest of us, he wouldn't lie on the *kang* before nighttime. He would spread something on the ground outside the billet and sit leaning against the wall and looking up at the sky. At times he would sing a little something, *ee-ee woo-woo*, couldn't tell what it was. That's how he died, sitting against the wall."

I asked where An was buried.

"You're joking!" Liu Wenhan said. "Who do you think had the strength to dig a hole? They were just hauled away and dumped in the wasteland. The Lanzhou-Xinjiang rail track is far enough away, well out of sight, but the passengers on the trains got whiffs of the stench, couldn't work out where it came from. When the balloon went up, Beijing said the Gansu Provincial Committee was to blame and sent a work team to sort things out. They began the salvage operation in December '60, and started sending people back where they came from. According to the work team's statistics, the combined population of the camp HQ, Mingshui sub-farm, and Jiabiangou sub-farm at that time was less than eleven hundred men. It wasn't easy to return people, either. Quite a lot had no home to go to by then, and quite a lot had been dismissed from their employment and no units would take them. Another year dragged by before the farms were closed down, in October '61. They say quite a lot more people died in that year, but how many I don't know."

6.

In 1978, twenty years later, rightists were "rehabilitated," got back their name, got back their work. It was called "being restored to one's profession." I profited from that fair wind and went to teach in the philosophy department of Lanzhou University. As soon as I got to Lanzhou I went to look up Liu Rong, An Zhaojun's wife, at Number Four Junior Middle School. She had remarried in 1965, and had left for parts unknown with her two children. Reports had it that she had gone to look for An Zhaojun in 1962, only to find when she got to Jiuquan that even the farm had ceased to exist.

At the end of 1978 I was sent on secondment to the Philosophy Institute of the Chinese Academy of Social Sciences in Beijing. In the three years I was there, I ran into the high tide of the masses pouring into the capital to present petitions. Victims of "unjust, false, and wrong charges" from all over the country crammed the railway station and slept in the streets. They formed long lines through the night at the windows as small as chessboards of the "Office for Receiving Letters and Petitions from the Masses" in the State Council, Ministry of Public Security, and other ministries and commissions, hoping to be granted a modicum of fairness and justice. Another lucky survivor from Jiabiangou, named Zhan Qingyuan, was among them. He had been a worker in the Xinhua Printing House and had been labeled a Bad Element. There was a Party policy at the time of the '57 Anti-Rightist Movement that workers who expressed rightist views were not called rightists but Bad Elements, the reason being that the working class was the revolutionary class, and theoretically there should not be rightists among them. He fell into that category. However, the Bad Element label was not simply designed for rightists: also under that umbrella were people who got into trouble over their womanizing, noncompliance with directions, fighting and causing disturbances, petty thievery. When rightists were rehabilitated, Bad Elements were decidedly not. In this way he lost out. With all doors closed against him locally, Zhan came to Beijing to seek justice.

Disappointingly, what he found was the iron wall of an impregnable bastion of bureaucracy. The paperwork relating to his appeal was rerouted to his original unit for it to deal with. Hearing I was at the Academy of Social Sciences, he came to see if I had any useful ideas. We talked a long time in a small café in Zongbu Lane. He had left Jiabiangou relatively late, returned to his unit by the work team. He said to begin with, the corpses were dumped far away, but as their numbers grew they were dumped nearer, and the final lot of dead men, including An Zhaojun, were dumped about two hundred yards from the headquarters gate, under the first sand ridge.

I returned to Lanzhou University in 1982. One day Yang Zibin, a colleague in my department who taught the history of Chinese philosophy (and was also a restored rightist), came to see me in a fury. He said he was going to protest against the Gansu Provincial Committee's autho-

rizing the Lanzhou Medical College to go to Jiabiangou to disinter complete skeletons for laboratory and teaching purposes. At the outset the
affair had been kept under close wraps, but the man in charge of supplies
at the college had initially agreed to pay piece-rate wages to the local
peasants, only to discover later that they didn't need to do any digging.
They could gather all the skeletons required from under the first sand
ridge in front of the remains of the main gate, which was just one day's
work. The supplies man felt he had made a bad bargain and demanded
the contract be revised, changed to payment according to time worked.
The peasants said he was welshing; he said the peasants were swindling.
With both sides at loggerheads, the secret came out and Yang Zibin got
wind of it. But the protest did not get off the ground, because nobody
was interested in that sort of thing.

It was quite possible that An Zhaojun's was among the skeletons
collected. Yet faced with piles of bones, who could tell hero from slave,
martyr from opportunist, honest man from fraudster, this man from that
man? Even if future forensic archaeologists were to examine genes, how
could they tell in which skeleton "The blood that fills the chest / Has boiled
over?" Let alone the fact that everybody gave up caring long ago.

Those masses of bones without graves had completely passed out of
mind, windblown, sunbaked, grass-entwined, sand-sheathed in the wilderness. They were thought of and uncovered only because a use had been
found for them. Thereupon memos flew, disinfectants steeped, pointers
stabbed, and they were free to be handled like zoological specimens.

At one stroke a history of blood and fire receded to the far horizon,
drowned in the shades of forgetfulness. And all those things that to this
day still nag at us, drain us, things that we hold fast in our memories
and passionately want to put right, have also, at the turn of a hand, been
transmogrified into indecipherable hieroglyphs. No one is interested in
restoring their meaning.

All that is left is these scraps and scintillas of memory scattered on
the four winds: An's protection, his discourse, his handshake, his stern

profile, his burning tears and lonesome song—not forgetting his *Work Site Express*, that pursuit of meaning, that will to challenge absolute zero. Only thanks to these was I able, for all that time when I was bereft of companionship and meat under a butcher's knife, to understand what is meant by the term "mother country." I got a sense of my connection with it, and my connection with history, with this entire culture and humankind. Never mind how tenuous or illusory—even the product of my imagination—this connection was, to a slave under the yoke it was the whole meaning of existence.

More than forty years have passed in a flash. I wonder where his sons, An Tai and An Shi, are now? Do they still remember their father? If nothing untoward has happened, they would be in their forties now. I wish them well from the bottom of my heart. They should know that their father was a man to be proud of, a true man.

ELEVEN

By Pale Moonlight

I had two chance encounters in Jiabiangou that I'll never forget.

The first was when I went to collect a postal parcel.

One day each month, they distributed these parcels at the farm headquarters. If a parcel had come for you, your name was written on a little blackboard, and if you saw your name when you came back from working, you could collect your parcel in the gap between the evening meal and the study session. The line was long; the parcel had to be inspected, so you had a long wait and were usually late for the study session, but that wasn't counted against you.

On the day in question, I had a parcel and joined many others along the wall outside the HQ office waiting for our names to be called. Some of us squatted, some sat, none spoke. Some dozed, some did some mending while the light lasted, some got together in small groups to smoke homemade cigarettes. As for me, I just sat there waiting, doing nothing. A late autumn wind gusted over the bare dry ground, sending dust and rubbish swirling dispiritedly. Sometimes an eddy would pass through the crowd of men, leaving a layer of dust on them.

An old bloke, probably in his fifties, wearing a beat-up army cap, was sitting beside me. The peak of his cap had crumpled and hung over his forehead. His gray beard was dirty and the big bags under his eyes sagged low and empty: a very picture of debility. He kept his mouth sewn tight. Time and again he looked at his hands, which were crazed with cracks, like pictographs. After it got dark he finally spoke to me: "What's your name?" I told him. "I've seen that name somewhere," he said. "Did you publish an article called 'On Beauty' in *New Construction*?" I admitted that I had. "The article had a fresh viewpoint, but fuzzy concepts and loose logic," he said. Then he told me that it didn't rate as a scientific paper— he'd read it only as a work of art. He even quoted some examples. I was amazed at how good his memory was, and how nimble his brain.

I asked, "Is aesthetics your line?"

"No, not at all, I'm just an amateur. I'm the curious type. I take an interest in everything, read a whole ragbag of things." He then told me he was a linguist by profession, and knew quite a lot of languages. The language he liked most was actually Tibetan. He said the expressive capability of Tibetan was in no way inferior to that of Chinese. The Tibetan translations of the Sanskrit sutras, and Kalidasa's works, and Tagore's poems in English as well, were all better than the Chinese translations.[1] They got the meaning over better, and captured the spirit. All kinds of ancient Tibetan works written in Tibetan, including the doctrines of the primitive Bon religion, could not really be appreciated in their depth and subtlety if you didn't understand Tibetan. I asked what Bing Xin's and Zheng Zhenduo's translations of Tagore were like. The old man said, "All right, but still a lot is lost. Poetry can't be paraphrased, Tagore's least of all."

He said Tagore had written a book, also called *On Beauty*, and asked me if I had read it. I said I didn't know English. "You should learn," he said. "You need to start early to learn a foreign language; it gets very hard when you are old." He went on to explain that book of Tagore's to me in great detail, but sadly I have forgotten what he said. I was not then what I had been; my interest in that field had waned. Rough and hard reality had buffed off a layer of tender skin, abraded my sensitive feelers, and made me, too, rough and hard. What I wanted was not the mirage and magic of poetry and beauty, but sufficient food, rest, and sleep. For me it was now fire and sword, barbaric yells, wild storms to rend the heavens and lift the lid off the earth. All dreamers, debaters, sentimentalists, and aesthetes, including my former self, were characters of another world. On this lifeless land, amid these loveless people, I was not entertained by a feeble old man discussing that other world.

Listening inattentively, looking at him inattentively, I had the vague feeling in the darkness that his intonation, his countenance, bore some tangential resemblance to my father's. Opposite us, the mud huts' walls were smeared with the sheen of pale moonlight, so pale it would have been invisible but for the contrast with the half of the walls that was in shadow. Nevertheless, the shine brought out the bleak chill of the row upon row of mud huts, terribly desolate, like empty buildings discarded and forgotten by the world. The space between the huts was a borderless wasteland, obscured and blurred like a sea of mist. That man's hoary, hoarse, yet ardent discourse sounded like this moonlight—dim, unreal, and distant as well.

Suddenly my name was called in the office. I jumped up and hurried inside. The parcel was thermal clothing from my mother, with a letter enclosed. By the time the disciplinary cadre had finished scrutinizing every item, it was a jumbled heap. Having no time to repack it, I scooped it all up and ran back to my billet, forgetting to acknowledge that old chap whose name I didn't know. It wasn't until the next day that I realized my discourtesy, which surely would have been hurtful to him. I could only hope for another opportunity to meet, when I could apologize and listen to him hold forth. But afterward conditions on the farm became more and more dire, young men weakened by the day, the old and frail died in droves, and this hope receded further and further.

The other unforgettable chance encounter occurred at the time of the summer harvest, a particularly hectic period in farming life. In the hurry to get the ripened grain in from the fields for threshing, all hands in country villages—men and women, old and young alike—set to and work day and night. The four brigades of our sub-farm were construction brigades, but at harvest time we all had to support the agricultural brigades of the base farm. It was a rush job that required work around the clock. The head of the sub-farm said in his mobilization speech: "The broad popular masses on the outside are engaged in the Great Leap Forward, not an inch of ground goes unplanted by the red flag, and every minute is fought for to carry forward the revolution. Many, many people take no sleep, battle on for days and nights on end. You need to atone for your wrongs with good deeds; there's no way you're going to exert yourselves less than the popular masses, is there?"

The farm's wheat fields were not very different from uncultivated land. The wheat grew small and straggly, in many places not at all. Many of the plants did not develop ears. No matter whether they had ears or not, our task was to pull them up, roots and all, bind them into sheaves, and carry them to the trackside for the horse carts of the agricultural brigades to haul away. There was no way to control progress. Sometimes a big field only required going through the motions; at other times you advanced inch by inch. Sometimes as you advanced you met up with another construction brigade and worked alongside them for a stretch, then split up again. We were not acquainted, yet were not strangers, either. But such casual encounters held little interest for us.

The sandy soil was loose, so it was easy to pull the stalks up and one shake would clear the roots of dirt. But you were weary from lack of sleep, and crouching for long periods made your back and knees ache painfully. To get some relief, you could kneel down and crawl forward. That required less effort, but then you would fall behind, so after crawling a bit you had to get up again and catch up by crouching for the next stretch. All that was hard to put up with, but it had its compensation: you could eat the wheat on the sly. You rubbed the grains you had dislodged from the ear in the palm of your hand, blew away the husks, and popped them in your mouth: a stolen pleasure. Everybody was hungry, everybody stole, so no one informed, just turned a blind eye. In this way an invisible bond seemed to be made between individuals who were separate, isolated, and opposed, which was also a pleasing thing.

The trouble was, if you ate uncooked wheat you would get the runs. For those few days, diarrhea was widespread. The farm had a good number of rightist doctors, who labored along with us. Only two were lucky enough to be assigned to the clinic and were authorized to see patients and dispense medicine. During the summer harvest they ran around the work site, medicine box over shoulder, going all night like us, and like us dog-tired. A lot of people to see to, a lot of ground to cover, attend to this one, miss that one. So your turn might not come around. If it did, you got some Terramycin pills, which were very effective.[2]

On the night in question our brigade joined up with another brigade on a rise in the ground, and sat resting at the edge of the field before transferring to our next site. Up came a doctor. We all swarmed over. He gave four prewrapped Terramycin pills to each one. Some men thought this was not enough and lined up again for another lot. The doctor couldn't remember who was who, and came across again. I thought I would follow suit and was about to stand up when a stranger next to me put his hand on my shoulder, saying this Terramycin was not good for you in large doses. He added, "I'm a doctor—you have to trust me."

I couldn't tell his age in the moonlight. I just had the impression of thick hair, full lips, and spectacles for extreme shortsightedness, like a bookworm's. When I took his advice and did not move, it seemed to give him a good opinion of me. He repeated, "I'm not having you on." That expression also reminded me of a bookworm.

He told me all mycin-type drugs were harmful. They killed not only invasive bacteria but also the body's own beneficial bacteria. He said that without the help of these beneficial bacteria, we could not fully digest food. In fact, as an indispensable component of our digestive organs, these bacteria were effectively part of our body. "This is like legume roots," he said. "Have you seen all those nodules on the roots of legumes? Those are made by nodule bacteria, but they're also the organ the plant uses to synthesize nutrients." He was confident, he told me, that every part of our body contained bacteria that were symbiotic with us. He suspected that our body, even our every cell, was no more than a composite of all kinds of microorganisms. "The activity of our cerebrum, our thoughts and feelings, is the resultant force produced by the combined action of many microorganisms."

He said he was shocked and dismayed to be told when he was small that over 70 percent of our body was made up of water, because that was not "me." The sight of a skeleton scared and disgusted him—he simply wouldn't believe it when told there was such a thing in his own body! It was only after he had gone to medical school and joined a research institute that he discovered that "me" was the summation of those things. Whether there was a "me" after all was a genuine question. He said that after he got out, he would definitely clear up that question.

Listening to this frightening and depressing discourse in the depths of the night in that wasteland, in that deep remoteness, with a hazy moon above and the Milky Way trailing down to Earth, I was profoundly shaken. But since I knew nothing, there was nothing I could say. We went our separate ways when the whistle sounded, and never met again. The questions he raised troubled me for a long time. Every time I thought of them, I thought of him. His surname was Yan, written with a character I didn't know. I concentrated so hard on remembering it that his first name slipped my mind, and I can't think of it for the life of me.

In the latter stage of the Cultural Revolution I was laboring in a May 7th Cadre School in the Jiuquan district when I heard about a survivor from Jiabiangou, then a clinic doctor in Subei Mongol Autonomous County, having been beaten to death in the course of the Cultural Revolution. He had this same rare surname, so I tend to think that could well have been him.

Thirty-nine years later, in the snowy winter of 1995, I saw a book in the Manchester Library of the University of New Hampshire in the United States that reviewed the scientific achievements of the past decade. It said that the mitochondria of cells in the human body were actually primitive bacteria which long ago penetrated our eukaryotes and remained inside. Together with many other microorganisms that reside in our body, they live according to their own fashion and reproduce according to their own DNA and RNA, which is different from ours. They drive the functioning of our cells, making it possible for our cells to use oxygen, enabling us to move and think. We cannot do without them. It is even said that our own DNA comes from the code of these symbionts. That is to say, even our genes were constructed from the coordinated mechanisms ordered by all these information sources. . . . The author of this book, the biologist Lewis Thomas, fellow of the American Academy of Sciences, makes the sweeping statement that our cells actually are an ecological system more complex than that of Jamaica Bay. In that case, I just hope they work for me, feel what I feel, think what I think!

Placing my fist on the book, I, or this ecological system called me, lean back in my chair and muse. This world has surely been too unfair to that doctor I once met on a moonlit night in the middle of nowhere.

TWELVE

The Blue Coat

Pe020le who live on saline-alkali soil are especially prone to haggardness, raggedness, and premature aging. Skin exposed to an alkaline wind will dry; feet immersed in alkaline water will chap; clothes covered with alkaline dust will fade and rot. After having stewed here for some time, we who had come from all corners of the country—and whether old, young, or middle-aged—could not be told one from the other. Among that grayish mass of humanity, it was obvious at a glance who was a newly arrived inmate: his clothes were comparatively in one piece and their colors distinct.

But there was an exception. Long Qingzhong, who belonged to the Fourth Team of the Third Company of the First Brigade, qualified as an old lag, but one garment of his had kept the brightness it had when he first came. Seen from a distance, it flashed against the gray and gooey background of the work site and was very eye-catching. He cared for that garment far more dearly than he cared for himself, and had become famous for that reason.

Long was by no means a slacker, but excessive concern for his clothes inevitably had an influence on his work, and he came in for his fair share of criticism at team meetings. Since he refused to change his ways, he had been brought up before company and brigade meetings. Camp

Commander Liu had actually referred to Long Qingzhong by name in one speech, asking if he had come to labor or to find a sweetheart. This quip was rewarded with weak laughter: In Commander Liu's mouth it did not rate as criticism. Indeed Liu went on to commend him, because while letters were being censored it was found that Long wrote to his mother that life on the farm was fine, and that he was very happy here. Commander Liu said this was loving the farm like one's home, and proved Long had made progress in his thought reform. Given these words of praise, there was no way they could get at him at team level.

I once ran into Long during a "reclamation challenge." This was a means of raising labor productivity. The camp headquarters marked out a big area of wasteland as the arena and sprinkled lime to mark out sixteen strips like runways side by side, each as broad as a highway and about 330 yards long. Each team deputized someone to till the soil, one man to a strip, all starting off together, to see who got to the end first. The competition was intense, but there were no spectators apart from a few disciplinary cadres. Everyone else was off digging ditches to drain the alkali in another work site. Every day the "Reports from the Battlefield" were published in the *Work Site Express*, and honors went to whichever team was out in front. The reward for the individuals concerned was more work and harder work—they sent you out again the next day.

Long wore glasses for extreme near sightedness and was as thin as a rake: he supported that eye-catching blue coat of his like a coat hanger. The bottom hung floppy, open to the wind. I said that problem would be solved if he tied a rope around his waist. He would have none of that: he said it was double-sided khaki cloth which would not take any rubbing. Any kind of rubbing left a white mark, so of course it could never stand up to being tied with a rope! As he spoke he pointed out one by one the patches on the cuff, shoulder, and elbow that were already white through having been rubbed. He was very distressed, and stroked those white marks as if they were wounds. His sleeves came down over his hands and got in the way for working, so he had to turn back the cuffs, exposing two rings of snow white wool. When sand fell on the wool it could not be brushed off: the more you brushed it, the deeper it got embedded. He kept taking off his glasses, and with his eyes glued to the wool, doggedly searched for the foreign bodies in it. He did not lie down in rest periods, just dozed sitting up. I watched him as I lay. His very thin neck, his deeply sunken cheeks, his drooping chin and open mouth, all bespoke an extreme degree of weakness and weariness. But he obstinately insisted on sitting up and could not be persuaded to lie down: the coat was the important thing.

If I slept, Long made not the slightest sound; when I could not get off to sleep, he was quite happy to talk to me. He had a slight stutter, but he took his time, pausing every now and again. It was hard to say if he believed I would keep on listening or if he did not care if I listened or not. He was an only son who had lost his father in childhood. In her widowhood his mother went through untold hardships to bring him up and pay for his schooling, right through university. His subject was biology, and after graduating he was assigned to the Lanzhou branch of the Chinese Academy of Sciences. He was often sent on field trips to study parasites on the plains. When back in his institute, it was a routine of eating in canteens and living in a collective dormitory; he was unmarried, though pushing thirty. He was bent on getting his mother to Lanzhou from their old home in Hebei, so that they could look after each other.

His mother's registered domicile was a farming village, and the system stipulated that she could not live in a city. Unworldly bookworm that he was, Long could not see the sense in that, and went about grumbling and showing his dissatisfaction. Then again, he was homesick, and he requested to be transferred back to Hebei. At that time the state was opening up the Northwest, and transfer of domicile from west to east was kept under clamps. Besides that, individuals had to submit to the needs of their unit. The leadership told him, "The Party and the state had a hard time training you: so much blood and sweat has been expended on you, yet at the end of the day you think only of your personal interest. Aren't you ashamed?" He had no answer to that, but still was not reconciled and continued to complain.

In the Anti-Rightist Movement his unit could not put together enough rightists to meet the quota, so they put his name on the list. Once the condemnation procedures were completed, he was shipped off to Jiabiangou. He did not dare tell his mother, and lied to her for the first time in his life. He told her that this field trip to the countryside might last quite a long time, and she should not worry herself. Just before he left, he received a parcel from his mother that contained the blue coat that made him so famous on the farm. It was old-fashioned, baggy, and not form-fitting, but as durable as could be. His mother had made it with her own hands. Her eyesight was bad and her fingers stiff, so the stitches were not very even, but they were doubled and redoubled, so the seams were tight and firm.

I was specially moved by his story because I too missed my mother. At the end of the "reclamation challenge," I had no more contact with Long, but I often thought of him. At that time people in Jiabiangou were falling down dead one after another. As his physique was frailer than other people's, I was worried that he would not be able to hold up, and consequently found myself looking more than usual over to where the First Brigade was working on the work site. When I saw the flash of that blue coat among the gray mass of humanity I was momentarily consoled. I believed it was mother's love that gave him the strength to survive. I think love is a force stronger than death.

One day the next year, at the turn of winter into spring, I went to the clinic to get a bandage changed, and passing through the basketball court in the dark, saw Long walking ahead of me. The surprising thing was, he had a rope tied around his waist. So at last he had come to his senses! I was very pleased and hurried to catch up with him. When he turned his head, I saw it was someone else wearing that blue coat. That man told me that Long Qingzhong was long dead, and the persons who took over the coat from him were dead along with him. By the time the coat had come into his hands, it had already changed owners several times.

THIRTEEN

Deaths of Soldiers

SHANGGUAN JINWEN

A rather unusual incident took place on the work site one day. The foreman of the Third Brigade, Shangguan Jinwen by name, was stripped of office on the spot by disciplinary cadre Officer Han, ordered to be bound, and thrown down on the ground.

Shangguan was an odd sort of character. He dressed in full military uniform, grass green in color, neither ragged nor dirty. Though only about fifty years old, he sported a beard and long drooping moustaches, like Ho Chi-Minh's. He had been a high-ranking officer in the People's Liberation Army before coming to the camp. How high he was, and how he had offended, I don't know; I just heard he had been on the 1,550-mile Long March and had been garrison commander at the PLA headquarters. When criticizing others he was apt to use Lenin's saying that immorality in private life was equivalent to immorality in political life, thus giving rise to the suspicion that he himself had come a cropper in connection with personal conduct. It must have been due to writing repeated confessions of behavioral problems that he elevated them to such a level, people thought. Another view was that he had taken poisoned bait—someone must have set him up—otherwise behavioral issues would have been no problem to someone of that stamp.

He had started to grow that beard of his on the day he came in, and declared he would not shave it off until he got out. As it grew he took on a grandfatherly look, rather stately, rather benevolent—in odd contrast to his military uniform. The disciplinary cadres also marked him out for special treatment, allowing him a fair amount of latitude and appointing him, to boot, foreman of the Third Brigade on our Xintiandun sub-farm. The Third Brigade was close by our Fourth Brigade: our billets were neighboring, on morning work parade our ranks were neighboring, and on the work site the sections we worked were usually neighboring too. We could often hear that voice of his, ringing with authority. In style and bearing he did indeed typify the brass hat. To lecture to long lines of men was his business; it came easily to him, and in lecturing, he was in his element. He was not a martinet, neither was he brutal; he just showed off, wanted face, liked to hear his own voice. Lecturing was what he enjoyed.

On the morning in question the ditches had frozen over, and we were all barefoot in the icy water shoveling mud. A lot of men in the Third Brigade were hanging back, afraid of getting their feet frozen. Shangguan demanded that they "stop acting like pansies." "In the old days," he said, "our Red Army had things a lot tougher than this on the Long March. No matter whether you were sick or wounded, you climbed snow-capped mountains and trekked over rough plains along with the rest, just taking them in your stride. If we were like you lot now, the revolution could not have been victorious. . . ."

Officer Han, squatting in our section, had been listening to all this, toothpick between his teeth, his ear cocked. He lifted his chin and called over: "Shangguan Jinwen, what's all this crap you're talking?" He paused, then continued. "It's no use telling others to get down into the water while you keep your boots and socks on yourself."

Because Shangguan was put to shame, he replied out of turn, delivering the riposte: "Haven't you got your boots and socks on, too?"

Officer Han removed his toothpick and slowly got to his feet. As he walked across, he said, "Tie this fellow up for me!"

The words were hardly out of his mouth before several Third Brigade men rushed forward to spring on Shangguan and force him to his knees. Others sprinted so fast to fetch rope that they ran out of breath. They tied Shangguan's hands behind him, crisscrossed the rope over his back, then tightened the rope knotted over his shoulders until it cut into his flesh. He squealed like a pig being slaughtered, an inhuman sound. His second cry was stopped in his throat before it could come quite out, and became a rasping *krr, krr, krr*. . . . The throttling turned his face the color of pig's liver, and the veins on his forehead and neck stood out like worms.

By this time Officer Han was squatting in Third Brigade's section, his toothpick once more between his teeth. He said: "We give you a little bit of importance and you get above yourself. You even forget who you are now!" Turning to address the body of men, he said: "Now listen up! Don't let this man give you the wrong ideas. Your problem is not whether or not you're pansies, not whether or not you're revolutionary. Your problem is whether or not you admit to yourself you've done wrong, whether or not you submit to correction." As he spoke, his toothpick joggled up and down in the corner of his mouth.

All the Third Brigade people were already down in the ditch by now. Someone standing in the water started up the chanting: "No reversing the verdict for class enemies!" "No shooting their mouths off, no getting out of line!" "Long live the people's democratic dictatorship!" "Long live the Communist Party!" "Long live Chairman Mao!" . . . The whole brigade took up the chants, thin arms stretched skyward in wave after wave, veins bulged on scrawny necks. Scarecrows though they were, the potency of so many voices raised in unison was still overpowering. Shangguan lay facedown on the ground, not moving a muscle. One foot was immersed in the icy water, complete with boot and sock, and his cotton-padded trousers were soaked halfway up one leg.

There was no telling whether Officer Han had handed out this punishment on the spur of the moment or the camp command had planned for it. At any rate, Shangguan Jinwen ceased to be brigade foreman and started to work as one of us. Because he could not stand up to the strain of laboring all day, he was subjected to a lot of goading on the work site. He got progressively weaker, cut his beard off, and left his face and hands unwashed. That imposing uniform of his got more and more tattered, and through the cumulative effect of mire and alkali, became indistinguishable in color, a nondescript dreary gray, like everyone else's clothing. One night after the small-team study session, he keeled over before undressing for bed.

GUO YONGHUAI

Shangguan Jinwen was not the only one on the farm to wear military uniform. There were two others, both in our First Team, Fourth Company, Fourth Brigade. One was called Guo Yonghuai, around thirty years old, short and slight of build, his face small too, very like the Qin dynasty general Bai Qi, who is described in Sima Qian's *Records of the Historian* as having a "small head and sharp face." His skin was dark with a yellowish tinge, and the whites of his eyes and his teeth were yellowish too. The yellowness was not the greenish yellow of jaundice but the coffee-tinted yellow of sandalwood. You got the impression from that that he was a tough nut, which in fact he was. He had fought in Korea, been wounded, and had the scars to prove it, like a hero's medals.

Guo was always the first to get up when the morning whistle blew, moving swiftly and nimbly. By the time we got dressed and lined up for grub, he was there ahead of us, waiting. It was the same story at the work site. At the end of every rest period he always bounced up at the first shrill of the whistle, and before you had dusted off the seat of your pants he was already holding shoulder pole and rope, waiting for you to go and carry baskets with him. When we were required to paddle in brine he paddled the longest, with the result that the maze of cracks in the skin of his feet were both denser and deeper than anybody else's. When we needed to plunge into icy water, he was the first to get his boots and socks off, forcing everyone to follow closely after him. These and umpteen other similar things did not endear him to us—in fact they made him hated.

In the farm system, we labored during the day and met to "study" in the evening. The latter involved mutual supervision and mutual criticism: "planting the red flag, uprooting the white flag, chopping down the black flag." The day's performance of every one of us was evaluated by the team as a whole. Generally speaking, the slackers, humbugs, and artful dodgers of the daytime were the most active and energetic speakers of the evening. They observed others most minutely, criticized others most severely. They could not fault Guo Yonghuai, but they never had a word of praise for him. The same was true of our team leader, Chen Hegen; by saying nothing he completely devalued all of Guo's efforts. Guo seemed not to let that bother him. In the evening he said nothing; in the daytime he labored for all his worth. He carried needle and thread with him and devoted the rest periods to repairing his clothes and footwear. His worn military uniform was full of patches, but it had no holes and was not dirty. Turned out so smartly, he looked even more like someone to be reckoned with.

Our team had three Bad Elements, namely Zhou Daofu, Wei Tingsong, and Lu Hongnian. They were outstanding in getting up to artful dodges, outstanding in making clever speeches, and outstanding in loathing and detesting Guo Yonghuai. Gradually an unspoken conspiracy formed among the majority of our team, with them at its core, to give him what for. Whoever filled the baskets filled his to overflowing. We all took turns carrying with him. Since he was short, he supported the front end of the shoulder pole, and the person behind always moved the basket rope up to his end, thus making him bear most of the weight. His slight frame swayed so much he could hardly keep on his feet, but in spite of that the one behind pushed him into a run. If he fell over on a slope, they chivvied him to get up so as not to hold up operations. Fortunately there were disciplinary cadres regularly patrolling the work site, so those people had to be circumspect and bide their time; otherwise there was no way Guo could have stood up to such treatment very long.

At the evening meetings they condemned Guo with one voice as a "sham activist," saying that when there were disciplinary cadres around he slaved away, but as soon as they left he loafed on the job. . . . He listened quietly to such recriminations, looking from one person to another, not saying a word. When the team leader told him to say his piece, he simply said he wasn't like that. Being unable to make an argument or to produce evidence, he only drew forth a stream of rebuttals and sanctimonious new accusations. This onslaught left him tongue-tied, but he didn't seem overly perturbed. The next day he worked flat-out as usual. No matter how hard you tried to grind him down, he rose to the challenge. He neither pleaded nor threw his hand in. Luckily he did not accuse anybody of anything in return, giving no handle to use against him, so the thing fizzled out. It was like treading on a stubborn pebble: regardless how hard you tread on it, you can't crush it, so you give up.

But if you didn't tread on him, he would tread on himself. As the old sage Zhuangzi said, "The trees on the mountain fell themselves, the spring steals its own water."[1] At that time, being hungry, tired, and short of sleep, every man's priority was to harbor his strength, whereas Guo exerted himself to an unbelievable degree. I was careful to keep clear of him, and when sometimes I had to partner with him, I was always busy thinking of ways to prevent him from dragging me into working until I dropped. For example, when we teamed up to carry baskets and there was a long way from where we filled a basket to where we emptied it, I always insisted that after emptying the soil, one of us should take back the shoulder pole, the other the basket. In that way I could take advantage of strolling back with an empty basket on my shoulder to have a breather. He could rush all he liked—he still had to wait until I arrived. He knew I was slacking, but he never said anything.

One day he could not hold himself back. He fell in with my slow pace, saying, "Friend Gao, we don't come here to play games, you know."

I anticipated what he was going to say by getting in quick with "I can't match your fitness."

"The shoe's on the other foot. I can't match *your* fitness, or anybody else's, come to that. My mum and dad died when I was little. I was a bare-arsed kid herding other people's cattle. All I had to look forward to every day was husks and greens—now, how can someone who grew up eating husks and greens match those who grew up on rice! Besides, you'd only be about twenty. I'm more than ten years older than you!"

"Therefore you need to look after yourself better."

"Working hard is exactly my way of looking after myself. See, it's the same as fighting in a war: the more scared you are of dying, the more likely you are to die. I've been in a war, and I've seen that loads of times."

Before I could work out what to reply, he went on: "All right, take the case of jumping down into the icy water. Afraid or not, you have to jump. If you're not afraid, it's not so painful. The more you fear, the more painful it is. The more you fear, the less you can stand it. Don't you agree?"

I thought for a while, and conceded he was right.

Nevertheless, he was still not able to stand up to the strain. While he was carrying a basket one cold, bright day in early spring, he suddenly dropped dead. Those who carried him away said they couldn't believe how little he weighed.

ZHANG YUANQIN

In contrast to Guo Yonghuai, Zhang Yuanqin was a strapping fellow. I am five foot ten, which was above average in our lineup. Zhang was at least half a head taller than me. He had broad shoulders, a massive chest, narrow waist, long legs, and big hands and feet: the very image of a Greek statue. He did not come in until the summer of '58, by which time we were very feeble, while he was extremely big and strong. Given his military uniform and giant size, he inspired us with awe.

Since he wouldn't have been much more than twenty, he could have been a new recruit. Or maybe not yet twenty, because there was a certain boyishness about his face, especially his mouth, which took on a lozenge shape, just like a child's. He had a strong chin, and a long and straight nose that went right up to meet his broad forehead. His "sword" eyebrows slanted upward and outward, the whites of his big eyes were clear, the eyes simple yet alert, the spirit of heroism showing through the childishness.

He was completely illiterate. "Watch out I don't give you a whacking!" was always ready on his lips, his voice like a bell. When you heard this pet phrase of his and looked at his great fists, you couldn't help shaking in your shoes. On the other hand he was a very fine singer. His voice was deep and penetrating, as if he had done exercises in resonance. I guessed he had belonged to an army entertainment troupe, but he had not. Neither had he done any voice training. He was in the engineers, and ever since joining up he had been in Tibet, building roads through the mountains.

Singing was not forbidden on the farm, but what singing there was, was restricted to the ritual passing of the song from brigade to brigade when all had assembled for a meeting. The old unchanging tunes sung at every mass rally since Liberation were transferred bodily to the farm. But outside that setting, joining in song was regarded as an "irregular situation." Full-throated singing by an individual was also prohibited: Have you gotten carried away? Are you staging a demonstration, or what? After Zhang Yuanqin had been sat on a few times like that for his love of singing, he did not dare to sing out loud on the work site, but he still often sang softly, especially when he got back to the billet after a day's work—then he never stopped. He sang as he lay on his bed with his hands cushioning his head; he sang half propped up against the wall looking up at the roof; he sang when he was sewing; he sang when he was rubbing the maze of cracks on his feet caused by their steeping in brine.

I don't know why, but those hackneyed old revolutionary songs took on a new charm when he sang them:

> *Er-yoo-oo Erlang Mountain*
> *High-yoo-oo a whole mile high*
> *Paths twisting-haa the going hard*
> *Giant boulders on the heights . . .*

Between the evening meal and the evening study meeting, a dozen men sat around in the gathering gloom listening, all affected by those plangent notes. No one spoke; no one even coughed loudly. When Chai Hegen eventually lit the little oil lamp and declared the meeting open, you could see with the aid of that lamplight the afterwaves of Zhang's song still rippling on the clouded faces: its sadness, its desolation, its longing for unattainable happiness.

At that time, "re-education through labor" had no set term. The story was that you got out whenever you were said to be reformed: if you were reformed by tomorrow, you got out tomorrow; if you failed to reform, you were there for a lifetime. Zhang Yuanqin took the promise as gospel. He did not know what was meant by being reformed, but he was desperate to get out, so he simply toiled like a slave. Being set among the half-dead, with his strength, he could do the work of ten men. As he worked he sang to himself:

> *Red Army men*
> *Men like iron*
> *Minds made up*
> *To go to Tibet*

In time with the singing, great shovelfuls of earth flew in salvos from the depths of the drainage ditches onto both banks. We all looked on coldly. The disciplinary cadres also looked on coldly. Working flat out was a show commonly put on by new arrivals, and everyone knew it couldn't last. What was surprising was that Zhang Yuanqin—this giant, this iron man—collapsed the quickest of all. It bore out the saying of Jack London: the hulks are the first to die. Actually there is nothing odd about that, for a goose can survive on a tuft of grass, but an ox certainly cannot. Existing on the same diet as the rest, he hungered sooner and wilted quicker than any of his workmates.

His singing tailed off and he started to loaf on the job. His way of loafing was very crude: simply to stand still. In the lingo of the camp, someone standing still was called a "telegraph pole." "Pulling up telegraph poles" was a lesson regularly read on the work site and was a standby for discussion at the evening team meetings, so standing still was the ploy least likely to succeed. He was hectored all day long, to the point that the chant of the basket carriers also taunted him:

> *Zhang Yuanqin-o*
> *hai-hai*
> *telegraph pole-o*
> *hai-hai.*

Stuck for any better idea, he resorted to going for a pee or a crap every five minutes. He went a long way off, stood or squatted for a long time, and walked back very slowly. This was a common practice for taking it easy, used with one accord by all. I myself used it every day. But we used it in moderation. Frequency, distance, duration, all had a limit. Just as the ancient sage Zhuangzi said, "If you would do ill, do not court punishment." Zhang did not understand the wisdom of the proverb "Draw on a stream sparingly and it will not dry up." Instead he itched to "kill the chicken to get at the eggs," so he immediately attracted notice.

The men of Jiabiangou were especially adept at "struggling against bad people and bad things." This was a sign that one had "reformed." Despite their being bags of bones, being dog-tired, being slow in movement and dull of expression, this facility was particularly highly developed. You might think nobody is up to a little dodge of yours, not even the fairies or pixies, but at the evening meeting everybody brings it up. This was a skill tempered in the crucible of long-term "reforming." It was not something that Zhang Yuanqin, a newcomer still wet behind the ears, could learn by osmosis. As he stood with his back to the work site, holding something in his hand, still as a statue, all eyes were focused on his back. One person noted down the time taken, while another, pretending to relieve himself, too, followed in his tracks to separate fact from fiction. Zhang was completely in the dark about all this surveillance, never even dreamed it was going on. After a while he thought it would have been forgotten that he had only just come back, and went off again.

Jiabiangou had a mimeographed newspaper called *Work Site Express*. It was run by the inmates, with the support of the camp HQ. One sheet a day, octavo size. It praised good people and good things, exposed and criticized bad people and bad things. In the end Zhang Yuanqin's name got into the paper, under the heading of "Resisting Labor." It published a concrete record of his respective excretions on a given day, giving frequency and duration. He did not appreciate what a serious business it was to become a byword in that way. When the *Work Site Express* was read out to him at the evening meeting, his eyes widened. He said, "It's the first time I've heard of not being allowed to go for a crap or a piss!"

Since he got no reply, he thought he had won the point. He answered in the same words when Officer Han gave him a dressing-down on the work site the next day. Han duly ordered him to be hogtied. Hogtying was a common enough thing on the farm for him to have seen it done, and he was very frightened. On hearing the order, Zhang's face went white, his mouth dropped open, and his eyes popped. Terror and pleading shone from eyes that darted about looking for help.

To this day I cannot understand how come those inmates who vied to carry out the task of hogtying Zhang—not having been taught how to do it, and being mostly office workers and half starved into the bargain—were so professional, so practiced, so nimble, so strong. Anyway, the rope was pulled so tight it sank into his flesh, and bright red blood oozed out straight away. Slowly it soaked the rope, and his clothing next to the rope. When at last they tore off the rope and stripped off his clothes, his swollen and bruised arms and the back of his hands had all turned a grayish white. He cried like a baby. Fortunately the camp doctor (himself an inmate) knew what he was about, and he saved the flesh from necrotizing. After some weeks Zhang was on the road to recovery.

When autumn came he received a parcel from his home in Shandong. It contained a cotton-padded vest, a pair of lined cotton mittens, and a pair of lined cotton socks. There was no cover letter. One postal parcel per month was allowed on the farm, to be collected always in the interval between the evening meal and the meeting that followed. The meeting had already started by the time he got back, and he didn't dare open his parcel. He placed it on his knees and first of all probed and felt it through the cloth wrapping, then set about pulling a corner of each item out through the hole made by the mail inspector to get a look at it. Though nothing could be seen properly because the light of the oil lamp was so feeble, he still tried. When that failed he rubbed the material between his knobby-jointed fingers; after rubbing one item he stuffed it back in and pulled out another. He kept this up until the meeting ended, when he quickly opened the parcel, shook out the contents, and turned them over and over to inspect them. He put them by his pillow when he went to bed, and kept touching them with his big, bony, chapped hand.

My bed space was right up against his. From his side I could catch the smell of new cotton, a country smell, a home smell, a smell that gave rise to many memories associated with my boyhood. As I was on the point of dozing off, I felt through my quilt that his back was trembling. The trembling grew more violent, and I heard that he was crying, the sound muffled by his burying his head in his bedding. Gradually his crying got louder, exactly like the wailing of a child. Someone in the darkness shouted, "Stop that noise!" The crying broke off abruptly. But the trembling of his back continued.

By the time his second parcel arrived, some months later, he was dead. In the "Parcels for Collection" column on the camp HQ's blackboard, his name lasted and lasted.

Correction: After Shangguan Jinwen collapsed, I went to Lanzhou. Since I heard that people had been dying like flies in Jiabiangou, I thought that was the end of him. More than forty years later, the writer Yang Xianhui told me that Shangguan had not died then, and was later released alive.

FOURTEEN

The Mark of Happiness

The men of Jiabiangou invented among themselves a mark of happiness, namely a matchless smile and a matchless jogging gait.

The potential for the invention accumulated over long years and months, but the setting in motion of the invention came down to a chance happening: some inspection party or other was expected.

The camp high command required us to make a basketball court and organize basketball teams, a dance troupe, a glee club, a folk art group, and a wall newspaper editorial office overnight. The day before the inspection party arrived, we stopped work early and were set to cleaning up, cutting our hair and shaving our beards. However, the disciplinary cadres said the most important thing was to "enliven the workplace atmosphere and display an impression of happiness."

The inspection party's visit was very perfunctory, and in its haste it did not get around to our workplace. We ate an unearned good meal of white-flour rolls, vegetables, and pork, with bigger portions than usual—in all, a meal to remember. The basketball team, folk art group, and so on, were not called upon to do their stuff and were just disbanded; yet the big wall newspapers produced by each of the four brigades were left on the walls to contend for artistic honors. Unless you saw those wall newspapers you would not have known how replete with talent

Jiabiangou was. All the layouts and designs were of professional quality. The hand-copied articles were in turn genuine calligraphy; the styles of the Tang masters Liu Gongquan and Yan Zhenqing, and the styles found on the Han- and Wei-dynasty steles were all represented, as well as the Song Emperor Huizong's skeletal strokes. The First Brigade drew on Liu Yuxi's poetry to make matching scrolls, reading "A thousand sails pass by the capsized boat / A myriad trees burgeon in front of a sick trunk." The fist-size characters were rugged and powerful, like Jin Nong's hand. You wouldn't see such fine script outside Jiabiangou.

The articles were for the most part critiques, of the "Refuting the Fallacy of the Party as Overlord" and "What Is 'Political Design Academy' Supposed to Mean?" variety. Their standpoint was manifest, their tone earnest. The poems were even more ardent. I remember one poem used three exclamation marks in its title: "Ah! Jiabiangou! Cradle of My New Life!"

The article that made the deepest impression on me was called "Refuting the Fallacy of 'Re-Education Through Labor Is Not as Good as Reform Through Labor.'" It argued that the reason why people took the quoted view was that reform carried a fixed term of imprisonment and re-education did not. If such people did not have an ulterior motive, it went on, they lacked the most elementary political sense. Reform through labor was dictatorship directed against an enemy, whereas re-education was a way of handling hostile contradictions in terms of "contradictions among the people," hence it stood for the generosity of the Party toward us. Not to fix a term was intended to help our remolding. If remolding was not complete, when you came out you might commit errors again. To wait until remolding was complete before being released reflected the Party's care and concern for us. To be ungrateful, and to go as far as to complain, was truly unconscionable . . . and so on in the same vein.

No one could tell if this was serious or humorous, truthful or mendacious. I believe the author himself could not say. No, it basically never occurred to anyone to make that distinction. This "non-differentiation" (to use a Buddhist expression) was a given: all problems resolved themselves in the great muddle; there was no need to take them seriously. Once you did, matters became complicated and nuisance ensued; everything got awkward and tangled, like the components of a machine being out of place. Just such a thing had already happened at Jiabiangou, but I shall have to explain that at some length.

Some time before this, Officer Wang was put in charge of our company. Wang had just transferred from the army and still wore his military uniform. He had had no education to speak of but was a decent sort. He walked back and forth over our work site, sucking on his bamboo pipe and saying very little. One day, after having squatted in our team's section for a long time, he looked at his watch and said, "Take a break—you're all tired." Everyone was indeed in dire need of a rest, but at the same time wanted to show keenness, so replied that no, they weren't tired and would carry on working.

Officer Wang's jaw dropped, his expression one of surprise and incomprehension. Wang Xiaoliang, who formerly had been head of the theory section of the propaganda department serving the Provincial Committee, stopped digging, pressed one hand to the small of his back, and supporting himself on the handle of his shovel with the other hand, stood painfully upright. In order to ingratiate himself with a witty remark, he said, "The leadership is falling behind the masses, ha-ha!" This was a well-worn saying employed by the leadership in the Great Leap Forward to encourage the masses, commonly seen in the press at that time.

Contrary to expectations, however, Officer Wang took it seriously; his eyes glinted with discomfiture, and he made no reply. Lowering his head, he poked a stem of dry grass through the barrel of his pipe to clean it, knocking out the debris intermittently on the sole of his boot, *rat-tat*. Having finished that he stood up, and without a backward glance, he dusted off the seat of his pants and went off. He left behind the smell of shag tobacco.

Everyone was still more discomfited than he was, felt they had been snubbed, and was very uneasy. The idea was to get in the man's good books, but the end result was to offend him. It was truly a case of "when a scholar meets a soldier, he can't make him see reason." How awkward! How complicated! Luckily Officer Wang was soon assigned elsewhere, and Officer Han took his place. Han was scheming and vicious, his face a saturnine mask, and he never looked you in the eye. He went all-out for Labor and Study, and relations were back on the familiar rails. Complexity and awkwardness gave way at once to simplicity and naturalness.

By the time the inspection party was to arrive, we were already in Officer Han's hands. He made a big thing of "enlivening the workplace atmosphere" and set about the job by targeting antipathy and resistance. In the daytime he stepped up mutual supervision; in the evening he stepped up exposure and criticism. So-and-so always had a sullen look: Who are you discontented with? So-and-so kept tight-lipped all day long: What devilish scheme are you cooking up? So-and-so carries his baskets of earth with a swagger: Who are you trying to impress? After all this informing on each other and criticizing each other, eventually we reached a consensus: Because we had not properly remolded our thought, to some extent we all harbored resentment and did not know when we were well off. Everyone made a self-criticism, undertook to put things right, and submitted himself to general supervision.

The workplace atmosphere changed very quickly. In each brigade, company, and team, everyone wore a smile. They smiled from morn till night, at all times and in all places. They smiled as they swung their pickaxes, smiled as they used their shovels, smiled as they carried their baskets up a bank, smiled as they trotted back down the bank. They chanted as they smiled and as they trotted. To begin with, they chanted *hai-hai, hai-hai* in time with the rhythm of trotting. Before long somebody built on this basis and created a work song with the same beat. A carrier at the rear would call out the words, and a carrier in the front would respond with the chant *hai-hai*. The words were all made up on the spot. For example, when a basket carrier trotted past the brigade foreman, Chen Zhibang, the song might go:

> *Chen Zhibang-o—hai,hai!*
> *Fine leader-o—hai, hai!*

Passing the slowpoke Zhang Yuanqin, the song might go:

> *Zhang Yuanqing-o—hai, hai!*
> *Telegraph pole-o—hai, hai!*

We are talking about 1958, and the Great Leap Forward was going on outside; competition among the popular masses in making poems, paintings, and folksongs was going great guns. I don't know what wind blew the elements of activism across the far-flung wastes and into our closely walled compound, but we Jiabiangou people did spontaneously begin to compete in work songs.

However, to our senses that had been honed to the sharpness of a dagger by mutual friction, the song words very often did not stand up to scrutiny. For example, it was pointed out the very same day that the brigade foreman was also undergoing re-education by labor, so it was inappropriate to call him a leader. Consequently that line was changed to "Fine example-o, hai, hai." Then it was objected that since he had not been released, it meant he had not been completely remolded, so could not be a fine example. Consequently it was changed again to "Driving force-o, hai, hai," which seemed to pass muster. Yet Chen Zhibang himself had pondered the question by this time and said it was improper to highlight an individual, so he stopped us calling out like that. In view of the great difficulty and high risk, the wave of creative enthusiasm receded, and we reverted to the simple and natural chant of *hai-hai*. That was fine, too: the fact that everyone on the work site smiled as they trotted to the *hai-hai* chant was sufficient to express our happiness.

All the same, our smiling and trotting was not of the normal kind. A precondition of the normal smile was cheerfulness; a precondition of normal trotting was strength. To smile and trot without those two things, we each had to carry on a hard and protracted struggle with ourselves. When you narrowed your eyes, the corners turned down; when you opened your lips, the corners curled up: through such studious contortions the lateral creases in the face outnumbered the lengthwise ones, and you got a smiling face. This took some effort. To keep up the smile for a long time required even greater effort. Because the smile bore evidence of this strenuous effort, it also somewhat resembled crying.

The trotting bit was harder still. To trot requires a spring in the tread of the back foot and a lift in the step of the front foot, so that both feet momentarily leave the ground at the same time, thus increasing the stride and speed. We lacked the strength to achieve that: we could only raise the back foot if we first put down the front foot, which was no different from walking. In order to avoid the appearance of walking, we bent both legs as far as possible, then abruptly straightened them like springing. With this sequence of repeated straightening, our bodies bobbed up and down, which made it look as if we were running. This form of trotting was slower than walking, and more tiring, but since we were not allowed to walk and hadn't the strength to really trot, we had no other option.

The business of the inspection party's visit was soon forgotten, but this smiling face and trotting gait persisted. Because the device of mutual supervision and the need to struggle for survival forced us to "persevere in progress and disallow regression," in time they became a habit and could hardly have been changed back if we had tried. The thousands of men on the work site all had narrowed their wide-open vacant eyes to a slit. As I bobbed along with my basket, threading my way with a *hai-hai* through a crowd of men all likewise bobbing along, I sometimes became mentally addled: I suddenly felt that these old acquaintances around me had turned into alien monsters. That went for myself, too.

On a morning the same as any other, I had just carried my first basket

of earth up on top of the newly heaped bank beside a ditch when I encountered a sunrise. The dark red sun that clung to the extremely long,
extremely straight horizon was big and round, and seemed to cast no
rays at all, yet there appeared lots of pale blue shadows on that desolate
and empty, rough and uneven planet's crust of ours. I could make out in
one long shadow a crowd of little grayish creatures scraping at the barren ground, bobbing back and forth and moving very slowly. As they got
farther away their outlines faded, until they disappeared into the primeval
background of prehistory. I experienced a sudden disorienting shock.

I thought that if an outsider who was not in the know was suddenly
faced with this exceptional scene, he would be so startled that his mouth
would drop open and stay open for a long time. I thought that those
countless faces fixed in a weird smile alone would be enough to give him
the willies. I further thought if an earthquake should occur now, and the
whole lot of us were buried and turned unaltered into fossils, archaeologists in future times would certainly be at a loss to explain the significance
of this matchless expression and gait.

I thought they might speculate that this was a mysterious ritual of an
irrational religious sect; perhaps they would imagine it was the lifestyle
trait or cultural metaphor of a long-extinct race in the back of beyond, like
the flattened skulls of Maya people or the weird and wonderful masks of
New Guinea. . . . But come what may, I believe, never ever would anyone
deduce that this was a mark of happiness.

FIFTEEN

Emerging from Death

That dawn we gathered together as usual in the weak sunlight, preparing to set out for work. It was very cold, and I wrapped my padded coat tightly about me, pulled in my head, thrust my hands in my sleeves, and stamped my feet as I waited in the file. All of a sudden I heard a shout: "Gao Ertai, step forward!" When I did so, Officer Han came up to me, looked me up and down, and said, "Go back inside."

I returned to my billet, lay down in my bed space, and cupping my head in my hands, looked at the speckled and flaking crust on the mud walls. Nothing went through my mind, neither thoughts nor fears. I did not know why I had been called out, but I knew that whatever happened to me, it couldn't be worse than my present state. Without intending to, I fell fast asleep.

I was awakened to find two policemen standing behind the commander of the sub-farm. A military jeep was parked outside. They told me to get in. Immediately I was told to get out again and fetch my luggage. I bundled up my rags and tatters, together with lice and straw, and stuffed it any old how next to my seat. The two policemen sat in front; I sat behind. This seating arrangement seemed to me a good sign, but I did not build up my hopes.

We drove across the huge Gobi, at times going like the wind, at other times bouncing up and down. It really was piercingly cold. I piled my rags over me and was lulled into sleep again. In my dreams I heard shots, which turned out to be my companions shooting at gazelles. They let off a whole volley, but missed. I slept fitfully for the rest of the journey.

When I finally woke up, dusk was closing in, the sun a blur in the west. We were nearing a small town. The heating flues of a few mud-built farmhouses scattered through the outskirts were sending up thick smoke from the stubble and dried dung the farmers burned. The smoke did not ascend—it accumulated in long, drawn-out, heavy clouds over the countryside that gradually merged with the evening mist, making the mist smutty and giving it a charred smell. Showing through this murk was the purpling of the night sky. On the ground I could dimly make out tussocks of wild grass, rows of white poplars, and raised field borders buttressed by yellow sand. Though there wasn't a hint of verdure, I was deeply moved. Seeing these diverse signs of human life, I felt like a traveler coming home after a long stay away. Instead of driving on into the town, we turned into a big high-walled compound where police were standing guard. There were watchtowers and barbed wire on the walls, and a sign over the gate that read "Gaotai Prison."

Caught in the last rays of the sun, the watchtowers were rosy red on one side, deep blue on the other. We got out of the jeep in deep blue shadow and were ushered into a room by policemen dressed in deep blue uniforms. In this badly lit room a stove glowed red, coal smoke, and tobacco smoke filled the air, and the stuffy heat was laced with a musty smell. The police were obviously old comrades, judging by the boisterous way they laughed and talked. Someone brought hot water for washing hands and feet—including some for me, to my surprise.

A sumptuous feast followed. A dozen people sat around the table, all Public Security men, both cadres and ordinary policemen. I was sandwiched between them. No one spoke to me. While they were playing drinking games, quaffing deeply, and talking at the top of their voices, I, half dead from hunger, tucked in by myself. Too impatient to chew the food, I swallowed big lumps of meat and boiled eggs practically whole. That night I couldn't sleep because of the awful pain in my swollen stomach.

Gaotai is a small station on the Lanzhou-Xinjiang line. On one side is the Qilian mountain range, on the other the Great Gobi. It is situated on an incline, which gives you distant views, but of a cheerless vista. We boarded a train here. It was not until I looked at the ticket that I knew the date was March 6, 1959, and we were heading east to Lanzhou.

When I had been escorted westward over a year before, there was a diner and a sleeper car on the train, but this time there was neither. The car attendant distributed pancakes twice a day, one per person. They were cold and hard, and there was nothing to go with them, but passengers stretched out their hands for these pancakes with great eagerness and held them as if they were treasures. I had been completely cut off from the world and hadn't an inkling that a nationwide famine had already begun. I was just aware that the atmosphere in the carriage was depressed, and that everyone looked gaunt and washed out.

We arrived in Lanzhou on the morning of the third day. The two policemen took me to the Public Security Department for Gansu Province, handed me over to two civil policemen belonging to the office of the head of department, and left. These two civil policemen were quite amiable. One was called Dong Lin, about forty, a history graduate from Lanzhou University. The other was Ding Shenghui, about thirty, a graduate of the law department of Northwest Institute of Political Science and Law. They told me that as its contribution to the celebration of the "First Decade of the New China," the Provincial Committee had decided to stage an "Exhibition of the Achievements of a Decade of Construction" and had built an exhibition center in the Qilihe district of Lanzhou (later to become the Gansu Provincial Museum). They needed some big oil paintings for it. My task was to complete these paintings by October 1, when the exhibition would open. I asked what was to be painted and how big the paintings should be. They didn't know; someone there would tell me, they said.

"I have to warn you," Dong Lin added, "the Provincial Committee transferred you here on temporary assignment because of the work that needs to be done here. It doesn't mean you are released from re-education through labor; even less does it mean your rightist tag is removed. There is a change in your work environment; there is no change in your status. The content of your work has changed; its nature hasn't. If you remember that, it will be to your good."

Ding Shenghui escorted me to Qilihe, handed me over to the exhibition planning office, and left. His parting words to me were: "The people here are all seconded from various bodies, and there's bound to be a lot of loose talk. You should be very careful what you say. At the same time, you've nothing to fear. Your relationship with anybody here is only a work relationship; your sole organizational relationship is with us. If anybody wants to get at you, they have to go through us. We'll come and see you in a few days, and you can tell us if there's anything wrong."

In the purely revolutionary lexical field of the time, these words of his, and Dong Lin's too, fell strangely on the ear. They'd addressed me as a human being, not as a political sign. That wasn't the language an organization used toward an individual; even less did it resemble the language used by an organ of brute force toward an object under its absolute control. There were no official formulas or jargon of the "remold thought," and "redeem transgressions through merits" kind. I was quite unused to hearing such a tone. Rather than being comforted, I was simply surprised.

This was the first time in my life that I discovered (for me it was a discovery) that there could be humanity even in the Communist Party police force. (I might add in passing that when I was arrested again thirty years later at Nanjing University and interrogated in Chengdu, I found that several policemen acted with humanity and had a sense of morality. Yet the language they used completely conformed to the norms of Party culture. The mechanisms used for getting meaning across were much more convoluted. The difference between earlier and later is symbolic of historical change, but we can't go into that here.)

The planning office assigned me to stay in the Friendship Hotel across the street. This was a luxuriously appointed hotel for the exclusive accommodation of Soviet experts. It was the first time I had stayed in a luxury hotel. There I was, thin as a skeleton and with scarcely any clothes to my back, placed in the midst of thick carpets, big wall hangings, heavy plush curtains, and glittering chandeliers: it was really weird, as if something was out of joint. Actually there was no mistake: the Soviet experts had all left because of the Sino-Soviet split, and the exhibition had taken over these rooms.

All the paintings I had to do were to sing the praises of the great achievements of New China, most importantly the General Line, the Great Leap Forward, and the People's Communes. Millions of people going without sleep to combat nature, move mountains, and make lakes; devotion to communal canteens as "imperishable foundations"; stupendous output, mountains of grain from a single acre, pigs as big as oxen; rustic blast furnaces blossoming all over and belching molten steel . . . all these great deeds that I was to highlight supposedly could not have been realized except under the leadership of the Party and Chairman Mao. The paintings had to pass a series of inspections and reach the point of "the leadership contented, the masses assenting" before they were judged finally acceptable.

They brought me a big pile of pictorial magazines that were full of photographs on these subjects. Since the contents were formulaic and only required meshing together, it wouldn't be hard to complete my commission. The job would still be physical, nothing to do with art. The good thing was that the intensity of the labor would be a lot less than that demanded for digging drainage ditches. My problem was my health. At that time my upper body was so thin that my bones stuck out, while my legs were swollen like tree trunks. I desired nothing more all day than to lie down, and when I did lie down I couldn't get up again; I had to turn on my face and slowly lever myself up with my arms. The paintings were huge, and I needed help to get up and down the scaffolding. On top of that, I could not stand for long to paint and needed continually to sit down. Nevertheless I gritted my teeth and summoned up my last reserves to stick it out. I knew that if I failed to satisfy, I would be sent back to Jiabiangou, to certain death. When Dong Lin said, "It will be to your good," that was the good in question. This was not about painting; it was about staying alive.

The food in the hotel was high class, came in many varieties, and what's more, was not limited in quantity. I very soon got fat through overeating, in fact a lot fatter than at any other time in my life. But a body of blubber gave no relief from exhaustion; my legs still felt as heavy as lead, and my reactions were still slow. When I walked around I was not agile enough to avoid bumping into people coming from the opposite direction. I still could not get used to seeing other people going off to enjoy themselves, wondering where they got the energy. After four or five months, though, I started to lose weight, and then I continued to slim down until I reached the level I was at prior to being imprisoned. At long last I felt my energy and vitality were getting back to normal. I was no longer afraid of climbing stairs or going on long walks. I reacted more alertly when something cropped up. I went up and down the scaffolding with more ease. At the same time I began to take an interest in things that did not immediately concern me, like the starry sky, the sound of the river, or a kite circling high in the heavens. I became fond of bookshops, losing all sense of time looking round them. And I was often visited by sexual urges, not being able to sleep again after waking in the middle of the night.

The work proceeded more and more smoothly. Having submitted various drafts for approval, I learned how to appeal to their tastes; having heard much prating and attitudinizing, I learned how to play to the gallery. I even heard from the Public Security Department that I was "acquitting myself very well." My painting titled "Commune Members' Home" was the best received. The subject was a canteen of a people's commune. The fish and meat on the table were crisp and swimming in oil; the faces of the men and women, oldsters and youngsters, were glowing with ruddy health; mouths gaped in wide smiles. Ironically, a great famine was spreading through the nation just at that time. My mind was fixed on producing results, my effort bent on making the details lifelike and the atmosphere jolly. It didn't occur to me that I was lying, that I was fueling the disaster by this pretense. No, occasionally it did occur to me, but it was no more than a fleeting thought that in no way affected my work.

As October 1—the day of completion of the assignment—got nearer and nearer, I became more and more worried. I hoped for the best, prepared for the worst. Every day I got up before dawn and went for a long run along the river, intending to get fit enough to stand up to another critical test. But the test did not come: after the exhibition opened, I was kept on to edit a picture album to commemorate the exhibition, and thus was allowed to stay in Lanzhou until the summer of 1960. By that time the Jiabiangou Farm was on the verge of extinction because too many people had died there, and, being left "homeless," I was sent to another reform-through-labor camp, the Jiahetan Farm in Jingyuan. The conditions of work and the natural environment there were both an improvement on Jiabiangou—besides which, my health had recovered, so I was not dismayed.

Looking back from the desolate countryside around Jiahetan, the luxury of the Lanzhou Friendship Hotel seemed like a dream. It came to me that in tandem with the resurrection of my physical body, my soul had actually advanced toward death. I had lost my self, become a pliant tool in others' hands, had become a thing. To be transformed into a thing was no different from being dead.

The will to live drove me to write. Secretly, using minuscule characters, I wrote on whatever scraps of paper came to hand. As time went by, those scraps grew too many to keep on my person, and I had to find a hiding place for them. That was dangerous, but the risk had to be taken.

In all my shuttling from place to place over the years, I have carried that ever-growing dangerous bundle with me. The bulk of the articles and books I published later had their source in that bundle. It was because it existed that I dared to believe I had emerged from the shadow of death.

SIXTEEN

Shifting Coal

Jiahetan Farm in the Jingyuan District was situated beside the Yellow River. Its population was made up of three groups. One was convicts, overseen by military police, called the Criminal Brigade. Another was convicts who had served their sentence, called the Occupational Brigade. The third group was made up of Public Security personnel sent down on rotation to harden themselves through labor, called the Cadre Brigade. I hadn't been sentenced by a court, so I was not classed as a criminal; but I had not been released from "re-education through labor," either, so could not take up employment. For convenience' sake I was enrolled in the Occupational Brigade. We labored collectively and ate and slept collectively, somewhat like the hands on an average farm.

One day the farm took a delivery of two truckloads of coal, but as the trucks could not get across the Yellow River, it was unloaded on a hill on the opposite bank. Because it was feared the local peasants would filch the coal, they sent me and Du Kaifa, another man from the Occupational Brigade, to move it over, giving us ten days to do the job. Du was a tough nut: small face, thick neck, broad chest, big hands and feet, hirsute, violent tempered. His clothes were filthy.

We set out that same day carrying shovels, gunnysacks, rope, haversacks, rations, cooking pots, and a goatskin raft. We took a shortcut to the Yellow River. Thunder rumbled in the background; in no time black masses of cloud were lowering threateningly on the horizon. The river was more than a hundred yards wide in its broad stretches, less than fifty at its narrows. Cliffs reared up on both sides; waves whipped the bare rock walls, giving off the growl of latent thunder.

We walked upstream for about a mile, lowered the goatskin raft into the water, loaded our things on it and lashed them securely, and jumped on board together. The raft dipped low in the water, then was lifted high by a big wave and slid down the wave's slope like a flimsy leaf. We slid so deep that I thought we would be submerged, but the next instant we were thrown high again. Du Kaifa plied his oar vigorously, his soaking-wet bronzed skin flashing in the sun, its gleam intimidating like that emitted by a brazen image.

When the black clouds swallowed the sun and darkness suddenly fell over the earth, a big wind rose, the gusts coming closer together. The raft lifted, sank, and tipped in this gloom, steadily nearing the opposite bank but at the same time being propelled downstream. Having described a sixty-degree course, the raft beached just right, at the point where the gorge started.

By this time we were wet through from the river water. We jumped off and unloaded our equally drenched things, dragged the raft to high ground, and tethered it safely to a rock. We hefted our stuff up the hill beyond the reach of flash floods, and found a cave to shelter in from the rain. The cave was on the cliff face, overlooking the river. It was shallow, but roomy and out of the wind. A rock ledge projected over it, just like the eaves of a loggia, and that would keep off the coming rain. Having put our things down, we went out and collected a big heap of firewood. Only then did we relax. We got a good fire going, stripped off our clothes and wrung them dry, then toasted ourselves, naked as the day we were born.

The rain began suddenly. In next to no time the air was filled with a sound like the washing of a tide. A lot of little yellow waterfalls spouted from our rocky eaves and swirled down into the river. The river surface was a blur, the raindrops kicking up a thick white mist. Our bonfire was going strong; steam was rising from our clothes and gunnysacks. We sat cross-legged by the fire, gnawing on a big flatbread, biting into a clove of garlic, drinking a mouthful of water, rejoicing that this downpour could not wet us.

While we were eating, Du Kaifa said, "If it wasn't for this weather, we could have got the coal down by tomorrow."

"Why so eager?" I asked. "Are you afraid our masters will forget about you?"

"It's not that. When the job's done, we can collect some rose-willow wands and weave baskets with them, and sell the baskets in the villages hereabouts."

"Is there any demand for them?"

"Baskets are in very short supply around here. They'll go like hotcakes at two to two and a half yuan apiece."

"I don't know how to weave."

"I'll teach you. If we put on a spurt, we can make five or six in one day."

"That's great. Let's give it our best shot!"

After we'd spent some time toasting ourselves, Du asked me about my family. A little while later he said that if only he could get back home, he would want nothing else in life. As he spoke he undid his belt pouch and took out a worn and grubby black cloth purse embroidered with red flowers and green leaves. From the purse he drew a paper packet and unfolded several layers of cigarette paper. Inside was a photograph. He turned sideways to look at it in the firelight, then handed it to me, at the same time rounding the fire to squat beside me and share the photograph with me.

It was an old snapshot, yellowed with age, only one inch square but showing three people. On top of that, it was blurred from wear and tear. The head and shoulders of a peasant woman and two girls could be faintly made out. A big dirty fingerprint in the bottom right-hand corner was much more distinct than the subjects' likenesses. He prodded it with his crooked, stiff, knobby finger. "This is my woman," he said. "This is my older lass; this is my younger lass."

I pretended to be interested, studied it attentively, and said, "They are both good kids, you can tell." To my surprise these insincere words, an empty form of courtesy, made him extremely grateful, and he became quite deferential. Without looking at him, I could feel he was affected. He took the photograph back with both hands, returned to his place on the other side of the fire, and carefully wrapped the photo and put it away. Once he got started talking about his kids, all sorts of itsy-bitsy minor things, no matter how tedious or trivial, were grist for his mill. I listened and listened until I slipped into a deep sleep. That night's flash flood and rock-splitting, earth-shaking thunder might never have happened as far as I was concerned: I was snoring my head off.

The sun was well up when I woke. A beautiful rainbow was suspended over the mist-filled river. The mist was flowing and shifting, disclosing and concealing deep blue mountain peaks. Kaifa had been up a long time, but he had not made a fire for fear of waking me. He was squatting there, sorting out some greens that he had just gathered. The greens were like pea shoots, but smaller. He said these were wild peas; they formed seeds in September, and the seeds were edible too. I asked if they were also called vetch, but he didn't know. I remembered looking the word up in the dictionary when I read a poem from the Wei Dynasty called "Gathering Vetch," and the dictionary said this vetch was also known as the wild pea. I thought that must indeed be what we had.

We soon found the coal by following the truck tracks in the gully. If we used haversacks to hump it down the hill, we reckoned it would take at least seven or eight days. So what we did was to fill the gunnysacks to the brim and shift them over to the edge of the escarpment; then Du let the sacks down by rope, and I caught them below. We did not pause except to drink water and munch a bun. By the time it got dark, the coal was all down on the river strand. We were black from head to foot and streams of sweat had made stripes, turning us into two monsters. The purpled furrows made by the straining rope and the scratches made by brambles throbbed and smarted, but we were inexpressibly joyful over finishing eight days' work in one day. Our red mouths were open in wide grins as we went back to our cave.

Now we would have eight days all to ourselves. Kaifa said we could use the money we got for selling the baskets to send back home, or maybe to buy some good provisions for a couple of bang-up meals. This evening already, he said, we could let ourselves go and make a big hole in our rations. So back in our cave we tucked into a washbasinful of noodles, flavored with vetch and garlic. It tasted wonderful.

First thing the next day, we set to work with a will. It was only the beginning of August—dandelions were scattering their fluffy white balls all over the ground, and in the bramble thickets wolfberries were already ripe, a juicy bright red. Clumps of rose willows were blooming with pale purple flowers. The roaring, roiling waters of the river glinted and sparkled through the foliage of flowering shrubs. A mountain eagle circled overhead; the sun shone resplendently on the river upstream of us.

Suddenly a black speck appeared against this glowing backdrop. Growing bigger and bigger, it emerged as a goatskin raft. Kaifu stared long and hard, shading his eyes against the sun. "Who's this, then?" he grumbled. "What do they want?"

The newcomer was Yang, the deputy head of the farm. We just managed to hide the willow wands before he came up. Someone had reported that there was a long row of sacks on the strand, and he had come to find what it was all about.

"Now that the sacks are down from the top, it'll be easy going," he said. "I'll have them send a couple of men over first thing tomorrow to help you get the coal across the river. The horse cart will be waiting, so you'd better look lively."

With that, he turned to go. Old Geng, who had rowed the goatskin raft for him, chased after him with Dongdong, Yang's son, on his back.

They came back fairly quickly, saying they had seen an eagle's nest on the escarpment, with chicks in it. Dongdong wanted the chicks caught so that he could play with them, but there was no way old Geng could manage the climb. Du was told to try.

I had discovered this eagle's nest the day before, and had wanted to go up and have a look, but Du wouldn't let me. He said the jagged cliff face was very dangerous. Some outcrops looked fine but gave way as soon as you stepped on them, and if that happened you were done for. He now repeated this objection, but Deputy Head Yang told him he could first test the rock with his foot, and rest his weight on it if it didn't fall.

After Du had gone on his way, Yang said to me: "We won't wait. Tell him when he has got hold of them to weave a cage with rose willow—he's an expert at weaving—and line it with some grass, and shut them up in it. Those little things are very delicate—tell him he mustn't go about it ham-fisted."

By the time I had hurried round to the cliff face, Du had already started on his climb, but he was still very far from the eagle's nest. One hand was wedged in a fissure of the rock wall; the other was gripping the stem of a plant. His legs were splayed wide, like a stick figure. That fierce eagle was circling agitatedly over his head, as if preparing to swoop down at any second. The mighty river boomed in a symphony of water and rock.

SEVENTEEN
Toward Life[1]

Just before spring planting in 1962, the Provincial Public Security Bureau notified Jiehetan Farm that I was to be released from re-education through labor on my own recognizance, but I wasn't informed until spring planting had been completed.

I was twenty-six years old, penniless, my clothes torn, my sole possession a shabby bedroll. My entire family was under the "dictatorship of the proletariat," so I couldn't return home, and with no other ties I suddenly had no place to go.

I asked Director Han, "What'll I do if I can't find anything outside?"

"Don't worry," he said, "you can stay on the farm. Staying here's also a way out."

That would be the end of everything, I thought. No matter what, I needed to get out as soon as possible.

At mealtime I used my extra meal tickets for steamed buns, which I wrapped in a cloth parcel. The next day I collected my thirty-four-yuan living allowance and coupons for twenty-eight jin of grain, shouldered my bedroll and parcel, grabbed a wooden walking stick, and set off. [2]

The bookkeeping clerk, Yang, asked, "Where're you going?"

"To the city. To look for work."

"What's your hurry? Better wait a few days for a lift!"

"No. No."

Even though spring was the windy season, that day there was no wind, but minute dust particles still hung in the air like a dry mist, and as I walked, the slowly undulating yellow earth of the great Northwest appeared more spacious and broad within this web of dust. The road followed the rippling terrain into the distant haze. I took long steps, and my shadow, blurry beneath the white sun, glided noiselessly over both deep and shallow vehicle ruts.

I didn't encounter a single cart or person until noon, when I followed the road through a village. Several short, low-beamed adobes with dirt-blackened porticoes and eaves, small wood-latticed windows, and saddle-shaped roofs were bunched haphazardly. The courtyards had common walls, and several families shared a well. By the well, shabbily clothed people washed vegetables or watered donkeys. As I passed, they stopped and stared; the whites of their eyes glared from their sun-blackened, work-worn faces.

On the low courtyard walls, slogans pasted up during the past years had peeled off, leaving mottled spots of color. Stumps from large trees were nearby, and if the dust was blown away, faint annual rings could still be distinguished. I imagined those bygone years when magnificent dark trees lifted to the sky and dense shade covered the ground. In '58 the trees were felled and burned in the village's steel refining furnace. The leaves were swept away, leaving strangely shaped mutilated stumps, and the magnificence was lost. Then the furnaces were abandoned and many saplings were planted. When I arrived, the apricot trees were beginning to flower, poplars revealed tender, goose-yellow young leaves, and stirring spring colors decked the hedges and tops of walls.

No one interrogated me about my identity, and I could sense the government's laxity. But I must have appeared alarming, because small children ran away when they saw me and adults stared with disgust and suspicion. A young girl sat sorting beans on a doorstep below the house eaves with a wicker basket on her lap. I went over and asked her for water.

Terrified, she dropped her basket and fled inside the house, scattering the beans. An old granny leaning on a walking stick came out to find out what I wanted. She gave me the water, filled my water bag, and told me to leave quickly before I frightened anyone else.

Beyond the village were wastelands and cultivated fields, but smoke from cooking or heating fires was still visible, and when the sky darkened, the light of faraway village lamps mingled with the stars. I was afraid of frightening the villagers and being driven away as a monster, so I spent the night in the fields on one of last year's abandoned haystacks. I blanketed myself deep in the hay, and amid the aroma I looked up at the stars, recognizing those my mother taught me to pick out as a child. They hadn't changed, and it was as if the world and I hadn't changed.

I awoke at midnight. Dew covering the ground had hardened into a thin layer of frost. The moonlight was silvery, crystal, and cold. For a moment I was afraid but didn't know why. Wilderness? Night? Loneliness? Reality? The future? It seemed all and none of them. Soon I fell asleep, and at daybreak I felt better.

I knew attending school was out of the question. I'd be lucky to find some corner far away from people and quietly pass my days, but in this China, which was entirely made up of communes and soldiers, this wish was an illusion. But I couldn't help wishing. After a while I thought about the tiny oasis in the vast desert, the Mogao Caves in Dunhuang. I wondered if I could find my refuge among the relics of the Wei, Sui, and Tang dynasties, just as Schiller had sought refuge in the Golden Age of Greece and Rome to escape the dark political reality of his contemporary Germany.

At dusk I arrived at the banks of the turbid and thundering Yellow River, where it raced below Jingyuan City's meandering earthen walls. In the faint crepuscular light, I couldn't make out a single person on the opposite bank. Above the wall, multicolored sun-lit clouds lingered, and through the crenellations, the city lights clustered or scattered in dots, interlaced into circle after circle of hazy halos like indistinct water-drop stains on coarse yellowish gray construction paper. I walked along the river toward the city gate. An old man ferried me across in his goatskin boat and pointed out a small lodging place near a coal dump that served mule- and horse-cart drivers.

The lodging consisted of a row of squat connected storerooms around a large courtyard. Smoke blackened the walls and ceilings, and the rooms reeked of burnt kerosene and human sweat. The brick beds had no quilts, just a large felt covering, but the three or four, or sometimes seven or eight, men crowded completely clothed on the beds with no need for blankets. They were muscular men, slow in speech, ingenuous and dutiful, with mud and coal dust clogged in their pores. I couldn't sleep because of the hoards of bedbugs and the neighing horses and braying donkeys in the courtyard. I stayed two days, waiting for the bus to Baiyin City, where I intended to transfer to Lanzhou.

The old city of Jingyuan, with its interlocking streets and alleyways, probably had had its moment of prosperity, but in these days of hunger, when the free markets were just beginning to open, the amount and variety of goods were as limited as they were in the village markets. During the busy noontimes, tea-boiled eggs and high-priced fried pancakes could be bought without ration coupons. At one yuan for each hundred grams of fried pancakes, I greedily used up my money. Other times, the dirt streets and alleyways were deserted and there was nowhere I could go, so I bought some pens and paper, crawled onto the brick heating stove in front of the *kang*, and wrote letters to my mother and my elder sister in Jiangsu and my younger sister in Sichuan.

Then I wrote a letter to the director of the Dunhuang Cultural Relics Research Institute, Mr. Chang Shuhong, explaining my ideas about Dunhuang art and research. I wrote that according to the reference materials I had read, it seemed that research at Dunhuang had stalled at the phase of verification, dating, sorting, and comparing data, and of writing descriptions and introductions. I went on: Other topics deserved to be developed, including the evolution of styles and the distinctive characteristics of art from different ages, and the mechanism by which central Chinese culture and western Asian culture converged. I said the authentic establishment of Dunhuang studies required the parallel progress of theoretical inquiry and archaeological verification. I was determined to do this, and if Mr. Chang was seriously interested, I would be willing to die in the sand dunes for it. I looked the letter over and felt it was too boastful, too unrestrained and unbridled, but I mailed it without rephrasing a word. I thought there was a very slight chance, so I forgot about it.

The day the bus was to depart, I discovered the tickets had been sold out for several days. I was nearly out of money and couldn't wait, so I shouldered my bedroll, went to the coal yard, and helped load and unload the coal trucks. I was stained pitch-black, but I was able to get a lift on a coal truck to Baiyin City.

Baiyin City was a newly emerging industrial city, with a population mainly of factory workers and their families. There wasn't a tree or a blade of grass in the entire city. A coin-thick layer of gray-black soot covered the roofs and the ground, but if the earth was scraped, conspicuous yellow sand appeared. Thick, mottled smoke poured from densely packed chimneys, while outside the city the gray-yellow, arid, and characterless mountains spread like rows of pyramids, one after another, into the distance. The entire day's bus journey from Baiyin to Lanzhou went past the same mountain after mountain. I was desperate with the monotony until I reached the outskirts of Lanzhou along the Yellow River and spotted a bit of green. At last I was relieved and thanked my fate that I could live somewhere beyond the reaches of Baiyin.

In Lanzhou, evidence of the government's relaxed policy could be noticed everywhere. Passers-by still had despondent expressions, but the streets were livelier and there were more goods in the shops. Through streets and alleyways, vendors hawked homemade wares, and highly priced food could be purchased at all times without meal ration coupons. The Orchard Garden Sports Stadium and the Workers' Cultural Palace in the city center often sponsored dances, where people crowded all night beneath flickering lights. Each work unit's weekend dance was open to the public, and no one was turned away; every dance was full. But the only rhythm was the perpetually unchangeable *one-two-three, one-two-three*, which no one got tired of. I went to look at the several fine-arts shops opened under the direction of the Department of Commerce and thought they could be a way to earn money if necessary.

To be employed, I still needed to go through the bureaucracy. My previous affiliation was with the Culture and Education Bureau, but after being named a rightist, I was expelled into re-education through labor and remanded under the Public Security Bureau. I wanted to go to Dunhuang, but that required that I return to the authority that expelled me, which regulations wouldn't allow. However, when Mr. Chang Shuhong read my letter, he insisted on recruiting me. Through great effort his two friends in the Provincial Public Security Bureau, Dong Lin and Ding Shenghui, overcame many obstacles, and the impossible became real. In early June that year, I took a bag, a bedroll, and a straw hat, and I arrived at Mogao Caves, Dunhuang Cultural Relics Research Institute.

EIGHTEEN

Dunhuang's Mogao Caves

To get to Mogao Caves, one must first go to Dunhuang City, which today is a destination for international tourism. Buildings stand thick as forest trees; the night markets stay busy until dawn; crowds of passengers shuttle through the newly constructed airport. Yet in 1962, there were only dirty brown adobes, one-storied and sometimes two, in haphazard clusters. Pedestrians were scarce along the pitted, manure-covered streets, on which clouds of yellowish dust swirled whenever a vehicle passed. Who could have imagined that Dunhuang was once a major stop on the Silk Road, that ancient land bridge that linked Europe and Asia? In that distant past, crowds of merchants arrived from many countries—border tribesmen, the Qiang and Hu, came and went; thousands of felt-canopied tents were pitched everywhere, and there were even more adobes; the streets were crowded with sobbing camels and spirited horses and red-skirted women; taverns served green liquor. The city flourished. It was fantastic.

Remnants of that past still lie in the desert outside the city: to the west, the ruins of the Han Dynasty's Yang Guan Fort and of the ancient city of Shazhou; to the north, the ruins of the Han Dynasty's Yu Men Guan Fort; and to the south, along the Shule River, a row of broken, uneven mounds of rubble, vestiges of the Great Wall's beacon towers. In the eastern plateau, wood and bamboo writing strips, farming tools, coins, arrowheads, and broken, sand-buried halberds with iron blades still not rusted away have been discovered, evidence that soldiers of the Eastern Han Dynasty and later once garrisoned there. The world-famous Mogao Caves are located on a steep southeast cliff face in the valley between Mingsha Mountain and Sanwei Mountain.

One can imagine that the Great Deluge's turbid and thundering waters carved the perpendicular, thousand-foot cliffs among the vast reaches of flowing sand. But why would that incessant, earthshaking, and everlasting wind, coming from so far, and those heavy yellow sands, flowing like water and leveling everything, stop at the cliff brink and accumulate into tall, ever-changing dunes but not enter this tiny valley?

The narrow valley stretches north to south for almost a mile. A stream emerges from the south end and flows underground again at the north end. Mid-valley, numerous dark, dense trees, hundreds of years old, stand stalwart; light and shadow play beneath them on several old temples. Cliffs of irregular height preserve more than 490 caves from ten dynasties: Sixteen States, Northern Wei, Western Wei, Northern Zhou, Sui, Tang, Five Dynasties, Song, Western Xia, and the Yuan. There are more than 50,000 square yards of wall paintings and 2,400 painted sculptures. The religious scrolls number in the tens of thousands; a few wooden cave eaves date from the Tang and Song dynasties. It's said that these caves are only a fraction of the more than 1,000 that existed at Dunhuang's peak. No one can know exactly. However, this couldn't have been accomplished by one person or by one dynasty; only the accumulated work of countless people over a thousand years, generation after generation, could conceivably create something so monumental. Without Buddhism coming east, without Indian and Persian culture, without Greek culture, brought by the Macedonians—all flowing with the caravans along the Silk Road—without the indigenous cultures of the Yue Zhi, Wu Sun, and Huns, without the Han Dynasty soldiers in their western incursions, and without the emigrants, demoted officials, and exiled men of letters importing central Chinese culture, all converging and intermingling to produce a wild vitality that activated channels for creativity, the potential of Dunhuang could never have been realized.

Therefore, if Mogao art is taken as an organic whole—synthesizing wall paintings, architecture, and sculpture—then history and nature must be said to have played a part. Doesn't the strange, numinous, and yet unprepossessing natural landscape add to the artistic fascination? And those traces of sediment that accumulated on the wall paintings over years, sometimes darkening colors, sometimes lightening them to a diffuse yellow tone, and those changes of color, the fading, peeling, and mottling that left distinct and indistinct depictions, all added to the richness and mystery. Even the dour and grotesque were made more striking than could be attained by a human hand, as those shiny and unbearably gaudy old sacrificial utensils developed a variegated green patina and changed into simple, dignified bronze relics.

Captivated by the torrents of colors, I walked up and down among this forest of wall paintings. I felt I had entered a dream. I thought how difficult it was, through the chaos of history and with so many contingencies needing to come together over so long a period of time, to allow for the creation of these works of art. I thought how much more difficult it was for them to endure through merciless time, through a thousand years of wind, dust, and the devastations caused by armies. And I thought about the impermanence of the world, how members of my family were dead or scattered and how I was brought back from death and was here face-to-face with this art; how extremely fortunate I was. I felt a grave and overflowing gratitude.

NINETEEN

The Story of the Stones

Against the dark, nightmarish backdrop of my memory, the Dunhuang Mogao Caves stand out mythlike, brilliant. During the first days after my arrival, I drifted confusedly in a dream between two worlds. I wore new but ill-fitting clothes, which my mother and sister had made and mailed to me from far away. I poked around everywhere. When I met anyone, I'd smile self-consciously.

I wasn't given any assignments but was told to first take a look at the caves. They were dark inside, and I could see only when rays of the the morning and noontime sun filtered in. The rest of the time I strolled around outside the caves, and for several days I wandered through the surrounding mountains.

The north was desert. Mingsha Mountain was to the west, and in the south was a chaotic array of higher unnamed mountains. Sanwei Mountain stood to the east. I climbed all of them. Except for Mingsha Mountain, which was sand, the peaks were rock: ash brown, purple-gold, metallic green, or earth yellow rock containing mica. They weren't hard and, because they were eroded by the severe winds, appeared hacked and chopped by an ax or knife. From far away they looked solid and rugged, but up close you could see that they were densely crisscrossed with fissures. You could break off a bit and crumble it in your hands into several flat pieces, which often contained marine fossils: corals, seaweed, conches, shells, or fish—sometimes embedded complete fish skeletons, distinctly outlined, lifelike, the same color as the stone. No, they *were* the stone.

I frequently sat alone on a mountain peak, silently facing this primordial universe, watching blue cloud shadows race endlessly across the vast, interminable desert, and listened to the wordless stones. They told me that hundreds of millions of years ago this was an ocean floor; they told me that hundreds of millions of years was only an instant; they told me that within the infinity of time and space an instant amounts to nothing; they told me that there's no instant or eternity but that everything and I myself were illusionary and transient shadows. They told me all this but refused to accept any of it and remained unmoved, obdurately existing in order to challenge obliteration. And no one could say that even to the end of time there wouldn't be anyone who could recognize you or there wouldn't be a chance encounter.

Facing the far-reaching, blazing wind, listening to these voiceless words, I knew that each cold, hard stone had a gentle, warm interior as quiet and motionless as a frozen flame. For tens of thousands of years they, like the inmates of the labor camps, watched each other and kept their suffering inside. And I thought that to suffer is better than not, because without feeling, what's the point of being in the world? However, desire burdens life and to accept the fate of all things is a rare wisdom.

I brought complete fossils back to the Mogao Caves. My colleagues laughed, told me I was naïve, these things weren't rare; from the northwest steppes to Inner Mongolia, Qinghai, and Xinjiang, they covered the ground. Even though this was true, I liked them, and on my room's empty bookshelves I kept rows and rows of stones. Sometimes the stones were like new friends, floating into my life like rootless duckweed, nevertheless bringing old, familiar feelings; sometimes they were like a philosophy or a religion that opened a window onto another world; sometimes they were like a simple form of art or what Clive Bell would call a "significant form":

each stone contained an unstoppable vitality and bore traces within of mountain winds, sea waves, and the chilly light of a fire, plundered savagely but also delicately and tenderly.

Later, books filled the shelves and I packed the stones one by one into cardboard boxes. Because there wasn't space in the room, I placed them under the eaves of the portico. When I moved, I left the boxes behind, and they disappeared during the Cultural Revolution. Sometimes it's better to let things you love go. The stones have returned to their primordial homeland, while I, drifting without freedom on the waters of history, wrote lines remembering Dunhuang.

Meditating deep into the night
My company, delicate stones

TWENTY

Quiet at the Sanqing Temple

I arrived in Dunhuang on June 2, 1962, and stayed at the hostel for a few days before I moved to the Lower Temple.

The Mogao Caves area originally had three temples. One was at the southernmost tip of the valley's long, narrow stretch. Formally called Leiyin Temple, it was now simply known as the Upper Temple. At the time of my arrival it had become the dormitory for family members of the Institute's staff, and in its sundry courtyards, household belongings were piled up, clothes were hung out to dry, and chickens and ducks scurried everywhere. Each family dumped puddles of filthy wash water in which the squalid ducks temporarily alleviated their homesickness.

Close by was the Middle Temple. Originally a Lama temple called Huangqing, it had been refurbished to house the Institute's offices, workshops, meeting rooms, hostel, kitchen, dining halls, and so on. There was calligraphy above the front gate: "Dunhuang Research Institute for Cultural Relics." It was by Mao Dun.[1] I thought the work was dry, stiff, and constrained. The Lama who remained—a man, Xu Si, and a woman, Bao Nai—were moved into the Upper Temple. Xu Si was more than seventy years old when I arrived. A tall, gaunt man, like Don Quixote in the illustrations, he tended the Institute's sheep, often remaining in the mountains for days at a time. Bao Nai, over eighty, still wore her dark purple vestments. Extremely skinny, hunchbacked, and only about three feet tall, she walked with a cane, leaning forward, tottering side to side, as if about to fall. She had a rasping voice but clear, sharp eyes. Often hordes of fierce-looking muscular men came across the desert to pay her homage; they called her "Lao Da" in reverence and awe.[2] In front of the door to her dark, low shanty, spirited, proud stallions belonging to those men were tied; the stallions snorted loudly, dug the ground with their forehooves, *de, de, de*, and rattled their bridles, *hua, lang, lang*, as they lifted and dropped their heads.

The Lower Temple, a Daoist temple still with its original name plaque, "Sanqing Temple," was located outside Mogao Caves Mountain Gate at the northernmost edge of the narrow, long forest about half a mile from the Upper and Middle Temples. It was said that in earlier times someone had been hanged inside, and that later a Dao priest had been beaten to death there by bandits. There were also legends of fox spirits and demons. It was a bit mysterious, a bit terrifying, and for a long time no one had lived there. Paint flaked from its porticoes, spiderwebs hung from dust-covered beams, leaves heaped in the courtyard, and weeds overgrew paths. Not far from the back door was the famous Cangjing Cave, where the vigorous and sturdy calligraphy of Zhang Daqian, in Zheng Banqiao's style, was to be found on an inner wall.[3] The Mountain Gate, which was just beyond the front gate, displayed three characters, *Mo Gao Ku*, by Yu Youren that had been scraped and brushed over with lime.[4] However, on close examination, the resolution of the brushstrokes, their weightings, their structure, their compelling, pure spirit, and, within their unrestrained ease, the vigor that shone through, could still be seen. About a third of a mile past the Mountain Gate there was an archway with fresh, brightly painted plaques on the front and back, each with four characters brushed by Guo Moruo.[5] The flashy, gilded characters and the blue background hurt the eyes, and I didn't like their attention-grabbing coquettishness.

I enjoyed the quiet at Sanqing Temple, so I asked to live there and the office agreed. I cleaned out a side wing, moved in, and remained for three years. Later the Institute decided to move their offices into the Lower Temple and began to refurbish it, so I was forced to move to the Upper Temple to be in proximity to others, to enjoy the noise of socialization and the joyful clamor of chickens, ducks, and children. Refurbishing completely changed the appearance of Sanqing Temple, but it never became offices, because immediately afterward, the Cultural Revolution broke out. I didn't like the Upper Temple, but I wasn't there long because once the Cultural Revolution arrived, they ransacked my living quarters and sealed them off and I had to take my bedroll and move into the Cowshed. The Cowshed was never in one place. However, the only fixed place I was nostalgic for was the Lower, Sanqing Temple with its dark moss and chilly dew.

The forty-nine people at the Institute were assigned to the Research, Cave Preservation, or the Administration departments. Research was subdivided into the Fine Arts Section, Archaeology Section, and the Reference Room. I was with Fine Arts. There were nine of us, including Li Fu, the former *biao hua* for Zheng Daqian.[6] Our main responsibility was to research the murals and paint copies. Work was assigned at the beginning of the year according to the annual plan and was distributed to each person. Everyone was responsible for his own work, and the seven or eight of us plus those in Archaeology, which made twenty people, were scattered among nearly five hundred caves. This gave us freedom. During the day I painted copies or leafed through books in the reference room, and after work I ate in the dining hall and went "home." Although the work didn't bore me, I enjoyed returning home, home to Sanqing Temple. It was a world belonging only to me, and the farther away from crowds I was, the wider this world was.

Outside my room's eastward-facing window, dozens of large trees sparsely occupied large tracts of land. It took two or more people to link their arms around the trunks, so they were called "The Devil Claps His Palms" by the locals. Beyond these sporadic stands of trees was the river, with its continuously flowing water. Several Sheli pagodas containing holy relics from ancient times were visible on the opposite bank, past the wild clumps of shrubbery higher on the slope. Sanwei Mountain was beyond. When I returned at early dusk and opened my door, the light of the setting sun, reflecting from the craggy red cliffs of Sanwei Mountain, was like a flame in which scintillating layers of gold, silver, purple, and red pranced. The rays dyed the river red and projected pale blue shadows from the trees onto the room's east wall. Now and then a bird flew, a fish jumped, and layer upon layer of bright ripples played along the wall. I often stood for a long time, motionless, by the window watching those flames gradually darken until the mountain was deep purple, and then I lit my old-style, glass-covered kerosene lamp and applied myself to the subjects I had been given. On the table were piles of old, yellow-paged, cord-bound volumes.

I realized that to research Dunhuang art at Dunhuang was a rare opportunity and that for my safety and benefit I needed to take advantage of it, to delve into these piles of old papers and become an expert. This was my primary motive for coming, and to be able to come was very fortunate. I was grateful to Mr. Chang Shuhong for helping me and anxious for him to know that I was the right person. Because of my own interest and desire for success, I threw myself into research and copying, and many times I'd spend days or even weeks trying to resolve a very minute problem, for example, the discrepancy between a line of Buddhist scripture and a variation, or the specific date of such-and-such an inscription in such-and-such a cave. I spent an entire year in cave number 465 painting copies of Yuan Dynasty Mizong murals, which I didn't like.[7]

Late one night I was thirsty and went back to cave 465 to retrieve my thermos bottle. The trees were huge, the forest dark, and in the moonlight, shadows spread over the ground. I could hear my footsteps distinctly. An intermittent tinkling came from the iron horses beneath the eaves of the Tang and Song caves, and even within the thick forest these ancient sounds seemed close by.[8] Larger sand particles falling from steep cliffs, hitting the wooden eaves and walkways, made the quiet seem quieter, quiet as the Gobi.[9] I walked down the long sandy path, climbed the high ladder, entered, and left the dark cave, submerged myself again in the empty, gloomy temple, and felt I had become a ghost along the way. I opened the door, saw the dim, yellow lamplight falling on the tabletop's old, decaying books, and suddenly had a horror of being buried. In the endless grave of silence the ancient dead seemed alive, and although I was living, it seemed I had died.

In the past I was tossed on waves of politics and thirsted for quiet, dreaming of a harbor to settle my body and mind, and now I had achieved quiet but at the same time realized it wasn't tranquility. This gentle, tender quiet had a cold, hard core. It was an intermediary between an instant and eternity, and a bridge to the void. I sensed this rather than thought it through, and began to want to escape.

I sorted out the pieces of miscellaneous paper on which I had written in very small letters everything I had seen, had heard, had thought while I was at Jiahetan Farm, and read them carefully. I felt I had returned to that former life of forced labor, starvation, and humiliation and felt even that life was better than the present one, in which I had become a walking corpse from an ancient grave. I read, and without being aware, began to write again. I wrote about the value of man, his alienation and restitution. I wrote about the pursuit of beauty and human freedom and that beauty is the symbol of freedom. I knew I was playing with fire but didn't care, because except for playing with fire, I couldn't find a connection to the outside world, to my time, to human history, and I needed that connection just as I had needed quiet and solitude. While I wrote, I felt the joy of being resurrected—but I lost the sense of safety, so I always latched my room from the inside. Sometimes the wind blew, the door rattled, and startled, I'd suddenly turn my head toward the door, my heart pounding.

Those writings were lost during the Cultural Revolution. Most fell into the hands of the "revolutionary masses" and were used as evidence against me, but I have no regrets. While I wrote, I was alive.

TWENTY-ONE

How Many Flowers Have Fallen[1]

The mention of Marc Aurel Stein, Paul Pelliet, Langdon Warner, and others, and of their "cultural imperialism" toward Dunhuang art, fills one with indignation.[2] Today some evidence of their plunder, meticulously preserved, is used as teaching material for patriotism and nationalism, but if we discard these "isms" and calmly weigh our loss, we can be more tolerant and accepting.

After Dunhuang art reached its peak during the Tang Dynasty, the brilliance and grandeur were gradually lost. No subsequent period equaled the preceding one. Song murals are comparatively coarse and slipshod. Not only is their structure loose, their brushstrokes lack artistic strength and rhythm. They're formulistic and conceptualized, every face identical, so that on entering a Song cave one feels a sense of dissatisfaction; however, their free, uninhibited use of color imparts its own style. The Yuan Dynasty, except for cave number 3, doesn't really have a style. When the theme of the Mizong, "to peel the skin, expose the tendon," was adopted, the paintings became unsightly.[3] There are almost no murals from the Qing, and the very few painted sculptures are gaudy, crass, with even less aesthetic value. From a broader perspective, the 1,600-year history of Dunhuang art is like a long, silent river that constantly changes, rises and falls, swirls—to use the ancient Egyptian description of the

Euphrates, a river that flows in two directions—until it reaches the vulgar world of the marketplace, where it ends and disappears. Why this loss? No one knows.

It is not unusual to find one period not the equal of the one before. Art of the European Middle Ages lagged behind the ancient Greek and Roman, and the standard of Soviet Union literature is lower than that of nineteenth-century Russia.[4] There are many such examples. Regardless of the reason, the decline of Dunhuang art isn't a unique phenomenon. What is surprising, however, is that the curve of this ongoing trajectory of decline matches for the most part that in central China, from the central plains in the north to the Yangtse delta in the south. For example, the caves of the Wei have a crude strength similar to the Jian'an "air and bone" style. The Hua Yan Buddhist splendor of the Tang caves has the same tone as that of the literature of the High Tang court.[5] In their use of "the purity and the void," the Song caves seem to have been influenced by the rational philosophy of the neo-Confucian scholars Cheng and Zhu. From the Yuan Dynasty down, there's been a gradual vulgarization of art in the caves that corresponds to the popularization of lyric songs and vernacular stories in central China. Politics and economics in Dunhuang, hanging as it does at the edge of the world, developed at a slower pace than the rest of China. Why the vicissitudes in the nature of Dunhuang art have been in step with the rest of China is a matter for more inquiry.[6]

In September 1962, the Deputy Minister of Culture, Xu Pingyu, led Liu Kaiqu, Wang Chaowen, and others to Mogao Caves to convene a conference of specialists in order to design an engineering project for cave stabilization. When they toured the caves, they discussed the Qing statues, decided they were ugly, and later at the conference resolved to remove and destroy them. I merely ran errands, so I was powerless and could only watch as the peasants enlisted for the task picked up piece after piece of smashed torsos and limbs, tossed them onto oxcarts, and dragged them into the Gobi Desert to be discarded. There, the statues deteriorated in wind and rain year after year, turning into dust.

The line of history of the art was cut off at its tail, yet it wasn't thought to be a problem. The looted relics put into the British Museum and similar places at least received proper protection and were put on public display, while those salvaged by the Chinese, which fell into the hands of petty or high-ranking officials, were lost along the way or were taken by the salvagers themselves, disappearing without a trace. Even the surviving scrolls, which were rescued and collected into the National Peking Library, according to Chen Yuan's "Records of Dunhuang Relics," were torn and pasted together; the most valuable parts had long before disappeared.

The day-by-day losses went unnoticed. Over the years people arrived to herd camels, chop firewood, worship at the temples, light incense, tie up donkeys, water horses, or stop their carts to spend the night. If they bumped against a statue and knocked off a finger or an arm, or rubbed away an eye or a face from the murals, it was never questioned. Of course this was unintentional and couldn't be considered vandalism, just as stepping on an ant couldn't be considered murder—but the effect on the ant is the same.

In 1922, the eleventh year of the Republic of China, the local government at Dunhuang settled more than five hundred White Russian refugees at Mogao Caves. The government gave them daily provisions and permitted them to set up beds, construct stoves, and start cooking fires. The refugees scraped, carved, drew over, and erased the murals. They knocked down the eaves that were built over the cave entrances during the Tang and Song dynasties, dismantled the wooden walkways that go from cave to cave, and used the wood for their cooking and heating fires. Large areas of many murals, including the famous illustrations in cave number 217, the "Lotus Sutra" and the "Guan Wu Liang Sutra," were blackened by smoke. They scraped the gold plate off many statues, leaving deep marks. Later, in 1939, the Guomindang troops of Ma Bufang camped in the caves and relentlessly dug trenches around them.[7] The loss is incalculable.

At the time of the War of Resistance against Japan, Zhang Daqian stayed at Dunhuang for two years and seven months, and made more than 270 copies of the murals. He codified the cave numbering system and tirelessly urged the government to construct protection walls, prohibit cooking, and assign custodians. When the copies were exhibited in Chongqing, they created a sensation, and the promulgation of Dunhuang art could no longer be neglected. However, Zhang's method of copying was to trace on thin, transparent paper placed directly over the murals, much the way children learn to write characters. There was unavoidable damage, especially to those murals that were friable with powdery pigment, or that were already peeling, crumbling, and worn. And because an expert chose which murals to copy, the most select ones were harmed. This problem was not only Zhang's fault; many painters and teachers and students from art colleges and schools did the same.

From '62 on, the Institute's regulations gradually became stricter. After the Cultural Revolution was over, Mogao Caves became a tourist attraction and the Research Institute was renamed the Research Academy.[8] Following the requirements for a for-profit landmark, the cave surroundings were rehabilitated and management was strengthened. Tickets were sold at the entrance. Guides were assigned to lead tours and specialists to give lectures, thereby avoiding the earlier problems that were caused solely by governmental neglect. But no one anticipated that the air pollution brought in by the crowds, and the ecological imbalance caused by the environmental change, would accelerate the crumbling, alkalization, peeling, and flaking of large areas of the murals, which is difficult to repair.

Unintentional losses are natural in history. We'd best not to concern ourselves, because in the past forty years, so many people's lives and livelihoods were lost throughout all of China and so much cultural vitality was dissolved into the floods of profiteering. And what can be done?

TWENTY-TWO

Initiation

When the National Research Institute for Dunhuang Art was established in 1944, the first director was the famous painter Chang Shuhong. In 1950, the second year of the new political regime, the Institute was taken over by the Cultural Relics Department of the Cultural Bureau of the Northwest Military Committee of the People's Republic, and its name changed to the Dunhuang Cultural Relics Research Institute. The existing personnel were kept on, and Chang Shuhong was reappointed as director.

When I got there in 1962, there were forty-odd people in the Institute, divided among the Research Department, the Administrative Department, and the Cave Preservation Department. The director, Chang Shuhong, was concurrently president of Lanzhou Arts College, and he did not spend much time at Dunhuang. The day-to-day business at Dunhuang was almost all undertaken by his wife, Li Chengxian, who was Party branch secretary and deputy director. At the same time Li Chengxian was head of the Research Department and was in charge of the professional work as well as personnel matters, services, and political thought work.

Li was a painter by vocation, and having spent some twenty years tracing wall paintings at Dunhuang, was highly competent professionally. She joined the ranks of the leadership after becoming a Party member;

she displayed exceptional enthusiasm for politics, making heavy demands on one and all. Impetuous by nature, she was blunt and sharp-tongued. When something came up, she could not contain herself; she had to enquire right away, investigate right away, and did not disguise her feelings. As her subordinate, you could read her face as a barometer of the political climate, which relieved you of trying to read riddles, and so was very welcome.

Nominally the Research Institute was directly answerable to the Ministry of Culture of the central government, but in practice the Party organization, which ran everything in the Institute, was a branch of the Propaganda Department of the Dunhuang County Committee, so in effect we came under the direction of that committee. Whenever the county took some action, the Institute was informed. The Institute had a medium-size bus, and our whole staff—Party members and non–Party members alike—often rode it to the county seat fifteen miles away to hear all kinds of reports: communicating the gist of a certain meeting, implementing some policy, mobilizing to emulate Daqing, or Dazhai, or the People's Liberation Army, or some hero or model or other, and so on.[1] When we got back, we discussed and followed through, cutting no corners.

For the ten or more years prior to my arrival, that had been the case. So although the Research Institute was an isolated island in the far reaches of a sea of sand, a place for the study of remote forms of ancient art, it was by no means cut off from the world. Successive political movements, like those used to suppress counter-revolutionaries, to eliminate counter-revolutionaries, and the Three-Anti, Five-Anti, Anti-Rightist, and Anti-Right-Deviationist struggles, had all gone on with great gusto. Sometimes the Institute was a bit slow getting off the mark, but it never simply went through the motions. Colleagues informed on each other and accumulated a lot of grudges. On the surface all was modesty and deference, pleasantry and openness, but at bottom they were all engaged in a trial of strength.

Having been sent to a reform-through-labor camp soon after graduating from university, I was not very clued in about the outside world, though I had experience that the others lacked. I thought I had found a haven of sweetness and light. In the presence of this vast array of wall paintings, "ancient trees and cold springs," and the company of all these cultured and affable gentlemen, I just felt I was dreaming, as if I had lost my bearings in a fog.

One morning as I was passing the reference room, I ran into Mr. Shi Weixiang. He was one of the most senior painters, having come in the 1940s. In 1957, he had been branded a rightist and was transferred from the fine arts team to the reference room, where he still was. On seeing me, he greeted me warmly and hurried to fish out his key and open the door. At the same time he told me why he was late (less than five minutes late), whereupon he stretched out his wrist and bade me look at his watch. Having never had a sense of time myself, I paid little attention and had no interest in looking. I just smiled foolishly to express goodwill. He obstinately insisted that I take a look, saying, "See, less than five minutes, you agree!" I said "Yes, yes" without understanding what difference it made if it were so, or what difference it made if it were not so.

Another day I ran into Ms. Shi Pingting of the archaeology team on the forest walk. She and her husband He Shizhe, deputy head of the Research Department, were both Party members with a military background. Shi had fought in Korea and taught at university. She had high political awareness, broad knowledge, and superior work competence; in fact she was one of the mainstays of professionalism in the Institute. When I encountered her on that occasion, she was carrying a stack of books in one hand and trailing a dry tree branch in the other. Having exchanged greetings and passed the time of day, she said the tree branch was already dead, had been blown down by the wind, and she had picked it up in passing. As that was obvious at a glance, I did not understand why an explanation was necessary.

Such things were not out of the ordinary.

In the discussions following reports, everyone was eager to have their say. The atmosphere was extremely lively when the topic was how to emulate heroic exploits. Everybody was moved to tears when Lei Feng's self-sacrifice was the lesson, the meeting room filled with the sound of sighing and sobbing.[2] Shi Pingting and He Shizhe took off their glasses and silently dried their tears. Duan Wenjie, head of the Fine Arts Department, wept even more loudly, wept until his eyes and nose were red, and was forever standing up to go outside and blow his nose, trumpeting as loudly as a foghorn. I had never seen such a display of prowess, and was just bemused. Afterward, Li Chengxian called me to the Institute office, saying, "Some people have reported that you have no class feeling: everyone else was moved to tears when studying those heroic exploits, while your eyes were swiveling around as if in greased sockets. Is that true? Yes? Then what was going through your mind?"

Li Chengxian called me in another time to tell me that someone had reported that when I went to the reading room, I always read *World Reports* before *People's Daily*. "Is that the fact?" she asked.

I told her I couldn't remember, that I picked up whichever paper came to hand.

She said, "How come it's always *World Reports* that comes first?"[3]

"We're not allowed to read *World Reports*?"

"It's not whether it's allowed. The question is why you are so interested in the reactionary propaganda of capitalist countries instead of wanting to hear the voice of the Party. Have you considered what kind of questions that raises? Go back and think things out. Don't let it drag you down, either; if you see the error of your ways, it will be all right."

A few days passed before she called me in again to say someone has reported that I was writing reactionary poetry. I told her I had not written any, and strongly denied it. She took out a sheet of paper on which was written "After awakening to the true faith I have kept aloof / The human path has been misted over these fourteen years." Underneath was added the time and place of discovery and the author's name, Gao Ertai. Li Chengxian folded the paper in two, to conceal the informer's name, but

I knew who it was: the handwriting was that of the head of the fine arts team, Duan Wenjie.

Two days before, I had gone to the print room to print an article, and had absentmindedly written two lines of Gong Zizhen's poetry with my finger on the dust-covered machine stand.[4] Obviously Duan had mistakenly thought they were my own work. I fetched the *Complete Works of Gong Zizhen* from the reference room, found the two lines, and showed Li. She said that as long as they weren't mine, that's all right, it's good to get the matter cleared up. "Now, don't you go blaming people for being suspicious," she told me. "In fact it's exactly fourteen years from 1949 till now [1963], and just at this time there's a campaign against humanism. What's more, you've been in trouble before in that connection, so it's very natural people might think you wrote those lines. Don't make a to-do over these things. If you have done nothing wrong, you can still strive to do better."

If I had done nothing wrong, I could still strive to do better; if I *had* done something wrong, I would have been in a right old pickle! Only now did I realize that Shi Weixiang's having me look at his watch, Shi Pingting's explaining the origin of the tree branch, and lots of things of the same kind were all perfectly natural and perfectly normal. It was because I had not been initiated that they had bothered me.

Later on, when we were called upon to learn from the self-sacrificing Wang Jie and Jiao Yulu, everybody was in tears again. I tried to copy them but couldn't manage, so I covered my face with my hands and lowered my head as far as I could. Peeking at the others through the gaps in my fingers, I discovered that quite a few pairs of eyes glittering with tears were glittering in my direction. I hurriedly lowered my head another notch, until it all but touched my knees.

TWENTY-THREE

Red and Black

From 1962 to 1966 the professional work at the Institute, including research, tracing, archaeological digs, and the stabilizing of the caves, was hurriedly abandoned in order to prepare for commemorative activities.

According to the account on a Tang Dynasty stele, construction on the Mogao caves in Dunhuang began in the second year of the Jianyuan reign of the Former Qin Dynasty, which is 366 CE. The 1,600th anniversary would occur in 1966. The Institute planned to hold a series of large-scale commemorative activities in Dunhuang in that year, to which would be invited scholars, experts, and members of religious orders from home and abroad, with the aim of furthering Dunhuang studies.

In 1964 there was more and more emphasis in the press on class struggle and giving priority to politics. Condemnation of human nature, humanism, pacifism, historicism, policies of concession, the philosophy of survival, the theory of "two combined into one," the theory of "profits in command," the theory that war was terrible, the theory of thinking in images, the deepening of realism, the zeitgeist as composed of various trends, and so on, rose to an earsplitting clamor. Chang Shuhong returned to Dunhuang from Beijing before the Mid-Autumn Festival to convey Mao Zedong's pejorative comments about the Ministry of Culture and literary circles. Chang held a series of meetings at which it was decided that the commemorative activities should give priority to politics, and he made a major addition to the agenda, namely to create a new cave for the socialist age.

After repeated discussion, it was resolved to recondition a large exist-ing cave that had no wall paintings or statues, to sculpt a statue of Chair-man Mao where a statue of the Buddha would traditionally have been, and on the west wall behind the statue, to paint a history of the Chinese Communist Party, entitled "Taking in Our Stride the Perils of Crag and Torrent." On the south wall was to be painted the histories of the wars against Japan and of liberation, entitled "Long Live the Victories of the People's Wars." On the north wall was to be painted the great achieve-ments of New China, entitled "600 Million in the Divine Land All Equal to the Ancient Sages," and on the roof of the cave the wonderful prospect of Communist paradise, entitled "The Hibiscus Land Bathed in Morning Sunlight." At the conclusion of the discussions, Chang Shuhong said that not an inch could be yielded in "planting the red flag": the new cave was precisely a red flag, and planting it in this age-old cave temple was exactly "a single red flower amidst dense foliage." Duan Wenjie, head of the fine-arts team, said this was a glorious political task that Director Chang had given us, and that we must ensure its completion. To study Party history through creative work, to raise our understanding through creative work, was a good opportunity to reform our thinking.

The project was big, the time pressing. The fine-arts team undertook the creation of the new wall paintings, the most demanding task. Chang and Li both took part in the team discussions. The requirements were to bring out the greatness of the Party using the method of the combination of revolutionary realism and revolutionary romanticism; also to be deco-rative, to bring out the special characteristics of wall painting. A decision having been arrived at collectively, I had the job of producing a proof, which would be revised and supplemented, then finalized. I worked flat out for two months to produce a number of designs. But no news came of a meeting to consider them.

Li Chengxian called me in to tell me that someone was trying to sabotage the new cave, but we would not back down. The matter brooked no delay, so if a meeting could not be called, we had to do without one: we would finalize the sketches when we ourselves were satisfied, then organize people to enlarge them and put them on the walls.

For the whole of 1965 I was kept busy on this task and produced five sketches for the four walls and roof. Each wall was to be peopled with several hundred characters, behaving differently but sharing the same form, the whole wall full of animation—by no means an easy job. But it turned out that pressing on with the painting was a wasted effort. Since I was totally absorbed in the painting, I was unaware that the times had changed and the power shifted. The thing was, the director had hung in his office a handwritten scroll presented to him by Deng Tuo, which read: "High cliffs, a thousand caves, shifting sands: toiling for twenty years in your far outpost, unearthing, excavating, searching the ashes of a past aeon, your heart is in protecting a land in blossom."[1] As soon as Deng Tuo was criticized by name in the press, people found fault. Before the launch of the Cultural Revolution, and before those who had been transferred to take part in the "Four Cleanups" had returned, people in the Institute went ahead and exposed "the brigand's inn of the Chang/Li couple." Meetings were held every day, first of all accusing Chang Shuhong of "putting professionalism in command" and "promoting only on the basis of talent"; then later on even such words as "having to dig out all covert Deng Tuo elements" were uttered.

The expression "Deng Tuo elements" was coined by the spokesman, He Shizhe. Unfortunately it was not taken up subsequently, but another phrase he used, "waving a red flag to oppose the red flag," was exactly the same as the phrase that later cropped up all over the country. He Shizhe said that it was not that politics were not in command in the Dunhuang

Research Institute, it was that bourgeois politics were in command. All the items in the plan for the 1,600-year anniversary were "black," all were playing up the feudal, bourgeois, revisionist ideology, as black as black could be. Realizing that there was trouble ahead, the new cave had been added at the last minute, said to be "a single red flower amid dense foliage," whereas actually it was waving a red flag to oppose the red flag, which was even blacker.

At this point in his speech, the normally urbane and courteous He suddenly pointed straight at me and said, "To tell whether it was a case of red or black, one only needs to see who is in charge of the creation of the new cave." He called upon all present to "examine this specimen, to see clearly from the outset the deep-rooted reactionary character of this person."

It was then the turn of all the others to stick their knives into me. The charges were that I was an anti-Party, anti-socialist extreme rightist, a savage wolf escaped from Jiabiangou; that my brain was petrified, all the papers I had written at the Institute had been poisonous weeds, and all my everyday words and deeds were resolutely reactionary. I was even accused of making a big X with a red brush on the statue of Chairman Mao. If that was confirmed, I would be a candidate for being shot.

I had just got married, my wife was pregnant, and we longed for security, so this made me extremely nervous. Chang Shuhong was not at the Institute. The impetuous Li Chengxian was surprisingly cool, not flustered by this reverse, and told me to keep my mind on my work. She asked me if the creation of the new cave was revolutionary art or not. I said it was. She said, "That's all right then—what are you worried about?" She said she had had a word a few days before with Dou Minghai (Provincial Party Secretary for Jiuquan and head of the Four Cleanups Task Force) and Dou had said that the red or black question would be judged by the verdict of the masses: we should believe in the masses, believe in the Party. He said that the opinions of a minority did not represent Party policy; she should not panic. Li said she knew that all along; there was no need to say so.

Her composure and confidence, and Dou's indication of support besides, reassured me not a little.

A month or so later, we went to the assembly hall of the Dunhuang County Committee to hear Dou Minghai make a report. This Dou Minghai, whom we knew as wearing a permanent smile, was out for blood on this occasion. Standing on the platform, shaking his fists, he said he would cut down the black flag and set up the red flag, "sweep away all cow demons and snake spirits." What was more, he made specific mention of "shattering the independent kingdom of the Dunhuang Research Institute."

I shot a sidelong glance at Li Chengxian, who was present. Her expression was impassive. I also turned my head for a quick glance at He Shizhi, sitting at the back. His expression was also impassive.

On the ride back to the Mogao Caves, everyone except Li Chengxian and me was very excited. Over and over they sang in unison:

> *The storm of revolution is engulfing the whole planet*
> *Cow demons and snake spirits are running in panic . . .*

The word "panic" was drawn out very long, in time with the rocking of the bus, and everyone's neck was also stretched very long. Heads wagged and feet stamped in perfect rhythm, and dust rose to fill the bus as feet pounded on its floor. Sitting beside me was the director's secretary, Li Yongning, a bit of a comedian given to loud guffaws. As he sang he had his arm around my shoulders, tightening and slackening and rocking and swaying with the beat. He was laughing so heartily that his whole face was deeply creased.

TWENTY-FOUR

Andante Cantabile

The first time I saw the name "Shi Pingting," it was on a door in the teachers' dormitory of Lanzhou Arts College. As her name suggested gracefulness, I imagined the person to be tall and pale-complexioned. When I later met her in Dunhuang, she turned out to be dark-skinned and stocky, and gave the impression of having knocked about a bit, which I couldn't help feeling didn't fit. At the general meetings of the Institute, she buried herself in an armchair up against the wall, crossed her arms over her chest, stretched her legs out, and propped her feet on a tea table in front of the chair. Her feet formed a V shape facing the rest of us. Left and right of the V were assembled her spectacles, tea mug, cigarette packet, ashtray, and notebook. When she spoke she closed her eyes and took her time, but her wits were as sharp as a needle. In criticizing the work of the Institute she was trenchant and eloquent at the same time.

Oddly enough, her husband He Shizhe, whose name suggested sage-hood, was truly fair-complexioned and tall. He wore heavy black-rimmed spectacles for acute shortsightedness, was thoughtful in manner, mild and cultivated in the style of a gentleman. He always sat upright at the conference table, his long musician's fingers cradling a small purple-sand teapot on the table. When he made a speech, his pitch was low and his pace slow, his words moderate and logical, his tone purely that of conferring among equals. But his viewpoint was exactly the same as his wife's, very trenchant. Hearing him speak, I often thought, Is this what they call "an iron hand in a velvet glove"?

They both had an army background and had laid their lives on the line in the Korean War, each having earned citations for valor. Later on they went to work in universities and research institutes and displayed originality in teaching and scholarship, their publications being both penetrating and meticulous. But the dustiness of books did not smother their martial spirit: at bottom they still emanated a dauntless militancy. They had no children, and their mental energies were devoted, apart from scholarship, to honing the edge of their intellect. In their studying they were skilled in analogical thinking; in discussion they neglected not even the smallest detail; in sizing people up they were penetrating; and in casual conversation they graduated from trivia to the level of meaning and value. Their conceptual capabilities were so good that I often felt it was a pity they did not take up philosophy instead of art history and archaeology.

In the autumn of 1962 a team of a dozen people from the Ministry of Culture met at Dunhuang to look into the consolidation of the caves. Shi Pingting and He Shizhi made a submission to the effect that the democratic revolution in the Dunhuang Cultural Relics Research Institute was not thoroughgoing, that the director before Liberation was still the director, that the old troupers had not been replaced, that there was no way of implementing Party policy, and that what they had was an independent kingdom in the desert. Their list of concrete items to be attended to made a thick book of several tens of thousands of words. They requested that the Party Central should send people to effect a radical shake-up. But the time was not ripe: it coincided with a temporary phase of relaxation, and Party policy stressed solidarity. Hence no action was taken.

Being a new boy, I was ignorant of all the matters referred to—except one. That matter made us friends. The two of them wanted to start up a periodical called *Dunhuang Studies*, and proposed I write an article for the first issue entitled "The Affinity to the People of Dunhuang Art." I said I didn't know what "affinity to the people" meant. They said there was plenty of stuff in the reference room. I said I had already skimmed through that, and it seemed that all articles on "heirship" had to refer to "affinity to the people," but the meaning of the term was never defined. It seemed to come from the Soviet Union, but reading Soviet treatises only left me more bemused.

At that time the breakdown in Sino-Soviet relations had not been made public, and Shi Pingting warned me, "You can't say that outside these four walls," while He Shizhe said with a smile, "I like the way you think for yourself." Shi said, "I do too, but you shouldn't go about blabbing. Watch out for people hoping to catch you out."

In the end I did not write the article. Instead I helped them with reviewing contributions and with the layout. But the magazine did not see the light of day because Chang Shuhong withheld his approval. In the material submitted to Xu Pingyu, He and Shi referred to this matter, claiming that Chang did not approve because he would not permit using Marxist and Maoist thought to critically study Dunhuang art. I said this was just speculation; supposition was not the same as fact. They laughed, saying "You don't understand the way things are."

One day over a meal in their home, the conversation turned to my experiences at the Jiabiangou education-through-labor camp. He Shizhe said that that was a valuable lesson in life, that I should be grateful for it. He said Lu Xun said there were two kinds of people one should eye with respect: those who had been to prison and those who had been on the battlefield, and in that he was right.[1]

"That sounds odd coming from you," I said.

Shi said, "You've already got us typecast, is that it? Tell us how you see us."

"I only meant it took me by surprise," I said.

"That implies we shouldn't surprise you, yes?"

"Don't take it like that," I said. "It was nothing, really. I've never gone to war. I couldn't cope."

"You can't imagine what it's like on the battlefield," Shi said.

"Why don't you try me?"

"You can't describe it; you can only say how it feels: cruel."

We fell silent. He Shizhe, stern-faced, reiterated solemnly, "War is cruel!"

"Yes," I agreed. "War is cruel."

Shi Pingting said, "When you say that and we say that, we mean different things. Just like a child saying life is a dream and an old graybeard saying life is a dream, they mean different things."

"I've been through a bit of war myself," I said. "Don't they say that politics is war without the bloodshed?"

"To be affected by politics is not the same as throwing yourself into politics," He said.

"I was only talking about what it felt like," I said. The three of us simultaneously burst out laughing. I had not laughed like that for many years. Perhaps I never had.

I hadn't been paid any wages for some years, and now I found myself getting eighty-three yuan per month at Dunhuang.[2] I sent it all to my mother, apart from a sum for my bed and board. He and Shi repeatedly advised against that, telling me I should send so much and keep so much. They said that as long as my family had enough to manage on at home, it would be all right, that I had to have a reserve. Buying books, some more clothes, getting some gear together, all took money. The monthly grain ration was 62 pounds; it didn't do to tough it out. For another thing, He and Shi added, one day I'd want to get married, and I'd need to have some savings put by. I used to get the same advice from my mother, and I was quite touched.

When the artwork for the new cave ran into political trouble, they were anxious for me, and at the same time they blamed me for taking too much on myself. They said it was not my personal business, so why should I get so het up? I said I was responsible for getting it done. They said that since I couldn't get it done, I shouldn't have taken it on in the first place—if you take on a task and can't get it done, you can't very well blame anyone else. I replied that I never thought it would have turned out like this, and they said I should have known. I asked them what I should do, and they answered that it was quite easy: just drop it. They also offered me a Zen koan: "Put down, and you find firm ground."

It was not until I went to see Li Chengxian to give up my job that I discovered that to drop or not to drop was a question of taking sides. From that point of view, many past things that I had not understood I now understood. Previously when He and Shi challenged Chang and Li, it was like ants trying to topple a tree; everyone distanced themselves from He and Shi. After Chairman Mao's two memos castigating the Ministry of Culture and the literary circles came down, and especially after Deng Tuo was criticized by name in the press, everyone discovered that Chang/Li's position was unsafe and He/Shi had had foresight, so instead they started to come over to He/Shi. Some people who normally kept Chang/Li informed now switched to reporting to He/Shi, or reported to both sides at once. It was no accident that the meeting to discuss the plan for the new cave paintings never came to pass.

This was the first time in my life that I faced the question of lining up behind somebody regardless of right and wrong. As I was deeply indebted to Chang, I could not fall in with the majority. I had no option but to do my utmost to finish off the new cave wall paintings. He Shizhe did not sympathize, and when the question of "Who is in charge of the creation of the new cave?" came up, all of a sudden I became the universal target, with everyone calling for my blood. Such was the fury that my slaughter was in imminent prospect. I had the feeling that I was falling into a pool of crocodiles.

It was not until the Cultural Revolution Task Force entered the Institute and proclaimed the start of the Cultural Revolution there that I felt some slight relief. The Task Force consisted of five people, two of them serving soldiers. Under their direction, a Cultural Revolution Leading Group was set up, headed by He Shizhe. Chang Shuhong was summoned back, as were those who had been sent elsewhere to do the Four Cleanups.[3]

Meetings were held every day; the temple courtyard was plastered with big-character posters, fingering the "black band of Chang, Li, Gao, and Wang." I was the Gao who was named; Wang was Wang Peizhong, third in command at the Institute. As he had just lately been unsparing in his efforts to denounce Chang/Li, I don't know how he got included.

I was the first culprit to be accused, as a bridgehead in the assault on Chang Shuhong. The denunciation began all over again, but it was all a rehash. The Task Force took most seriously the allegation that I'd made an X on the statue of Chairman Mao. They regarded it as a case of active counter-revolution and pursued it in deadly earnest. But that was the one charge that was baseless: the testimony of the informer Duan Wenjie was contradictory, and it was left out when the Task Force closed the file. Later on, when the tide turned against the Task Force, this was held up as an example of how it protected class enemies, but that tale is for later.

Chang, Li, and Wang were next in the dock, while I was banished to my room to write my self-criticism. One of the mistakes I admitted to was opposition to the head of the Cultural Revolution Group, He Shizhe. I explained that in public he accused me of being out-and-out reactionary, but in private praised me for thinking for myself; in public he denounced pacifism and the line that war was terrible, but in private said that war was cruel; in public he accused Chang Shuhong of not supporting him in publishing *Dunhuang Research* in order to suppress censure of feudalist, capitalist, revisionist culture, while the contents of the first issue were all feudalist, capitalist, revisionist. To back up my claim, I wrote from memory a table of contents of the first issue and an abstract of each article. All this I handed over to the head of the Task Force, the air-force officer Yu Jiasheng.

That same evening on my way to the toilet, I ran into Chang Shuhong. When I told him what I had done, he was greatly alarmed and reproached me repeatedly for being too rash. He said that if they got going on class vengeance, I'd set myself up as a typical case. Thinking things over, I too was a bit afraid and strongly regretted my action. Two weeks later I met

Chang again and told him there had been no reaction at all from the other side: it looked as if He was entirely in the dark, which signified that the Task Force did not trust him. Chang said, "If they really are going to put the screws on him, it won't be just because of that bit of material of yours; there must be a lot more against him."

Another two weeks later, one day in August, there was a general meeting of the Institute, and we four were told to attend as well. I learned only when I got there that He Shizhe and I were to confront each other. I could see that everyone was in the same boat as me, totally unprepared. But quite a few people immediately sensed the implication of confronting the head of the Cultural Revolution Group with someone already classed as "cow demon and snake spirit." They not only fell over themselves to back me up, they also disclosed a large number of He's problems that I was unaware of. They said he was a careerist, a plotter, a two-facer, a time bomb, a Khrushchev-type person . . . His crimes were said to be even more serious than mine.

He Shizhe was not fazed by his reversal of fortune; his manner was still serene. He argued logically and forcefully, his words stern with conviction. After every few sentences, however, he was interrupted, and as soon as he paused they shouted at him to get on with it. At first he shot a glance at me, then at the Task Force. The Task Force said nothing from start to finish, and their faces stayed expressionless. Eventually he became tense, repeatedly brushing his fingers through his hair more vigorously than was necessary. Time and again he took off his glasses to wipe the lenses, never completing the job to his satisfaction, and with trembling hands too. I looked across at Shi Pingting in her armchair: she kept shifting her sitting position and looking right and left. She more clearly betrayed that she was suffering a wave of deep-seated fear.

Oh, so the brave warriors were also afraid.

Instantly the joy of revenge raced through my veins; then it was gone just as rapidly. The residue left was a deep sadness, for myself and for them.

TWENTY-FIVE

Alien Tears

One day toward the end of October we were summoned to another meeting. The assembly room was elaborately decorated; on a big red banner had been pasted fifteen big white characters in the style of the Song Dynasty: "Mass Meeting to Celebrate the Victory of the Proletarian Great Cultural Revolution." On both sides of the Chairman's statue there were several red flags. There were some strangers in attendance, presumably high-ups of some sort.

The head of the Task Force announced the verdicts on us at the outset of the meeting: Chang Shuhong was to wear the hat of "counter-revolutionary," was expelled from the Party, was relieved of his post, and was to stay at the Institute to labor under supervision. Li Chengxian was expelled from the Party, and her salary was reduced by six grades. Wang Peizhong's salary was reduced by one grade and he remained in the Party on trial. He Shizhe was not allowed to renew his registration (i.e., would leave the Party in accordance with "purifying the ranks"). My salary was reduced by three grades. Shi Pingting and a few other people were exempted from penalty. And some other people were judged not to have been in the wrong: they were to put the matter behind them and progress with a clear record.

The head said the Party policy was to be stern in criticism and lenient in handling. This was, he declared, a victorious assembly, a uniting assembly, signifying the new birth of the Dunhuang Research Institute. Now we can hand over to our successors, he went on, with all uniting around the revolutionary leading group headed by Comrade He Shan, and advance boldly in close conformity with the strategic plan of the Party and Chairman Mao!

He Shan was a student of the wall painting department of Central Industrial Arts College. He had been assigned to the Institute not long before, on graduating. Very militant, he had joined the Party in the heat of battle, and replaced He Shizhe as head of the Cultural Revolution Group. He said our Institute had now got back on the socialist rails; that it was from now on determined to carry on the revolution in terms of the dictatorship of the proletariat and to perpetuate Mao Zedong thought for a thousand ages. The atmosphere of the meeting was enthusiastic; people swarmed onto the podium, protesting their loyalty and pledging their determination, mouths gaping in smiles, tears wetting their sleeves. I was rather puzzled. I had read the newspapers posted on the bulletin board while sweeping the yard, and it seemed that in Beijing they were throwing out the Task Forces, yet we still had this scene here. I couldn't figure out what was going on. Looking at some of them rejoicing, others worried, I was reminded of that occasion some months previously, how they had sung in the bus on the way back from hearing Dou Minghai's report, and still felt shivers run down my spine. Given the present outcome, there was still some room for celebration.

The day the Task Force departed, we were cutting grass in the Lower Temple. As their van came down from the Upper Temple it traveled very slowly, very slowly. Thirty-odd people were hemming the vehicle in, all stretching their arms out and scrambling along sideways, competing to shake hands with and speak to those inside. And having achieved a handshake, they were holding on for an eternity: they could never get to the end of what they wanted to say. Then they had to repeat what they said, going from one to another to say the same thing. Those crowding around wanted to have their say, too. Amid the babble of voices, and with much pushing and shoving, they staggered and lurched along with the van. The five passengers inside were hanging half out of the windows, their arms at full length, grasping one after another of the forest of hands. When one hand was held fast, they used their other hand to grasp another person's hand. I don't know how they managed to hear anyone clearly, given several mouths speaking at the same time.

In this way the van and the crowd moved on together at a snail's pace for a long, long way. Not until it had passed through the outer gate and was nearing the copse that acted as a windbreak did the van gradually pick up speed and start raising dust. The people in the dust cloud began to trot, eventually breaking into a run. At last they could not keep up, and the van sped off. Only then did they straggle to a halt, panting, waving their hand-kerchiefs, lifting their heads to peer into the distance. They waited until the dust cloud dispersed and there were only shadows cast by clouds on the vast Gobi Desert before they disconsolately make their way back. When they passed by where we were, they did not see us. One and all had swollen eyes, red noses, tear-streaked cheeks, and were sobbing wordlessly.

After the Task Force left, we were sent to a village to work, board with a peasant family, and receive re-education from the poor and lower-middle peasant class. In winter the days were short and the nights long, and there were few jobs to do on the land. In the evening we gathered in the schoolroom of the brigade headquarters, and by the flickering light of a lantern studied Chairman Mao's sayings, were lectured to by the Branch Secretary, got our orders from the team leader, and sang, "The sky is big, the earth is big, bigger still is the kindness of the Party. Dad and mom are not as dear as Chairman Mao." Meeting over, we went back and slept. As it was freezing cold everywhere, only the heated sleeping platform was warm. Day after day passed in this fashion. We had no idea what changes in the landscape were taking place over our horizon. Despite the fact that the memory of swords drawn was still fresh, it seemed to belong to another world.

A van suddenly came for us at the end of the year, to take us back to the Mogao Caves. As soon as we got out, we saw overlapping layers of big-character posters on which two factions were engaged in a slanging match. The language used was out-and-out murderous. One faction was headed by He Shan and was called the Revolutionary Alliance; the other was headed by Fang Xinggang, like He Shan a graduate of Industrial Arts College. This faction was called the Revolutionary Headquarters. Both competed in loyalty to Chairman Mao, and each accused the other of opposing Chairman Mao. Like fire and water, they could not coexist; one had to go down to extinction. It was held that the Task Force had implemented the capitalist-reactionary line of Liu Shaoqi and Deng Xiaoping, and had sabotaged Chairman Mao's great battle plan.[1] So the two rival factions were united in opposing the Task Force, and both painted big-character slogans: "We Demand That the Task Force Be Dragged Out and Struggled Against."

Individual big-character posters were even more vehement, especially those of the people whom the Task Force most trusted and most liked, those who stuck most closely to them. They all said their "lungs were bursting with anger," demanded "boiling xxx in oil," "beating the dog's head xxx to pulp," "flaying and burning xxx." (The xxx's represent the names of members of the Task Force.) When I recalled the send-off some of those same people got some months before, I was truly baffled.

The two factions separately pasted up big-character posters ordering that the four class enemies, namely Chang, Li, Gao, and Wang, had to toe the line and were forbidden to speak or act out of turn. They called upon the others who had been denounced to rise up and expose the monstrous crimes of the Task Force. I had no idea how the line between friend and foe was drawn, or why the hostile factions were so in agreement. As soon as He Shizhe came back, he took over the leadership of the Revolutionary Headquarters.[2] He was, as before, mild and cultivated and thoughtful in manner, never using violent language, behaving like a Confucian-style general. The majority put their trust in him and placed themselves at his beck and call, and He Shan's Revolutionary Alliance faction was put in the shade.

The members of the Task Force had long since returned to their individual units, so there was no way to "ferret them out." We four became the common enemy of the two factions; they took turns raiding our homes and attacking us. In the past the attacks had been verbal; now they became physical. Both factions competed in revolutionary ardor, which equated with competition in hatred, competition in who was more brutal in beating people. Chang Shuhong and Li Chengxian were regularly beaten till they lay squirming on the ground, covered in blood. And those who beat them most brutally were precisely those who had previously enjoyed their greatest trust and greatest affection and were their closest followers.

TWENTY-SIX

Curious Tales from the Cowshed

1.

In those years utter chaos reigned at the Institute. Nobody could make head or tail of what went on. The cow demons and snake spirits had no source of information; those of us in the cowshed were looking at the sky from the bottom of a well, as it were, so the scene was even more blurred.[1] In the two-faction struggle, the underdog Revolutionary Alliance defeated the top-dog Revolutionary Headquarters. New faces kept appearing. The Soldiers Propaganda Team, Workers Propaganda Team, Peasants Propaganda Team, Help-the-Left Brigade, Mao Zedong Thought Propaganda Team—all came and went, no one being able to keep up with who came first, who came after, or who was who. Our two factions of revolutionary masses went out to link up; Red Guards from outside came in to link up. The more they linked up, the fiercer the struggle became. On the one hand they were in a fight to the death; on the other they "brought about the great union," established "the revolutionary committee." Just when you thought order had come at last, what would you know, things got even more chaotic, more class enemies were revealed, there had to be a "purging of the class ranks . . ."

"Hats" flew fast and furious.[2] Chang Shuhong was called a capitalist roader, a Three-Anti's element; Li Chengxian was called a landowner; Fan Xinggang was an evil boss man, an active counter-revolutionary; He Shizhe was a right-winger who had slipped through the net, a sinister mastermind, a reverser of verdicts; Shi Pingting was a chameleon, a little reptile; Shi Weixiang, Li Qijing, and Sun Ruxian were called old rightists, like me; Li Zhenbo, who had overseas connections, was called a spy; Duan Wenjie was called a hoodlum, and because he had left the Party, a rebel. The rest of the distinguished company were reactionary authorities, or representatives of the black line in literature, or historical counter-revolutionaries, or class dissidents, or economic criminals, or leftover dregs of the Nationalist Party, filial descendants of the landed bourgeoisie: all were given their appropriate place in the stocks.[3]

Unlike us four, they had all participated in the Big Linkup before they entered the Cowshed, which had them chasing all over the country, and they were all half dead from fatigue. At that time they had no choice but to go, but now they were asked why they had wormed their way into the linkup ranks, what counter-revolutionary linkups of their own they had got up to. On top of that, they were required to reimburse the price of the "state" railway tickets according to the distance traveled. Since their salaries had been withdrawn, the amounts were deducted in installments from their subsistence allowance.

The cow demons and snake spirits were divided into two groups by gender and were housed apart. There were quite a few married couples among them: besides Chang and Li, and He and Shi, the wives of Sun Ruxian, Zhang Ersha, and Wan Gengyu were also detained. The husbands and wives were able to see each other three times daily: at "penance" sessions, mealtimes, and evening "political study." If Red Guards from outside came to link up, there were bound to be struggle meetings, in which case husband and wife would be sure to see each other undergo a beating.[4]

Every day before our meals, we gathered in front of the portrait of

Chairman Mao in the canteen. We formed two lines and chanted in unison a dozen or so sayings from Mao's Red Book, like "It is a rule that reactionary things will not fall unless you beat them down," "The popular masses will not rejoice until counter-revolutionary elements suffer," "They will not be reconciled as long as they live," and such stuff. Then we bowed three times to Chairman Mao's portrait and yelled out three times: "We ask to do penance before Chairman Mao!" Chang Shuhong could not stand upright, as a result of his many beatings, so he knelt to ask to do penance. Some of the revolutionary masses sat behind us at the six round tables, eating their food. At the end of the morning penance session we crowded around the table at which sat Kong Jin, who was in charge of production, and received from him our various work assignments for the day.

At eight in the evening we reassembled in the canteen to study Mao's *Selected Works*, and to expose and criticize each other. At the beginning, when those who had beaten people found themselves sitting with the people they had beaten, they were visibly embarrassed. It was even more awkward when they had to damn themselves as reactionary in front of those they had beaten. As time went by, though, their skins thickened and they stopped caring. Still, the business of attacking others while defending themselves against attack was quite a strain on the nerves, and a couple of hours of that left them all exhausted.

After we had gone to bed, the driver Wang Jiesan often rousted us out to unload his truck. Sometimes when he went to fetch coal and got back after midnight, he had us sweep out and wash the truck down after we had unloaded the coal. Having missed our sleep, we still had to get up on time the next day to work, which was hard to take. We once all suggested that he get together with Kong Jin to coordinate tasks. Wang glowered and said, "What's the point of going through him? The working class has to exercise leadership over everything, don't you know that? You study Mao's *Selected Works* every day, don't you? Call that studying!"

2.

As a matter of fact, other people besides him liked to call on us when they wanted something done. The electrician Hou Xing was the Institute's model student of Mao's *Selected Works*. In order to demonstrate that workers-peasants-soldiers were able to do everything, he used material in the sculpture center to sculpt a statue of Chairman Mao in the courtyard. Plinth included, it was over ten feet tall. The figure stood at attention with the shoulders square and the body straight and the torso, upper limbs, and lower limbs side by side in a vertical plane, like five round pillars. The fingers, which were pressed symmetrically against both legs, were also of the same thickness and length. The head was somewhat recognizable, but as small as a basketball. When the scaffolding was removed, it was a shock to behold. The work completed, Hou rounded us all up to take turns with the paint sprayer.

The spraying machine was heavily rusted, and it took a lot of strength to work the plunger. We could manage only five to six presses each, and the weaker among us only two to three presses. The twenty-odd of us formed a circle around the statue and moved slowly clockwise, taking turns working the plunger. As Chang Shuhong could not stand up, he crawled along and managed one press when it was his turn. Hou Xing went up and down his ladder with the spray nozzle, his eyes gleaming; every so often he would roar, "Put some vim into it!" Obviously he had gotten to know for himself the happiness of having his creation see the light of day.

Hou sprayed on one coat after another, and as he turned the nozzle, from time to time it would sweep its spray over us, leaving a thin layer of white specks on our bodies, including our faces, that could not be washed off. I covered my head with my jacket, and looked out on the world through a small aperture on those nationally and internationally renowned artists who, heads down, waists bent, were working like dogs—as if I were viewing a peepshow.

3.

I spent those years viewing a peep show. It was not simply that there was plenty of entertainment to see—the events themselves lengthened the distance between myself and my surroundings. At first I was in the thick of it, a target for all arrows and an indispensable supporting player on the stage of revolution. Later on, the leading actors started to fight among themselves and the supporting players were sidelined; so I became a bystander, able to watch the show.

Initially I was the only enemy; the rest were all "the people." Afterward, more and more were ferreted out and the ranks of us enemies expanded by the day: the number grew from one to four, from four to twenty-five. Those doing penance became a mighty host, more than half the personnel of the Institute.

On the day that Dunhuang County established its Revolutionary Committee, a mass meeting was convened in the city. We were dragged along too, and in common with the class enemies of the whole county, we wore high hats, were hung with black placards, and stood on both sides of the Command Platform to be pilloried: long serried ranks, their forest of high hats dense and depressing. In our row, besides Chang, Li, He, and Shi, there was Dou Minghai, Party committee secretary for Jiuquan Prefecture; Wang Zhanchang, secretary of the Dunhuang County Committee; and a load of other Party and government officials. It was bizarre and absurd to see them all lumped together with me.

The constant refrain of the speeches from the platform was that we should be knocked flat, trodden down, and not allowed to stand up again as long as we lived. But I knew that could not be done. Given that the offensive was on so wide a front, I felt fairly safe in the thought that "one person can hide in a crowd of ten thousand." I believed that my own fate would hardly be any worse than that of the masses who at that time packed the city square, sitting squashed together on the yellow earth, shaking their fists at us and yelling slogans.

The weather was very fine that day. Red flags fluttered like waves of the sea; the shouts of thousands made the earth shake and the mountains tremble. "My humble self subservient to the mass will," I dreamed a beautiful daydream and actually experienced the joyous sense of attending a festival.

4.

Since we could not make sense of what was going on, our only course was to pay no attention. In any case, we did what we were told to do and settled for waiting to see how we would be dealt with. At the end of the political study session, we just went back and slept.

There was a time when we were frequently awakened in the dead of night by the sound of firecrackers, drums, and cymbals. It was the revolutionary intellectuals celebrating and publicizing the fact that Chairman Mao had issued a "newest and highest directive." The newest and highest directives variously told them to go and settle in the countryside; to go to cadre schools to reform themselves; to combine with the old cadres they had overthrown to form a new leadership . . . These "wonderfully welcome news" items made them frantic with joy; they banged drums and cymbals and let off firecrackers as they sang and danced.

In order to keep close in step, in order that others could also keep close in step, they had to spread the news to all and sundry with the greatest speed. At whatever time they heard the announcement over the radio, they would set about celebrating and propagating, with not a minute to be lost. Because of the time difference with Beijing, they often had to rouse each other in the depth of night and spring into action.

I remember once we were unloading coal at two in the morning when their celebrating and propagating procession passed nearby. It was led by two men who were holding up a blackboard on which the newest and highest directive was written; behind them came some people banging drums and cymbals; behind them a dozen or so people doing the "loyalty dance." We couldn't see their steps very clearly, but they seemed vaguely to resemble the dance for celebrating an official's promotion in Peking opera, though to keep time with the drumbeat, the rhythm was more urgent:

Loyal loyal loyal to Chairman Mao.
Boundless boundless boundless forever forever forever.

Every seventy or eighty yards, they came to a halt. Cymbals, drums, song, and dance stopped together, and a man shone a flashlight on the blackboard and read the words out in a loud voice. Following that came a burst of firecrackers, and simultaneously cymbals and drums started up again and the procession continued. Stopping and starting in this way, they set out from the Middle Temple, went around the Upper Temple, down to the Lower Temple, and turned back again: all this took two to three hours at least. After unloading the coal we went back; only after we had gone to bed did we hear the faint sound of cymbals and drums coming from the Lower Temple, and growing in volume.

I was perplexed. There was no one at all in that vicinity, only still night, empty hills, deep woods, black stones. To whom were they spreading the word? Mulling things over on my pillow, I decided this must be uniform orders from above, to be carried out in towns and villages alike. They did not dare to fall short, so they did a circuit of the woods. I had a vision of those creatures of the night—foxes, jerboas, owls, and so on—turning around after they had made a safe escape and tilting their heads to inspect this crowd that was making a row to wake the dead. When the noise had died down they would certainly, like me, be quite unable to figure out what it had been in aid of.

5.

In line with the newest and highest directive, the Dunhuang Cultural Relics Research Institute set up a Revolutionary Committee. Due to the lack of old cadres to unite with, the position of head was temporarily unfilled. The head of the original Cultural Revolution Team, He Shan, became deputy head of the Revolutionary Committee and took charge of everything. Thenceforth the whole of the work of the Institute—apart from continuing with movements like "Purifying the Class Ranks" and "One-Hit and Three-Anti's,"—was responding to the call of "Three Loyal-tos, Four Unboundeds," "Grasp Revolution, Speed Up Production," and "Be Prepared Against War, Prepared Against Natural Disasters," with the Ninth Plenary Session of the Party in mind.

The "Three Loyal-tos" were "loyal to the leadership of the Communist Party; loyal to Mao Zedong thought; loyal to the proletarian revolutionary line of Chairman Mao." The "Four Unboundeds" were "unbounded love, unbounded faith, unbounded worship, unbounded devotion to Chairman Mao." This activity was ritualized. They painted the four walls of the assembly room an orange color, and on the east wall painted a radiating red sun. On the sun was painted a head of the Chairman, with an army cap and red collar tabs. Below that was a row of sunflowers supporting three red hearts, and on each of the three red hearts was written in yellow the character for "loyal." Every morning and evening they would all gather there, stand to attention, and facing the yellow "loyalty" characters with the precious Red Book clasped to their hearts, shout in unison: "We respectfully wish our great leader, great commander-in-chief, great teacher, great helmsman Chairman Mao life without end! Life without end!! Life without end!!!" That done three times, they went on to three times respectfully wish Deputy Commander-in-Chief Lin Biao eternal good health. Following that they sang the Mao Sayings song, recited the Sayings, and studied Mao's *Selected Works*. The answer as to what should be done today was sought in the *Selected Works*—in other words, asking Chairman Mao for instructions. This ceremony was therefore called "morning call for instructions."

Next came "Grasp Revolution, Speed Up Production." Those who investigated cases investigated cases, those who disinfected, disinfected.

They had a lot on their plate. The religious culture of Dunhuang was supposedly an opium which poisoned the people, and if it remained, it had to be disinfected. Disinfection was revolution, and at the same time it was production. The completion of the work of disinfection would be a tribute paid to the Ninth Plenum. Everybody cut fiber boards into newspaper-size pieces, nailed them onto a frame, painted them red, then wrote quotations from Chairman Mao on them in yellow square characters and hung them at the entrance to the caves to disinfect them. Since there were hundreds of caves, the work involved was huge.

The quotations were not copied from the Mao Sayings book but were sought directly from his *Selected Works*, and were to the point. For example, to counter the picture of Saduona feeding the tiger in cave 254, they chose the passage on "Emulate Wu Song on the Jingyang Ridge"; to counter the picture of the five hundred robbers becoming Buddhas in cave 285, they chose the passage "You can know their present from their past."[5] They ransacked the *Selected Works* to find a good match, and debated over and over. Sometimes they argued until they were red in the face over which quotation was more suitable for which cave: it was a must that future visitors should be effectively inoculated before entering any cave.

When I went to sweep the caves, I saw a gradual increase in these finely crafted quotation placards at the entrances, and admired their care and patience. Of course there were still quite a lot of repetitions, strained connections, even complete mismatches. One could not blame them, for the wall paintings were so plentiful: it was a highly commendable achievement to do as much as they did.

6.

Another kind of regular work at the Institute was to "prepare against war." We played a part in that, digging the air-raid shelters. The others underwent people's militia training in the afternoon, which was quite tough too. Before their shift was over they also had to go to the assembly room and report the day's work to the image of Chairman Mao. This ceremony was called the "evening report."

The procedure for the "evening report" was the same as that for the "morning call for instruction," except that the study of the *Selected Works* was replaced by insights gained from the study. The lessons learned in the morning had been applied during the day: What had been improved? What achievements had there been? What problems had been encountered? What intelligence of the enemy had been discovered? What things had not been done well? Criticism and self-criticism had to be carried out. By the time this program was finished, supper time was normally long past, while we cow demons and snake spirits had completed our penance ritual, had eaten, and were preparing for our evening political study session.

That winter, after I had come back from the hills and "opening up the wilderness," I had the job of supplying water for the kitchen, besides sweeping the caves. First thing in the morning I carried my bucket, pick-axe, shovel, and iron borer to the frozen river on the other side of the woods to break the ice and fetch water. While the frozen river and the snow-covered hills opposite changed color successively from the blue of predawn to violet and then to silvery red, I carted water to fill the kitchen cistern. By the end a layer of frost had formed on my beard, eyebrows, and hat brim, while the rest of me was sweating and steaming all over. After sitting in front of the kitchen stove for a while to toast myself dry, I had to lock up and return the key to the caretaker before repairing to the caves.

The caretaker took part in the "morning call for instructions" in the assembly room. The red-hot stove in there sent out steaming waves of heat, and the room was packed full of people, creating a thick fug. As soon as I opened the door there was a blast of fetid air, saturated with body odor, coal gas, cigarette smoke, and a strong smell of paint—so thick you could cut it with a knife, like a solid. Each time the door closed, I made a leap to get clear and thought, "It's lucky I don't belong to the revolutionary masses."

TWENTY-SEVEN

Facing Walls

I was in Dunhuang for ten years, from 1962 until 1972, but I worked on my art projects for only four years. When the Cultural Revolution erupted in '66, I was dragged out for "struggle and criticism" and put under supervised labor. I remained under supervised labor until I left Dunhuang in 1972.

The Cultural Revolution changed not only the daily lives of the people at the Institute but also the way they looked and acted. Overnight those gentle, reserved people turned into fierce beasts and violently leaped and hollered, suddenly sang at the tops of their voices, suddenly burst into tears, slapped themselves, rose at midnight and yelled "Long Life," or banged gongs and drums to disseminate the thoughts of the "Great Man." [1] In the whole Mogao Caves area, only those icons of Buddha and bodhisattvas maintained their dignity and self-possession.

After more and more people were dragged out for denunciation, I was cast aside as a "dead tiger" and often sent to clean the caves. My job, to sweep out the sand that fell from the cliffs, drifted in, and accumulated into thick or thin layers, was impossible to assess because those cliffs contained four to five stories of over 490 caves, and no one could tell where the sand had entered. If I hadn't swept a cave, I simply said that more sand had just drifted in.

I spent years doing this. Every day, alone, I leaned on my broom, gazed up at the walls, and roamed in my imagination with the immortals and Buddha, as if I lived in another world. After dark, when I couldn't see clearly, I went out onto the wooden walkway and looked into the distance "leaning on the railing, there was no one else," a unique, poignant experience.[2] Beyond the ocean of trees, a strip of light from the setting sun fell on the Earth amid ten thousand hectares of primordial wilderness, and often in my reverie I didn't even know what year it was.

I had seen these murals before, but what I saw while leaning on a broom was different from what I saw while I held a data card or a paintbrush in my hand. Within the framework of Buddhist doctrine, the material displayed was extremely rich, especially in its depiction of all aspects of social life and its illustrations of the previous reincarnations of Buddha and Buddha's moral tales. The murals pictured hundreds of activites, including farming, silk-worm cultivation, weaving, building, hunting, fishing, husbandry, marriage, funerals, pedagogy, commerce, pottery making, blacksmithing, harnessing and driving, milling, cooking, warfare, begging, butchery, martial arts, singing and dancing, acrobatics, morning court scenes, banquets, imperial tours and hunting, tonsuring, and trials. Also illustrated were palaces, moats, pavilions and towers, bridges and ponds, boats and carriages, schools and shops, rest stations and wine shops, costumes and jewelry, and utensils for religious rituals. Useful material could be found for researchers from many disciplines.

When I held data cards, the murals were information; when I held a paintbrush, models. But now, with a broom in my hands, as I awaited punishment and had the time to take a leisurely look, the murals, one after the other, became a spiritual history and a space for the expansion of my thought.

Everyone said Tang art was the best and most beautiful, but I preferred the Wei Dynasty caves. Human figures in the Sixteen States caves were short, sturdy, and plain, while those of the Tang were full-figured and dignified. Only during the Wei and Jin dynasties did the figures become graceful, with a vivid, elegant bearing, broad foreheads and narrow cheeks and brows, and eyes set far apart, with simple, distinct facial features, illustrating exactly what was written in *Worldly Stories Retold*—"elegant outlines and pure images"—and in *Famous Paintings of Different Dynasties*—"transformations give rise to strange effects."[3] The colors were not those of the actual objects: green horses, blue horses, black mountains, white mountains floating in space, blue people, green people, and red people, all with white eyes and white noses, none of which could be seen in the human realm. Crowds of figures swarmed from black or earth-red backgrounds, giving a mystical and mysterious effect.

I lingered most in cave number 285 of the Western Wei. The cosmos was represented, transparent and clear, by a simple whitewashed wall. The Milky Way flowed in a torrent; tenuous clouds scudded through the air, and the vast emptiness mingled with the supreme purity. There were the multiple heavens of Buddhism: the Heaven of the Sun; the Heaven of the Moon; the Heaven of Weiniu, of Pinayejia, and of Jiumoluo; the Heaven of the Eight Degrees, and so forth. There were also subjects found not in Buddhist scriptures but only in ancient Chinese mythology: Fuxi, the sun god; Nuwa, goddess of the moon; the gods of the four directions, Zhu Que, Xuan Wu, Qing Long, and Bai Hu; Lord of Thunder and Rain; Fei Lian, the Feathered Man; King of the East; Queen of the West; and monsters from the "Ask the Heavens" section in the *Chu Songs* surged and chased each other throughout the sky.[4] Some rode thunderclouds and lightning; some rode flying wheels. Spiritual pennants fluttered; a magnificent canopy was suspended in the sky; flags furled and unfurled; ribbons flowed from clothing like rainbows, and you could feel the swirling wind as if it rushed from the wall.

All the decorative markings throughout the cave, including those on the embellished ceilings and niche lintels, were composed of lines. Countless lines, thin yet strong, tensile as metal wires, slender, long, and pliant as wandering spider threads, interpenetrated the unfathomable, precarious, and strangely lighted blocks of color and followed one another, chased one another, sometimes converged, sometimes flew apart, lightly descended, abruptly soared, extended leisurely and abruptly shrank; they merged, interlocked, swirled, seemed about to tangle but suddenly rose, scattered but still corresponded and met in unexpected places. Like music, with a flute's modulating flow but not its feebleness, with a drum's cadence but not it's wildness, they took their time, without urgency and with a tinge of sadness, but in this sadness there was self-confidence—not the terror of fate, not a tragic loftiness, not a self-deprecating submissiveness or a hesitation about where to go.

The art in the Tang caves, especially in those caves between the Zhen Guan and Kai Yuan periods, had the characteristics of the Hua Yan sutra: splendor, magnificence, and sublime beauty.[5] The colors were contrasting, vivid and rich, and the brushstrokes diversified. They demonstrated the "middle touch technique," dipping the brush halfway into paint, sometimes using the tip, sometimes the side, so the effect was a modulation between light and heavy, fast and slow, rarified and substantial, thick and thin. The Orchid Leaf style, elegant and curved; the Iron Wire style, forceful with clear edges; the Wandering Thread style, soft and fluid; the Master Cao style and the Master Wu style—all were intermingled yet distinct. The bodhisattvas and their attendants were arrayed in colorful textured clothes in the Master Zhou style, with curved eyebrows, plump cheeks, glowing flesh, full bodies, long hair flowing down to their shoulders, bared upper torsos, with pearl beads and precious jewelry, luxurious and dazzling. Some stood still, some danced and sang, some flew, others sat still and meditated, but they were all vivacious, engaging, yet dignified and self-composed. The art did not depict either the repression of the senses or reckless abandonment to the senses; the solemnity of the Buddhist kingdom was transformed into human affections, and the paintings became magnanimous, profound.

Within the Tang caves I admired the statues most, especially those in caves 205 and 194 and a few others. The statues were all of Buddhist deities, each with his or her own personality: Anan was pure and simple,

Jiaye worn with worldly care, while the bodhisattva Guan Yin was innocent and benevolent. They were barefoot, as if they had just emerged from
the desert's burning winds and flaming sands after many hardships; they
faced the coming day calmly with neither fear nor grievance, regarded the
future as if it were the past, and conquered misfortune without noticing.
The reclining Buddha of cave 138 was the portrayal of Sakyamuni nearing death. He had a relaxed and natural posture, an unworldly, serene
countenance. As if awakening from a dream, as if opening like a lotus,
he regarded his end as his beginning and overcame death without being
aware.

Seeing death depicted as a triumph of life, I remembered that those
statues from Western art that took death as their theme (for example,
"Laocoon") were tragic. Broad chests, bulging muscles, drastic movements, tense expressions, were symbols of the struggle against fear and
desperation. In contrast, these effeminate, peaceful, and serene statues in
the caves had more force. This difference cannot be explained by ready-
made concepts, such as the opposition of masculine and feminine, or the
Christian metaphor of the cross or the Daoist diagram of the yin and yang.
Their hidden message was a door to a different world.

Facing the walls in these tiny stone caves, I had a sense of openness. It
was a pity when it got dark and I had to return to the outside, along with
those others dragged out to make confessions before the icon of Chairman Mao, sing propaganda songs, listen to exhortations, denounce and
criticize one another, and make self-denunciations and self-criticisms.
And just like the ghosts penned by Dante that bit, gnawed, and tore one
another, we had nowhere to hide. Walls were everywhere.

TWENTY-EIGHT

Sunset on Barren Mountain

1.

To the north of Dunhuang are Yiwu, Jiji Mesa, Akesai; to the east Yumen, Jiuquan, Jiayuguan; to the south, after crossing the Shule River, are the perennially snow-capped Qilian Mountains; and to the west there are Loulan, Luntai, and Bailongdui, while farther west there's Luobibo. The seven- to eight-day journey by camelback from any of these areas to an adjacent one goes through a desolate landscape, over endless flowing gravel and sand without a trace of a human being.

The world-famous treasure house, Mogao Caves, commonly known as the Thousand Buddha Caves, is located in a tiny oasis occupying less than half a square mile within that expansive desert. There were no work units in the area except for the Dunhuang Cultural Relics Research Institute, and no inhabitants except for the Institute's families. During the Cultural Revolution, the forty-nine people of the Institute were put in and out of detention in the Cowshed, and at the Revolution's peak more than twenty were confined. Those who remained outside split into two clashing factions. Later, they told us, the two factions reconciled and the Institute planned to establish a "May 7 Cadre School." [1] In the winter of

1968 they sent seven of us from the Cowshed into the mountains to clear land for cultivation.

Having a burdensome work quota while facing the severe northern cold of these desolate, deep, and uninhabited mountains would of course be harsh, but we who had been assigned were inwardly delighted. The struggle sessions, exhortations, confession rituals, supervised labor, and late-night study sessions, where we tore at and ripped into each other, had left us exhausted, but once in the mountains we had the hope that these conditions would change, or at least that for a time we could free ourselves from anxiety and settle our overly strained nerves. Those left in the Cowshed already looked at us with envy.

There were seven in our group. One was an illiterate, forthright gardener named Wu Xingshan, who, since he was a Daoist priest at the Thousand Buddha Caves before Liberation, was naturally considered one of the "monsters and demons." Another was Zhou Dexiong, who was illiterate but intelligent, capable, and had first-class cooking skills, but because he had once opened a restaurant, had "flirted" with capitalism. The other five were professionals within the research section. Mr. Huo Xiliang specialized in cave and temple research and was the archaeology section leader. Mr. Shi Weixiang was an expert in the regional history of Gua Zhou and Sha Zhou and a knowledgeable authority on Central Asian civilization. His excellent calligraphy in the classical Jingti style had the flavor of that of the Wei and Jin dynasties. Mr. Duan Wenjie was my direct superior at the Institute. Before he was "exposed," he was deputy director of the research department and group leader of the fine arts department, and afterward became leader of the "exposed" group. After the Cultural Revolution, he replaced Chang Shuhong as the Institute's director. These three had followed Mr. Chang to Dunhuang before the Liberation and never left. Because they were erudite Dunhuang scholars, they were all well equipped to be my teachers. Mr. Li Zhenbo, originally an instructor at Central Conservatory of the Arts, had been at the Institute for over ten years. That year I was thirty-one. I had just come in '62, and was the youngest and the least qualified of this group.

At the Institute, we seldom had anything to do with one another and, except for the weekly political study sessions, rarely met. Even after we were "exposed" and were under the "dictatorship of the proletariat" by day and huddled in one bed by night, we didn't share our thoughts. On the contrary, due to the continual close contact, we were afraid that someone might grab onto something and use it against us, so we shut ourselves off, and each one of us, always fearful and scrupulously attentive, couldn't find rest even in sleep. I was the same: frightened I'd say something in my dreams that would betray me.

Ten or more people slept on one long platform bed; Chang Shuhong was on my left and Shi Weixiang on my right. As soon as Shi Weixiang lay down, he started to snore. I was envious but later found out that it was an act to show he felt at ease and harbored no contrariness. And he did give that impression. I wanted to follow his example but found it difficult. First, it was exhausting; second, I couldn't imitate my own snoring because I never heard it; third, I couldn't stop unless I pretended to wake up again; and fourth, I had to assume that someone in the dark was paying attention, otherwise the effort would have been for nothing. I tried a few times but it was extremely taxing, extremely uncomfortable, and I gave it up. One midnight, Shi Weixiang, Sun Rujian, and I were ordered to unload coal. When we returned, we heard Duan Wenjie cry out in his sleep, "Chairman Mao! Long Life!" We thought it was curious, but not until the next day during labor, when Old Duan tried all sorts of tricks to get a reaction from us, did we realize it was a ruse. We knew pretending to talk while asleep was harder than pretending to snore, but we wouldn't play along, and without consulting each other, we all told him we heard nothing.

Everyone was happy now that we were about to enter the mountains, but happiness depended on the fact that they were sending one of the "revolutionary masses" to escort, oversee, and manage us. Otherwise it would have gone badly, because we would have been forced to spy on and judge one another, to supervise, guard, and tear at one another, and the torment we inflicted on ourselves would have been far crueler than at the Institute.

Our team leader, Fan Hua, was about fifty. A poor peasant from birth, he had done odd jobs at the Institute for more than thirty years. He was honest his entire life, worked with unwavering diligence and cordiality, and never said more than a few words. Following Liberation the political movements were unrelenting, but he, a destitute working-class peasant who never harmed anyone, attracted no attention. During the famine five years earlier, he had come upon an ugly starving cur abandoned by a shepherd; he fed it a few times but never thought the dog would follow him. People were starving and he fed a dog. Everyone advised him to slaughter it to supplement his diet, but he couldn't; he just kept complaining as he fed the dog. It was a big joke.

Assigning Fan Hua to be team leader was purely serendipitous: since it was a strenuous job that no one else was willing to take, it fell to him. It was fortunate for us, because only he wouldn't tyrannize us, only he would be able to work with us on an equal basis, and only he would *dare* work with us on an equal basis. When he told us to prepare to depart, we enthusiastically, happily obliged and quickly gathered up the tools needed to clear the land. However, there were no personal belongings: our homes had been "sealed off" and all each of us had was chopsticks, a bowl, and a bedroll.

The next morning we set out.

2.

A stream surges from the earth and flows through the Thousand Buddha Caves area, forming a small desert oasis, before it disappears underground again. The source of this water is in the southern mountains. These smaller mountains, which are the foothills of the Qilian Range, billow up and down into the Gobi Desert until they disappear into the infinite dry ocean of sand. Our task was to climb to the water source, clear the land, and lay the foundations for the Institute's May 7 Cadre School.

Wang Jiesan drove the eight of us in a Liberation model truck to the mountain pass, where we unloaded hoes, spades, saws, provisions, cooking utensils, and eight bedrolls. After we packed everything onto a handcart, we entered the mountains. I pulled the cart while the others pushed; in this way we forged ahead, stepping over gray-yellow gravel, following the gray-yellow ravine. The big sky and vast earth made us feel insignificant. Because of the gentle grade I didn't notice we were climbing, until I incidentally turned my head and saw how high we were. No one spoke; only the gravel pressed beneath our feet made a sound—*xi suo, xi suo*—while the wheels emitted tenuous, rhythmic noises, as if saying *ee—nuff, ee-nuff.*

That evening we spread our bedrolls at Bitter Mouth Spring, and by the afternoon of the second day we entered a comparatively broad ravine. Beneath the cliffs, variegated with grayish yellow, rust brown, light coffee colors, and deep reds, reedy, soil-covered knolls appeared. As we walked, the terrain became open, the cliffs and rock outcroppings fewer and the rolling hills more. At dusk we arrived at our destination, Big Spring.

Big Spring was a flat, broad riverbed deep in the desolate, chaotic range of mountains. Clumps of red willow grew along the riverbank; their branches intertwined into a vast flat sheet that meandered along slopes swarming with an endless fluff of golden rushes. From a distance in the summer, the willows looked like a blue ocean of trees beneath the brush of the Russian painter Shiskin. In autumn, blossoming flowers turned everything pink. But then it was winter; the flowers and leaves had withered and fallen, and beneath the reflecting evening sun, the slender, pliant, and densely packed red-willow stems turned a silver-gray blended with gold and red, light, soft as a cloud of smoke. Seen from afar, the willows mingled with each other, then merged with the hills and ridges into a purple haze. Suspended above, the distant unbroken silhouette of snow-blanketed mountains sparkled amber within the dusk.

Water gushed from the ground at different places along the riverbed, forming various-sized bogs and lakes that flashed sunlight among the red-willow shrubs. Because of the warm soil temperature, the water never froze and remained limpid, clear, the year round. On the submerged egg-shaped rocks, slippery green moss grew thick as swans down, while flocks of waterfowl sported on the surface, sometimes startling and flying away making *ga, ga* calls.

A half-dilapidated clay brick adobe, without planks for door or floor, sat on the side of a rock-covered hill near a pond. Inside it was empty except for a long sleeping platform on the left and a broken-down cooking stove in the right corner. It had been a station house for camel drivers, but because a new highway had been built, it had been abandoned and had lain forgotten for many years.

We stopped the cart at the foot of the hill, transported our supplies item by item into the hut on the slope, and spent the night. The next day we fixed the cooking stove, set up the chopping board, cleaned ashes from the cavity beneath the sleeping platform, repaired holes in the walls and roof, and then split up to collect either firewood or camel dung. Wu Xingshan simply sealed the frameless window with clay, while Fan Hua draped burlap over the doorway. An opening was left in the roof for light and air and to vent smoke. The hemp string that suspended an oil lamp from the ceiling was rotted, so Zhou Dexiong ripped threads from a burlap bag and twisted a new cord. A brightly polished ink bottle served as a kerosene lamp, and by nighttime the room felt surprisingly cozy and orderly. We blew out the lamp, started a fire in the brazier, and without a word gathered round and warmed ourselves awhile. And then, as if it were entirely natural, we climbed onto the bed without "confessing to Chairman Mao" and fell asleep.

On the third day we started reclaiming the surrounding virgin land, which, due to several previous eruptions of floods, was alluvial: flat, loose-soiled, and not difficult to work. We only needed to excavate the willow shrubs, make furrows following the terrain, level the soil, and dig an irrigation ditch to draw in the bog water, and the land would then be ready for next spring's plowing and seeding. According to Fan Hua's "handed-down" message, this would be the Institute's first achievement in carrying out Chairman Mao's May 7 Directive.

With Fan Hua as team leader, Duan Wenjie wasn't in charge, so the whole system of daily political rituals, so stringently carried out at the Institute, wasn't mentioned at all. We worked hard by day, but during the dark, secluding nights, we warmed ourselves for a while by the brazier, climbed onto the platform bed, made snug by the burning camel manure beneath, and slept. When it was still too early and I couldn't sleep, I lay there, weighing things over in my mind or smoking a hand-rolled cigarette. Duan Wenjie didn't talk in his sleep. Shi Weixiang didn't pretend to snore. I felt that the almost audible silence meant we were truly liberated. And I thought about the fact that there were no study sessions in which we self-scrutinized and denounced each other; that no one could wake us at midnight to unload coal; that we didn't have to line up before daybreak, bow to an image of Chairman Mao, and self-confess; and that here there wasn't even an image of Chairman Mao. I was completely happy, especially when the wind's keening sounds above the hut reminded us of the freezing, gloomy night and we curled into our warm, dry quilts and couldn't help but thank our fate.

The only problem was a paucity of food. At the Institute we had fixed rations but could always supplement our diet with wild vegetables. However, the mountains had no wild vegetables and we couldn't even think of meat. Therefore the turnips we brought along became precious. We chopped small pieces into thin slivers and sprinkled them on top of soup to give it a little taste. A fixed ration of twenty-eight jin was hard to bear, but for people like us (I don't know what Fan Hua thought), if we didn't suffer one thing we suffered another, and who could be happy without a cost? We exchanged humiliation for hunger and felt it was worth it.

3.

At the Institute we worked every Sunday, but here we rested and washed or patched our clothes, blankets, shoes, and socks, or closed our eyes, folded our arms, and leaned against the south wall of the hut to take in the sun. One Sunday Fan Hua unwrapped a white cloth parcel containing a complete barber's set and gave us each a haircut. Early that morning Wu Xingshan had set out to the mountainside, where he filled the straw basket on his back with *suoyang*; he then gave everyone some "to improve life." *Suoyang* is a penis-shaped tuber, which when dried is used as an herbal medicine for blood circulation, diuresis, strengthening the kidneys, and enhancing virility. It was very precious and scarce near the Institute, but plentiful here. Zhou Dexiong washed them, boiled them until soft, and then blended them with corn flour to make a slightly sweet cake. We ate our fill.

Afterward we sat around the fire, lost in thought, enjoying the feeling of satiation. It wasn't late, yet the room had become dark. No one spoke. Occasionally someone coughed. The wood in the fire crackled intermittently and popped a shower of sparks. Zhou Dexiong puffed and puffed on his pipe.

"Urumqi is really very rich," Fan Hua suddenly blurted.

No one answered. The reflected firelight played and flickered with the shadows on eight contemplative faces.

After a long pause, Li Zhenbo asked, "Have you been to Urumqi?"

"Just once," Fan Hua said. "In 1962 for a specialist conference. Li Chengxian sent me to buy food. They had everything there . . ."

"Xinjiang is a minority area. They should be treated specially," Wu Xingshan said.

"Once you get to Urumqi, it's like a foreign country. Nothing's the same," Fan Hua continued in a low voice, as if talking to himself. "The houses are different. Some have pointed roofs, some domes; some roofs are flat; some have railings on four sides, some holes for smoke. The people are different, too. They have high-bridged noses and deep-set eyes. Some have pencil moustaches, some full beards, some goatees, some sharp-tipped moustaches pointing downward or sharp-tipped moustaches pointing upward, some three-tufted beards or five-tufted like the God of War. People bump shoulders on the street. The watermelons are very big! The grapes are very big! Everywhere there are little grills for lamb kebabs. Ten cents buys two kebabs. They sizzle and drip oil in your hands."

He paused, stoked the fire. The fire brightened, dimmed, leaving a lingering shadow of gloom on eight faces.

"There are crowds of people wearing different clothing in bright colors. How well the colors go together," Fan Hua continued in a dreary tone as if the gloom had infected him. "Some wear colored hats and riding boots; some wear white hats and long gowns. Some gowns are pure black, some all white, quite unusual. Some girls wear green sleeveless jackets with white embroidery or purplish red jackets with silver embroidery, some black jackets with gold embroidery, and these go with skirts of all colors, some light yellow, some apricot yellow, some deep red, some sky blue, and all very short. Their legs are bare and they wear boots. They're high-spirited. They like to hum. Singing fills the streets . . ."

"Shh, shh," Zhou Dexiong urged, putting his finger to his lips.

We listened. Barely audible in the deep silence came a faint *ding, dong* sound.

"Those are camel bells," Wu Xingshan said. "A team's coming."

We went outside but couldn't see anything. The hazy evening sun dyed layers of clouds and mountain crests a golden red, and the countless snow-covered peaks glimmered like a chain of precious stones embedded in the firmament. Coming from the murky, stale-aired little hut and suddenly faced with this sublimity, we were stunned and couldn't speak for a while.

The bells became louder, clearer. Then seven camels loomed like shadows out of the dusk and kneeled in a row by a pond under the cliff. Two men alighted and unloaded large parcels. Afterward one coaxed the camels up and watered them, while the other carried a leather coat uphill. Zhou Dexiong went to meet him, took the man's coat, and led him into the hut.

The man was about seventy; a missing front tooth gave him a

ludicrous smile, but he was full-spirited, with a strong, sonorous voice that emanated from deep inside. His weathered, deeply wrinkled face, cramped between a huge nondescriptly colored beard and a large leather hat, had a healthy, ruddy glow. A single riveting eye scanned the room, noticing everything.

"Damn! Cold as hell!" he said. He sat by the fire, rolled back the brim of his hat, and brushed the frost from his beard and eyebrows.

Zhou Dexiong lit the cooking fire, put water on to boil.

A strapping, fierce-looking, sullen young man came in carrying a bag of flour. Without looking at anyone, he tossed the bag on the chopping board with a thud.

He said to the old man, "What are you going to do with this?"

"Don't be in a hurry," the old man said. "They're boiling water!"

"You can use some water to wash up or to cook with," Zhou Dexiong said complaisantly.

Zhou, who previously owned a restaurant, knew how to treat people. At the Institute he was clean and neat and cooked delicious food that was well liked. But after we were "exposed and denounced," he bullied us by withholding food; if we resisted, he would ask us if we were unhappy with the Party's rationing policy. Once "exposed" himself, however, he became companionable.

As he boiled the water, he said to the young man, "Warm by the fire while I cook for you. Do you have anything I can make into a meal? "

"No," the young man said.

"We still have a couple of turnips; I can cook something for you," Fan Hua said as he picked up two cornmeal cakes. "First eat a little of this. We mixed it with *suoyang*."

"Thanks." The old man was obviously moved. He asked the young man, "Where's the antelope meat?"

"Down below," the young man said.

"Go fetch it!"

The young man left. "Where did you get it?" Zhou Dexiong asked as he rolled dough into noodles.

"We hunted it . . . gazelle."

Zhou Dexiong stopped rolling the dough and asked intently, "How did you hunt it?"

"A steel trap."

"What kind of steel trap?"

"Haven't you ever seen one?" The old man stood, lifted the door curtain, and shouted down the mountain, "Hey, bring back a steel trap!"

They were Anxi peasants carrying firewood back to their production brigade, and in the future they would have to return to the mountains to gather more. Fan Hua asked how things were and the old man said it depended, sometimes good and sometimes not, but his brigade was all right. As he spoke the young man carried in a skinned antelope carcass, frozen hard as steel, and a black triangular steel trap.

The old man took the trap, opened it, and placed it on the ground. He stepped on the middle spring and said to Wu Xingshan, who was standing alongside, "Pull this back. Use some muscle!"

Wu Xingshan pulled two curved iron bars back, which opened into a circle. The old man hooked the bars in place, carefully lifted his foot, and then picked up a stick about as thick as a thumb and lightly touched the trap. *Pow!* The trap jumped fiercely, snapping the stick in two. Everyone jumped backward.

After eating, we climbed onto the platform bed. The old man took down the kerosene lamp and put it on the edge of the bed. He and Zhou Dexiong ignited the lamp and lit their pipes; then the old man related stories about the gazelle, its habits and its natural terrain, and his hunting techniques . . . until the morning hours.

They left early next day. Zhou blatantly asked to borrow a trap and a gazelle leg and agreed to return the trap when they came back and present them with a gazelle.

4.

It takes two people to catch a gazelle. Since I was the youngest, I had to be one of them. The scholars weren't mobile, Fan was in charge, and Zhou had to cook, so it was decided that Wu Xingshan would join me.

The herds stayed clear of our area because of our presence. According to the old man, there were four other water holes besides the one we used. We chose the nearest, set the trap by the waterside, where there were the most gazelle tracks, covered the trap lightly with twigs and reeds, sprinkled sand over it, and then brushed the sand smooth and using the hoof, stamped prints on top, intermingling them with the surrounding prints. As we withdrew, we swept our own tracks clear and covered the earth with more gazelle hoofprints. Then we left, thrilled by the accomplishment of this deceitful, dirty little job. The following day we watched from a distance; there was no movement, and I began to suspect that we had done something wrong.

We checked the traps daily and, without my realizing it, it was Sunday again. While the others rested, Old Wu and I set out early—and found the trap gone and a depression left in its place. We figured a gazelle had been caught and carried the trap away. We bent over and tried to find its tracks, which should have been different from the others covering the riverbed and valley, until our backs ached. Just when we were about to lose hope, on a hillside about a hundred yards away, we found a depression that looked as if it had been gouged out by a spade.

It was as we expected: the gazelle ran away with its trapped leg lifted, which was why there were no distinctive tracks in the immediate area. The gazelle, gradually unable to support the weight, dropped its leg and the trap made that depression. We followed the trail and found a similar depression not far away. The farther we went, the more closely spaced and wider the depressions became, which meant the trap was wrenched into a level position. Finally the depressions cut a continuous narrow trench, streaked with fresh blood, through the sand. With our eyes on the ground, we followed this trench as it twisted, turned, climbed up and down through the hills. I didn't know how far we had gone when we found the blood-streaked trap on a slope, the trap still gripping the gazelle's severed lower leg. This wild animal was escaping on only three legs.

I once read in a book that if a hunter approaches a trapped fox from upwind, it immediately bites off its leg and runs away; this three-legged fox is then even more savage and more cunning. All carnivores have this ability, but since a gazelle has no sharp teeth or claws, it must wait until its leg is dragged off before it can free itself—and how much more it must suffer. The gazelle can run up to seventy miles an hour. Only the cheetah can run faster, but the endurance of the gazelle far exceeds that of the cheetah. Even though it was fleeing on three legs, I didn't think we could catch it. I thought we should return.

Wu Xingshan sat on a rock sweating, gasping, and repeating over and over, "Oh, what a pity! What a pity!" His big red face was redder than usual.

I could see the rippling crests and furrows of countless mountains and ravines, and beyond, the blue cloud shadows swirling and racing over the light purple Gobi Desert, while the biting, cold wind swept the silver sagebrush. I paused and looked awhile. Then I urged Wu Xingshan to return. When I put the trap over my shoulder, I realized how much weight the wild animal had carried for such a long distance in its bitter struggle to survive.

There was no vegetation, due to the high elevation—only the rust-colored rocky terrain—so we could hardly distinguish one direction from another. It was disheartening.

As we were walking, Wu Xingshan said, "Wait, I'll go back and get the leg."

He turned around and climbed the hill. I sat and waited. When he returned, he held up the blood-speckled leg and said, "Wait till they see this. What a large gazelle!" I didn't respond. After a pause he repeated, "Ah, what a pity!"

We reached the adobe at Big Spring by afternoon. Everyone sat quietly and listened to Wu Xingshan's narration. Wu passed the leg around; each person turned it over in his hands, sighed, and said it was a pity. As Zhou Dexiong expertly rolled the noodles, he asked for every detail; the kneading board creaked beneath his hands.

"This gazelle can be caught," he said resolutely.

Everyone straightened up and stared at him.

He didn't turn, just continued kneading. "The old man said some really large gazelles are capable of throwing off a trap. But as the gazelle loses strength, it'll find a nearby corner to lie down. If it finds someone is still chasing it, it'll get up and run. But the second time it lies down, it can't get up again. Eat your fill before you go. It'll definitely be caught!" The noodles were already in the pot.

Everyone talked excitedly at once: "It'll be caught." "Eat your fill and rest awhile." "Increase your strength." "Catch that gazelle."

Huo Xiliang's sonorous Shandong voice came from deep in his chest. "We must act as Chairman Mao instructed: be resolute, don't fear sacrifice, overcome obstacles, strive for victory!"

Shi Weixiang added in his heavy Sichuan accent, "A man who hasn't arrived at the Great Wall is not a true man!"

Li Zhenbo, in a Beijing accent, alluded to one of Mao's poems: "To cross ten thousand rivers, one thousand mountains, is an easy task."

Duan Wenjie waved his hand, told them not to worry, and said it would be all right. "If you want to recognize a hero, go to a harsh place; this is Hu Qiaomu's poem, right?" Then he turned to me, patted me gently on the shoulder, and said warmly, "That's right, isn't it? We can count on you."

Fan Hua threw an old lambskin overcoat over Wu Xingshan, who had been sprawled on the platform bed since we entered, and said, "You're sweating—don't catch cold." He draped a cotton-padded jacket over my shoulders as I sat by the fire, then sat down and quietly listened to our conversation. He waited until we finished eating and said, "You have a tough job to do. Can you still run?"

Wu Xingshan answered, "I can't, not even a little!"

"If you can't run, don't go," Fan Hua said. "Soon it will be dark and the mountains are big. You don't know what's out there. If you come across something dangerous, it would be bad."

"You rest. I'll go," Zhou Dexiong said. He quickly tied his pants tightly around the ankles with a string, looped a thick hemp rope several times around his waist, grabbed a wooden pole and an electrician's knife, and then waited for me to finish eating.

We climbed through the mountains until we came to that hill where we had found the trap and the gazelle and the severed lower leg of the gazelle. We made out its tracks among the rocks and shrubs, and followed them into a muddy, reed-covered valley, where they merged with many other prints.

The energy of this gazelle was astonishing. And now we started a chase that tested our own endurance. After we were discouraged by going in several circles, we came upon a fresh track that looked as if it had been scraped by a stick and decided it was made by the gazelle's broken leg bone. We followed and soon came upon another scrape. The farther we went, the more the scrapes extended and the deeper they were cut into the ground. Among the red willows in the ravine, they finally joined into a continuous long line.

It wasn't a straight line: it trembled, twisted, and turned, bent into a broad, sweeping arc, and sometimes looped into an irregular circle; and at one place two unequal-sized circles appeared. This trembling, crooked, and occasionally looping tracery was a vivid portrayal of the wounded beast's agony and pain—especially the circles, which were the traces of despair that momentarily flashed through its simple mind.

Splotches of blood showed where this exhausted, weakening gazelle had rested while it watched vigilantly, listening for our movements. Then gathering strength, it staggered forward to escape.

I followed, reading the path of the animal's struggle, and became so shaken that I didn't realize I had already lost Zhou Dexiong in the distance.

Suddenly in front of me a donkeylike animal with wolfish fur sprang from behind a boulder and surged forward. I was stunned and stood up, frozen. This thing stood still. We faced each other—no more than a hundred feet between us—each of us terrified.

I didn't know how much time had passed when I heard from far behind Zhou Dexiong's yell, "Gazelle!"

The loud cry startled the bewildered animal; it reared its head and ran. I immediately followed and the struggle for life and death was renewed. It jumped over a rock; I jumped over a rock. It crashed through red willows; I crashed through red willows. When I climbed a hill, it headed down. When I reached the ravine, it was on the opposite bank. But it was slowing, and I was approaching closer and closer. Then it looked as if it almost stopped. I closed in.

Its broken hind leg was a pulpy mass, and the other hind leg had dragged to the ground after so much running. As I watched, the back part of its body gradually became paralyzed and collapsed. It used its two forelegs, step by step, to pull forward. It wasn't walking but a labored, slow, and intrepid forward movement, but the gazelle absolutely would not stop. The blood-spattered hind legs, buttocks, and lower belly were abraded by the gravel. I could see muscle and white bone through the blood and mud, like meat in a butcher shop. And it still hauled itself forward step by step.

I followed slowly. This animal, with no sharp teeth or claws, had never shown malice or had done any harm to any other animal. Running away was its only self-defense, and now it couldn't run. It crawled to an outcropping, couldn't get over it, and stopped. Suddenly its forelegs crumpled; it knelt, toppled over, and couldn't rise. Its body stretched out. Blood continually seeped into the sand. Its back part was a mass of mutilated flesh, but the clean, bright fur of its shoulders and head glittered with a silky luster. It raised its childlike head; its snow-white large ears didn't move as it stared in panic; it looked at me with its big innocent, bright eyes, like the eyes of a healthy infant.

I looked at it. I sensed a glimmer of light in its eyes, a light I could understand, and for a second there was mutual recognition.

Slowly it raised its head; with a thud the head fell again. It stirred, as if it wanted to rise, but gave up. Its belly moved up and down; its nostrils flared and closed. In the harsh cold, puffs of white mist gently blew the sand, grass, and leaves that had fallen near its nostrils and on its face.

I sat down. It hadn't expected such a sudden movement; it jerked its head and twisted violently. I thought what a savage, frightening, and bloodthirsty monster I must seem. And the truth of it saddened me.

Beams of slanting sunlight flashed through the crags, turning the valley gorge a golden color, and for a moment, not only the gazelle but also the nearby crags, red willows, reeds, and every piece of gravel beneath me was suffused with gold. A wavering blue shadow extended to my feet. Zhou Dexiong arrived, gasping hard, his pale face soaked in sweat, his lips trembling.

"The gazelle?" he asked.

I looked to the ground.

His face brightened. He yelled, "Oh, it's huge!"

Zhou pounced on the gazelle, fixing it to the ground. The gazelle struggled, emitting a strange, sorrowful noise. Zhou Dexiong pressed his knees down, untied the hemp rope from his waist, and tied the gazelle's four legs together, not caring whether they were injured or not, and pushed the pole through the rope. He stood up, brushed the dirt off his body, and said, "If that other leg wasn't broken, we could have led it back on three legs. Now we can only carry it."

I didn't say anything. He found a rock, sat down, took a deep breath, and said, "Have a smoke."

I shook my head no. As he lit a cigarette he said, "This damn running is too much. At least it wasn't for nothing. Gazelles are fat in the winter. The hide's also good. Too bad the back part's ruined."

I had never seen him so happy.

5.

The gorge was already submerged in shadows, leaving an antique-copper evening glow on the stark red peaks. We lifted the gazelle and were about to return when it quivered violently and twisted, letting out strange, pathetic noises. I put down my end of the pole and suggested to Zhou Dexiong that we slaughter it. He emphatically refused and said that if we slaughtered the gazelle, it would freeze stiff and wouldn't taste good after it thawed. Besides, then it couldn't be skinned for its hide.

"But it's in great pain," I said.

"What pain! It's food. If you're afraid, lift the front end."

We switched, lifted the gazelle, and not far along, it kicked in the ropes, groaned, and died. I sighed with relief, as if I were no longer guilty and my burden had lightened. Our pace quickened.

The glow of dusk still lingered. As the large deep red moon climbed high into the sky, its brutal, harsh light reflected throughout the wilderness, adding to the mystery. I saw shadows lurking in the east. In the west the luminance of the moon joined that of the sun, and for a moment it seemed the polarities of yin and yang were mixed and ambiguous.

"Old Gao," Zhou Dexiong yelled from behind, "stop looking around, all right? This thing reeks of blood. If a wolf or bear picks up the scent, we're in trouble."

We pressed on through the dark mountain shadows. After we walked for I wasn't sure how long, we reached "home." Everyone was fast asleep, but soon as we arrived they sprang to their feet. Overjoyed, they kindled the brazier fire and lit three oil lamps. The lamp and fire glowed together even more brilliantly. Sparks flew and danced, while thick clouds of smoke rolled and tumbled like an inverted Yellow River over our heads.

Some people skinned the gazelle; others carried water, tended the cooking fire, or kneaded dough. . . . Zhou Dexiong and I did nothing. We sat like guests warming ourselves by the fire. In an instant someone carried over water for washing our feet; in another instant someone brought over freshly brewed tea. After a few sips, someone else rushed over and refilled our cups. Zhou Dexiong excitedly related his account of the hunt, entirely forgetting his fatigue. As they busied themselves, they asked questions without letting a single detail go.

After the meat was cooked, it was sliced into chunks and put into a washbasin, which was placed in the middle of the platform bed. Eight people sat cross-legged in a circle, eating with their hands. Under the bright light, we could see plenty of meat still sizzling in the pot. Everyone talked cheerfully, without restraint, their faces half-covered with grease.

Huo Xiliang regretted there was no wine.

Li Zhenbo said that during the War of Resistance against Japan, he had drunk a kind of liquor in Shanxi called "maiden wine." According to local custom, when a daughter was born, relatives and neighbors sent rice as a congratulatory gift. The head of the family used the rice to make wine, and then buried it underground. They'd dig it up for the daughter's wedding and serve it to guests.

"You can't buy that wine anywhere," he continued. "I drank it once: pure red, translucent, and thick as glue. If you pick it up with chopsticks, it stretches into long threads."

Shi Weixiang said that speaking of customs, the people in this area used to "hit iron sparks": On New Year's Eve they placed a red-hot iron on an anvil and competed to see who could strike the most, the brightest, the highest, and the farthest-flying sparks. Old people, children, and young women gathered around to watch; the atmosphere was lively and exhilarating. He said he suspected Li Bai's lines "The blacksmith's fire reflects against the sky and earth, red sparks of stars raveled in purple smoke" was written about this. Li Bai was from Central Asia; he should have been familiar with this area. Shi said he had looked for proof in the Tang murals but couldn't find any.

Duan Wenjie added that he had observed this custom; it was practiced regularly until the Liberation. "And over New Year they eat dumplings, fried pancakes, and steamed bread. In the Northwest the staple foods are important, but not the other dishes. The same kind of wheat flour can be made into more than ten different kinds of meals, but there's not much else. The farther south you go, the greater the diversity. Look at what the Cantonese eat: snakes, frogs, raw monkey brain, live donkey meat, everything; they even eat worms and fried maggots, but not the northerners."

Huo Xiliang retorted, "No? We people from Shangdong and Hubei eat locusts. We eat them fried. If anyone loses his livelihood, people would say they're having fried locust at home."

Our habit of not speaking was suddenly broken. We talked about everything easily, without holding back, until the brazier fire gradually dwindled, cooled, and was covered with a white layer of ash. One after another, we climbed into bed and slept. Through the roof vent filtered the silvery blue light of dawn.

Everyone slept until noon.

From then on, we often hunted gazelles. It was always a job for Wu Xingshan and me. As I gained more and more hunting experience, I became colder and harder. And I had in truth turned into a carnivorous beast. On the other hand, life became easier, and the animosity and malice between people lessened.

From beastliness something human emerged.

6.

Two months passed quickly. Wang Jieshan was about to come to pick us up at the mountain pass, and we couldn't put off returning to the Institute by a single day.

Fan Hua said that after we return we should propose that other areas along the river also be opened up for cultivation. "That way we can come back."

Everyone supported him. We guessed the people at the Institute would agree: first, the more land we reclaimed, the more merit for them; second, the work was hard and they thought we deserved hardship; and third, there weren't many jobs at the Institute and they felt our presence was a nuisance. Although we were all thinking the same thing, no one dared say it openly. Zhou Dexiong was already planning what he'd bring: soy sauce, vinegar, ginger, garlic, fennel, cinnamon bark, wild pepper seeds, star anise, dried chile, cooking wine, and if possible, some liquor. These items were available only in the kitchen, and he would have to depend on Fan Hua's influence.

That day after supper, while we were warming by the fire, Fan Hua said, "Don't let anyone know about hunting gazelles. We'd catch hell if they found out! I won't bring it up, and don't you either."

Wu Xingshan's eyes grew wider and wider as he exclaimed, "No way can we let them know! If they know, it'll be bad. I won't say a word."

No one made a sound.

Those confidential thoughts blurted out without deliberation by a simple, honest man suddenly instilled great fear in us, just as if he had unintentionally dropped a bomb. When the smoke cleared, everything was different. Who could really guarantee they wouldn't know? Could we trust everyone here? Let alone people like us! Zhou Dexiong said that as long as no one else said anything, he'd keep quiet, but that could mean he expected other people to talk. I figured he might take the initiative, and his words could be construed as a preemptive declaration. Those who make declarations are to be feared, but not as much as those who don't say anything.

As expected, early the next morning before we left for work, Duan Wenjie, who, like the rest of us, hadn't touched a copy of *Quotations from Chairman Mao* after coming into the mountains, was now engrossed in reading a copy. Everyone immediately tensed up. This use of body language to make a "declaration of independence" was far more significant than the matter of hunting. But first we had to face the problem of the gazelle. We all used any means possible to shed responsibility. At every opportunity we would bring the subject up and hint at our innocence. A few words slipped here and there seemed casual enough, but on reflection intimated something deeper. Like the Eight Immortals who crossed the ocean, each one of us manifested his individual powers to protect himself.

Wu Xingshan, who had no ability to protect himself, was in no great danger because he was coaxed to go on the hunts. The only two who couldn't avoid responsibility were Fan Hua and myself. He had more culpability as our leader, but he was one of the revolutionary masses and had a working-class identity. Most likely for him a large matter would turn into a small one and a small one into nothing. On the other hand I was a rightist, a member of the "black gang," and even nothing could become something. They could say my actions were "resisting personal reform," "resisting labor," or even a "sabotage of production" and of the May 7 Directives. It's not that they could say it; they definitely *would* say it. And these people here around me would be the first to speak.

Suddenly the situation became nasty. I looked around at everyone's cold eyes: the sinister eyes of Duan Wenjie beneath sparse eyebrows, the sharp raptorlike eyes of Zhou Dexiong set deep in the sockets under dense eyebrows, the beady eyes of Huo Xiliang entrapped in flesh, the large eyes of Li Weixiang encircled with purple against his pale face, and even the myopic eyes of Li Zhenbo, whose glasses had been smashed, seemed to have a stealthy glare.

I kept thinking, "What now?"

One day I chose a suitable time and said hunting is a form of production and proposed we bring back a gazelle to the Institute "to improve everyone's life."

Wu Xingshan was dumbfounded. "What would that do!"

Fan Hua felt I had sold him out. He said, "But if they find out, it'll be bad for us."

I answered, "Precisely because we're away from of the Institute, we need to conscientiously reform ourselves; we should report all our movements to Chairman Mao. Catching a gazelle is trivial and not a political offense, but if we collude to be silent about it, then it will be significant and become a political offense."

No one said anything.

Fan Hua lifted his eyes and shot a glance at me. I looked back. Our eyes met and for a moment I saw the same light that had trembled in the eyes of the gazelle.

I was taken aback, then saddened, and wanted to say something to bridge the painful distance between us. But I quickly sobered up, understood that would be madness. Could I tell him that I didn't mean what I said? That I was grieved? That we shared the same thinking, the same feelings? That I liked him, respected him, and appreciated him? He'd find that sort of inept candor not only dangerous but also incomprehensible.

For some unknown reason, the old man and the youngster didn't come again to gather firewood, and we had to leave.

The little cabin in the mountain pass that witnessed the changing world was again abandoned to these wild mountains and valleys. I looked back. Its two boarded-up windows, like eyes, looked at us first with bewilderment, then astonishment, then with indifference, and then receded gradually into the dimensionless world of a dream.

The journey downhill was easier. Since all our provisions had been used up, the cart was lighter. But our footsteps were heavier.

Just as when we came, we silently trod gray-yellow gravel and followed a gray-yellow gorge. The gravel pressed beneath our feet made a *xi suo*, *xi suo* noise, keeping rhythm with the axle and wheels' sharp, prolonged creaks: *"Where to? . . . Where to? . . ."*

TWENTY-NINE

Dou Zhanbiao

During the Cultural Revolution, as one of the "monsters and demons" at the Dunhuang Research Institute, I cleaned out caves under supervised labor. Once I was inside any of the approximately five hundred caves, no one could find me. Whenever the Red Guard were mobilized, the "revolutionary masses" rounded up the "monsters and demons" within the Institute for a beating. These "On-the-Spot Criticism and Denunciation Sessions" were set up as a reception for the Red Guard. I was in the caves and missed most of those severe beatings.

On occasion I had the pleasant duty to do odd jobs for Dou Zhanbiao.

The old worker, Dou Zhanbiao, of the Cave Preservation Department, was an extraordinary man.[1] He had a long, narrow face and an exceptionally large head and protuberant chin. Short, skinny, with a bent posture, he walked with a slight limp and resembled the Lohans painted by my teacher Lu Fengzi.[2] Although taciturn, slow in response, and without formal education, he had many skills and was highly intelligent. For more than ten years he gave many suggestions during the cave preservation and stabilization project, solving problems that had confounded specialists. Everyone at the Institute spoke of him with respect.

In this place where "intellectuals piled up," the Cultural Revolution was especially cruel. The few working-class within the staff flaunted their authority; only Old Dou was the same as always: steady, taciturn. He kept out of everyone's way. During heated struggle sessions, he dozed in a distant corner of the room. From 1966 on, he never offered a word, never pasted up big-character posters, and always played along as a member of the team.

No one dared hit anyone else in front of him, except during a struggle session. Old Dou was puny, but for some unknown reason, when he quietly sat watching from the side, everyone felt too self-conscious to lift a hand.

Even the heavy-set and muscular Wang Jiesan, twice Dou's size, was inhibited. Wang loved to hit people. Once Wang complained that I hadn't scrubbed his truck clean; just as he raised his fist, he spotted Old Dou, who said, "Hi." Wang Jiesan touched his head with his raised hand, combed his hair with his fingers, turned, and congenially said, "Old Dou, where're you off to?"

One day, the entire Institute was sent to labor in the countryside. We were required to take along a blackboard covered with Mao's slogans and put it in a convenient place for study. This was a sacred object, which the "monsters and demons" couldn't touch. At first, none of the revolutionary masses were willing to handle it because it was too bulky and cumbersome; they left it on the ground and climbed into the truck. The driver didn't dare drive away, but stayed there as the truck rattled and shook, puffing exhaust. We all looked at the Red Books on our knees without making a sound. Finally, Old Dou slowly climbed down, picked up the blackboard, and lifted it onto the truck.

When we arrived, it was Old Dou who took the blackboard down; he carried it on his back again and again when we moved from one workplace to another. Due to recent irrigation, the ground was wet and there was nowhere to sit or lie down during the noon rest period. Some squatted, others stood, while others sat uncomfortably on spade shafts they had arranged together. Old Dou found four rocks, turned the blackboard over, propped it up on the rocks, and then sprawled out on top. Everyone stared fearfully at this irreverence.

He calmly sat up, looked around, and said, "My back's tired."

He lay down again and, under everyone's eyes, quickly began to snore.

When I did jobs for Old Dou, he taught me many skills. Whatever we had to do, he taught enthusiastically and patiently. I learned to build a hearth and a cooking stove, lay bricks for a wall, do woodwork for doors and windows, drive mules, nail horseshoes, change wheels, mend tires and, even in the wilderness, without a kneading board and cutting knife, make a pot of delicious pulled noodles.

In the summer of '68, we were commanded to construct small walls, each about twelve square feet, along the highway from the Mogao Caves to Dunhuang City. Mao quotations were to be written on them. These were called "quotation tablets," and this "glorious political mission" was given to Old Dou. He was required to build the walls sturdy enough so they could be "transmitted down one thousand autumns and ten thousand generations." I assisted in preparing the bricks, clay, cement and limestone, which I transported to the work site by horse cart. Old Dou instructed me to take my time, so I took my time. At that very moment when the two factions were fighting without resolution and the "monsters and demons" were terrorized, I drove a horse cart back and forth through the vast and empty desert, whistling and gazing into the distance from beneath the brim of a straw hat. In the clear air as far as one could see, whirlwinds, one after another, stirred dust and sand, and like moving, gold-sparkling little trees amid the flowing cloud shadows and mirages, they revolved and chased one another, sometimes fading and sometimes looming large. Occasionally a truck filled with Red Guard soldiers rushed past and disappeared into the barren, prehistoric backdrop, and I knew there was another struggle session.

Old Dou laid the bricks quickly. In those summer days the desert was an oven. The sun baked our heads, and the hot sand was a frying pan beneath our feet. There was no shelter, and still we labored, constantly panting; our sweat dried immediately. Water was limited and evaporated quickly, making it difficult to mix the mortar smoothly. Old Dou told me not to bother. He built the walls without mortar; then he smoothed the façade evenly and straight, and was finished. I was worried that a strong wind could blow them over and they'd say we had cheated on workmanship and materials. Old Dou said that it didn't matter; the walls wouldn't collapse for several years. But I worried what would happen when they did collapse. He said no one would care. After a while he added, "How many years can these things be considered sacred?"

This was the last time I worked for him. The next year, I left Dunhuang for Jiuquan to work on the exhibition, and I remained there. I never met Old Dou again or got in contact by letter. After my wife died, when I was at the May 7 Cadre School with my three-year-old daughter, Gao Lin, someone brought me a large bag of dried apricots and a small bag of shelled roasted peanuts, and told me Old Dou had sent them for the child. At that time these were scarce commodities that I had no way to buy.

One day after twenty years (I can't remember the exact date), I suddenly had a strange feeling and vividly recalled Old Dou as if he were standing before me. Xiaoyu and I talked about him for a long time.[3] Ten days later the *Guangming Daily* reported his death, which had occurred on the same day I had that feeling. A chill came over me. The newspaper said that during his wake at the Dunhuang Institute, many people wept. I believe they did.

THIRTY

Companion

In the autumn of 1978, shortly after I arrived in Lanzhou, a husky young man from Dunhuang came to visit me. As he was leaving, he gave me a bag of red dates, which, he said, was from his father, Wang Jiesan.

Wang Jiesan was the Dunhuang Research Institute's driver. Stout, powerfully built, with hair scattered over his chest, abdomen, arms, legs, and extending up to his cheeks, he had something of a daring outlaw's air of toughness and bravado. Formerly the driver for Division Commander Liao of the Guomindang's occupation army, he had, as a follower of Commander Liao, power over others. Anyone who met him was intimidated. Whenever Commander Liao didn't like a restaurant's food, Wang would knock over the table. In '49, after Commander Liao was shot by the new government, Wang spent a year in prison. Following his release, he couldn't make a living until Chang Shuhong, picking him out for his driving ability, had him come to the Institute and be its driver. So Wang became a member of the working class. In '62, when I arrived at the Institute, he had already been there ten years. Diligent, responsible, he treated people considerately and attentively, was always ready to help, loved to visit and talk, and was liked by everyone. I liked him, too.

At home, however, he beat his wife relentlessly, and so was subject to criticism. This wasn't a political or an economic matter, and he was, after all, a worker unscathed by previous political movements, so besides criticizing him now and again, there was nothing anyone could do. They could only give to his wife, perpetually covered as she was with bruises, their continuous sympathy.

During the Cultural Revolution, members of the working class were the unquestioned leaders in all things, and sowherever "intellectuals piled up," workers, soldiers, and peasants were sent in. This was called "mixing in sand." The few original workers at the Institute became recruiting targets for two factions; some stood with one side, some with the other, some with neither. Wang Jiesan? Both factions favored him. After a few struggle sessions, he discovered that in addition to his wife, he could beat others with impunity. Immensely happy and on an emotional high, his face radiated; he became a new man.

Intellectuals, with their delicate arms, small fists, lofty ideology, and endless fury, didn't beat people the same way Wang did. He approached what he was to do without emotion and without a word, as if slaughtering a pig or skinning a lamb. With his especially powerful legs, he kicked the old director, Chang, back and forth over the ground until Chang crawled dripping with blood. Wang didn't limit himself to the struggle sessions, but used his fists and legs at will and without restraint. Of course, those beaten were the "monsters and demons" already dragged into the open. They were under supervised labor and did everything they were told, but what they feared most was being assigned to Wang to clean his truck.

Despite this, when the Institute ran out of coal, Wang had to drive his truck to Yanguo Gorge to replenish the supply. He could order no one to do it for him. It was always after two or three in the morning when he returned, furious and indignant. As soon as he got down from the truck, he'd savagely kick my door and keep kicking until I got out of bed and opened it. Then he'd growl, "Unload the coal," and leave. He took it upon himself to give this extra work to me and to no one else. It wasn't because of a grudge, but because he passed directly in front of my sleeping quarters on his return from the coal dump. Tired late at night, he didn't want to waste energy making a detour to get someone else.

At that time, my wife, Cilin, was pregnant with Gao Lin. In constant anxiety about me by day, and startled awake by loud noises at night, she couldn't sleep. Alone and frightened, she would turn the light on and wait until I returned, which was usually at daybreak. Blackened by the coal from head to foot, I hastily boiled water, washed, changed clothes, and rushed to attend the "monsters and demons" morning confessional ritual; then waited for Kongjin, who supervised the laborers, to assign the day's jobs. Cilin, at home, again boiled water and washed my clothes. She had to wash them several times to get them clean.

Not until our home was closed off, Cilin went back to her parents, and I entered the collective Cowshed did my situation change. Wang Jiesan still did not go through Kongjin for permission, and ordered us to unload coal late at night. However, he usually got three to five people, which made the load lighter, and I no longer had that deep sense of guilt because my pregnant wife and unborn child were involved in an uproar. So the work was less tiring.

In the winter of 1968, when the Institute made plans to establish a May 7 Cadre School and sent us to clear land in the mountains, Wang drove us to the mountain pass. Halfway there, the truck slid into a sand pit and became stuck. We needed something to put under the tires for traction, so everyone scattered. I walked with Wang Jiesan. Hunched deep into our coats against a freezing wind, hands in sleeves, we followed the riverbank higher into the pass.

The farther we went, the higher the terrain. Looking back, the truck was very small, almost imperceptible, and that strip of water that issued from Bitter Mouth Spring, ice crusting on its banks, swelled, a blurry white, now wide, now narrow; it twisted and turned right and left through the iron gray Gobi and lay like a scar upon the Earth.

Wang didn't look worried, but walked confidently, without hesitation, step by step, over several sand-covered hills until he found a place that was sheltered from the wind, where he squatted, pulled out a small square of newspaper and a tobacco pouch from his coat, adroitly rolled a cigarette and took a puff; his eyes narrowed in pleasure amidst the smoke. I was even less anxious. After all, there was nothing good waiting for me and time was meaningless, so I squatted alongside him and protected myself from the wind.

He turned and threw me a glance. "Go on. Keep looking."

I didn't move. He said again, each time louder and louder, "You hear me? You hear me? Speak. D'you hear me?" He paused. Suddenly, lowering his voice, smiling slightly, he pressed closer and said slowly, "You pretending to be deaf and dumb? We just left and already you're out of line. Let me tell you, it's better to give in; if I tell you to jump, you jump! The working class leads in all things. Y'know that? Get going!" He paused and suddenly yelled, "You going? Y'know who I am? Don't you know who I am? What are you looking at?" As he spoke, he flicked his half-finished cigarette some distance away and abruptly stood.

I also stood. He was standing on a higher spot than I was; behind me was a deep, precipitous slope of loose sand. He threw a punch and missed, his feet gave way, and he fell, sputtering, all the way to the ravine bottom. He crawled up against the heavily shifting sand, repeatedly slipping, then crawling again, until he was in front of me, completely out of breath. He quickly sat on his behind, gasping. I sat alongside. We quietly looked off into the distance.

Without warning, he pushed me sharply with his foot, but before I rolled down the slope I had enough time to grab his foot and drag him along. The two of us, grappling, rolled the whole way down. I was furious. I lost all reason. I straddled his chest and slapped his face. While he was defenseless and couldn't hit back, I hit him with everything I had. He was a heavily bearded man, and the stubble on his recently shaved face burned my palms, but I didn't give a damn. As soon as I stopped, I'd think how he kicked my door at night and slap him again.

I hit him, stopped, hit him, stopped; I didn't know how to end it.

Gradually, I cooled down, thought about the consequences, became frightened, and pulled him to his feet. I patted him, straightened his hair and clothing, retrieved his hat, put it on his head, looked at it from the right and left, and made a funny face, thinking to make a joke out of the whole thing, but I couldn't. No matter how much I tried to show conciliation, he didn't buy it, mumbling deep in his throat to himself, "Good for you . . . Class revenge, huh . . . We'll see how that goes . . ."

We turned back without a word. His clouded expression worried me. Walking along, I called, "Wang Shifu."[1] No response. After a few steps, I called again, "Wang Shifu." Still no response. "Today I did a wrong thing. When we get back I'll make a self-criticism, a revolution deep within my soul . . ." He smiled coldly, quickening his pace as if he was anxious to put distance between us.

I caught up, followed at his side. "Wang Shifu, I was persuaded by a rumor. I heard you were Commander Liao's driver and were a counter-revolutionary running dog. This assertion is obviously a venomous attack on the great working class. But my thinking hasn't been reformed. My revolutionary vigilance isn't high. In my confusion I believed the rumor. I thought you were an enemy that had infiltrated the working class, and I hit you because you were a counter-revolutionary in their ranks. Didn't Chairman Mao say 'humans and devils, right and wrong, are confounded'? My mistake is too serious. Attention must be paid to it. When I get back, I'm going to self-criticize before the army propaganda team, the workers' propaganda team, and before all the revolutionary masses."

Still he ignored me and gloomily went on. After he walked some distance, he suddenly said, "Let me tell you, self-criticism will do you no good."

"But I made such a great error, how can I consider my own good? I want to cut away my past; I can't be afraid of pain."

He stopped, turned. "You think you self-criticize and it's over? The more you talk, the worse it gets. It's better not to bring anything up. I'm telling you, let it go. It's for your own good."

I told him, "I know Wang Shifu has only concern for me in mind, and I'm very grateful, but what should I do if they find out?"

"How can they? This is the Gobi. Heaven knows, Earth knows, you know, and I know. Who else can know?"

"Then I'll listen to Wang Shifu."

He was pleased. "It's for your own good."

We reached the truck and found that they had already stuffed gnarled red willow roots beneath the tires and had been waiting for some time.

We unloaded provisions at the mountain pass, and I moved on with the others into the hills. Wang Jiesan drove back to the Institute. I thought he'd keep his mouth shut, but I couldn't be sure and felt uneasy. In the two months we spent in the mountains, it never occurred to me that he was more troubled than I was. He even went to the city, sought out my wife, and asked her to advise me not to self-criticize.

I also didn't expect that, careful as he was, when the Cultural Revolution reached its climax, Wang would also be put into the Cowshed. At the end of 1968, after purifying class ranks, they also purified financial and economic ranks. In the Cowshed, beside formerly and newly identified "rightists," "defectors," "spies," "capitalist roaders," "dregs of the Guomindang," "chameleons," "little creeping insects," "puny bosses mixed into mass organizations," and so forth, another group was added: the "economic crime elements" who "undermined the wall of socialism," bringing the number of people up to twenty-four. Our Institute altogether had forty-nine people, and I often thought, "Add one more to the Cowshed and there'll be more than half inside, which would be really amusing." But I didn't think that one would be him. Someone accused Wang of black-market trafficking, using his position as a driver; more charges were quickly added, and he became one of us.

I was one of the first to be put in the Cowshed and he was one of the last. Those who had arrived one by one before him, and who had beaten or persecuted me, experienced a moment of awkwardness when we met. Others put on airs, as if they were unjustly accused heroes and I was the one who deserved punishment. But not Wang Jiesan. He ran over to me, patted my chest, and said, "Little guy, you're going to be my friend."

He had just come when "Prepare for War, Prepare for Natural Disaster" started. Day and night, shelters were dug in and around the Institute. Like the clearing of wilderness for the May 7 Cadre School, the shelter digging was given to the "monsters and demons." The shelters were deep and narrow; no one could straighten inside. There was room enough for only two people to work at one time. We cooperated, entering the pit in shifts. Our shift worked through the night. We supervised each other, so no one could slack off.

Wang Jiesan didn't care if we broke the rules. If, during work, I mended my clothes, wrote letters, or even covered my head and slept, it was all right. He was not like the others, who'd run the next day and make a report. While I slept, he didn't make a sound; when I awoke, we talked; there was nothing we couldn't say. I asked if he was like this with others; he told me it depended on the person. The intellectuals wanted only to gain favor and were the most feared. If they couldn't drag out material for criticism, they'd be so sad they wanted to die, and if they could find something to incriminate you, they'd die of happiness.

Once, during the night shift, Wang gave me a few large red dates the size of apricots. They had delicate skin, small pits, thick and firm flesh, and were sweet and juicy. He asked if they were good. I said, "Delicious," and with his large, hairy face, he grinned like a child.

Large red dates were Dunhuang's special produce, famous everywhere. After I left, I never had another chance to eat one. I have heard that industrial pollution, due to the rise of commercialization and the use of fertilizers and pesticides, changed the taste of produce from many parts of the country. I don't know about Dunhuang red dates. Good still? Wang Jiesan, who gave me those dates, must be over seventy now. Strong still?

THIRTY-ONE

Chang Shuhong

I was very saddened by the news of Mr. Chang Shuhong's death. Even in my distress, I wanted to write of my respect and gratitude to him and also of my shame and regret.

Chang Shuhong studied in France at an early age. His oil paintings frequently received international awards, and for a time his reputation flourished. He was deeply shaken when he saw art from Dunhuang scattered overseas, and so he returned with his sculptor wife, determined to preserve that art and conduct research. He found the necessary support, and in 1944, as war spread everywhere, he established the National Research Institute of Dunhuang Art at the Mogao Caves. He rode in with a group of people on camelback and became the director.

In the vast desert, the winds yellowed with sand, life was difficult but work harsher. His wife couldn't take it and finally left him. In 1949, after the Communist regime took power, the Institute's name was changed to the Dunhuang Cultural Relics Research Institute. Chang was authorized to continue as director. His second wife, Li Chengxian, a painter and the Institute's Party Branch Secretary, was appointed assistant director. Soon after, Chang joined the Communist Party and became a member of the National Political Consultation Committee and Representivite of the People's Congress.

I was more than thirty years younger and had no relationship with him, but what I knew of him from newspapers and magazines left an impression. In 1962, I had come out of the labor camp with no friend or family and with nothing to look forward to. Except for a shabby blanket, I had no belongings; except for taking odd jobs, I had no path I could follow. Dirty-faced, disheveled, I was a beggar on the road. In an inn, where they also housed mule and horse carts, at the Jingyuan county seat, I sprawled across a *kang* and wrote a letter, telling Mr. Chang my views on art, art history, and Dunhuang research, and recommended myself for work.

It was an attempt without much hope. On the envelope I wrote to "Mr. Chang Shuhong, Dunhuang Research Institute," without even a return address. I didn't expect he would get the letter, let alone painstakingly read it through. Afterward he contacted the Gansu Province Public Security Bureau for a review of my personal files, then asked someone to search out my paintings, my published articles, and the criticisms of those articles. After this, he again called the Gansu Public Security Bureau, told them he'd like to use me, and asked their support. The person who answered the phone, Dong Lin, said, "As long as there's no problem on your end, we haven't any."

But as expected, the problem came from the bureaucratic system of Culture and Education. My rightist identity, my history of being restricted from holding a public position and being in a labor camp, all precluded my going.[1] My case dragged on for a long time, but Mr. Chang was determined and garnered support from the deputy minister of culture, Xu Pingyu. The Public Security Bureau removed my "rightist" label and said that if my work record before my dismissal was expunged and I entered the workforce anew, the problem could be resolved. From then on my life's road took a huge turn, opening wide before me.

Mr. Chang was concurrently head of Lanzhou School of Art and was at that time in Lanzhou. Before I went to Dunhuang, he summoned me twice to talk. Only then did I understand these twists and turns.

He said, "The country has been hard-pressed for a few years, but things have loosened up now. There is much that needs to be done. Dunhuang research has to be restarted. Just when we need talented people, I didn't expect it would be still so difficult. We should be grateful to the two in the Public Security Bureau, because without their vigorous support nothing could have been accomplished."

"We need also to thank Xu Pingyu," I said.

"That's not the same. Xu said only a few words. If you want to get talented people, you must speak up."[2]

Then he continued. "At Dunhuang, you need to first conduct a comprehensive survey of the caves and compile many data cards. Buddhism is profound and multilayered, and you have to understand it thoroughly. You need to completely familiarize yourself with the history of the cultural exchanges with Central Asia and the history of the Guasha area. There are many scriptures and documents that must be reviewed. From your letter I sensed your youthful impatience and exuberance. I'm afraid you want quick success but haven't the perserverance. You need to focus. Painting's the same. You need the skills that are specific to Dunhuang painting; you can't sketch their likeness and think it will do. You must think things through and gain a solid basis, which takes several years of hard work. Discipline yourself and don't rush things."

Once at Dunhuang, we were too busy and had no further opportunity to talk. Mr. Chang had ambitiously initiated a series of international academic conferences commemorating the first cave's construction 1,600 years earlier (366–1966). The preparation of academic papers wasn't easy, let alone editing and printing *The Dunhuang Compendium*. However, as things developed, politics came to the fore, and with our busy schedule we had the added responsibility of digging a new cave and creating new murals to celebrate the Revolution. The project of shoring up the stone caves, for which the Ministry of Culture allocated several million yuan, was already under way while more than three hundred civil engineers sent by the Ministry of Railroads were hectically working night and day. With many details to attend to, Mr. Chang rushed back and forth. Meeting with him was difficult, and when we met, speaking with him was also difficult.

Differences in age and social position, the relationship between leader and the led, all preclude deeper ties; that's natural and normal, but many who arrived earlier than I did also kept their distance. For about a decade, there had been continuous political movements, and Mr. Chang and his wife, as leaders of the Institute, had to carry out party policies. Each time there was a new movement, they had to discipline some of their people. The people at the Institute were few, so once the political movements became more frequent, almost everyone was accused of something. Resentment deepened for months. When the Cultural Revolution arrived, the resentment, continually simmering under the surface, exploded into the open.

Everyone became one of the revolutionary masses and Mr. Chang their target. Transferring me with my "rightist" label to Dunhuang was used to prove he was a counter-revolutionary. He had arranged for me to come, and that made my problem his. Everyone charged through this breach to expose his greater and more manifold "crimes." He was knocked to the ground and called "ox demon."[3] Li Chengxian was called a "snake demon." The Dunhuang Institute was the "Chang/Li black den," and I was their "evil accomplice." Sometimes I was dragged along to the struggle sessions and was of course beaten, but much less often and less severely than they were.

Those who beat Mr. Chang most viciously weren't those he previously had disciplined but rather those he had personally cultivated and promoted. In the past, whenever he went abroad to direct exhibitions, he always took along someone named Sun. Later Mr. Chang sent him to Central Beijing School of Art for advanced study in sculpture. At one struggle session this person, with tears in his eyes, asked, "Why did you use your high position to make such underhanded bribes just so you could corrupt young people?" When there was no answer, he struck. A large man, Sun raised his fist without pity. With one swing of his hand, blood trickled down the corner of Mr. Chang's mouth; with another blow, an eye immediately puffed up. Gradually the eye swelled until it resembled a small, round, dark purple eggplant. The revolutionary masses were stunned. For a time it was absolutely quiet.

As in the rest of the country, the Institute's revolutionary masses split into two opposing factions, each claiming loyalty to Mao and accusing their rivals of disloyalty. To compete for loyalty was to compete for brutality. They competed in denouncing Mr. Chang and took turns ransacking his home. Chang and his wife were banished to a small, narrow, deserted warehouse. Searching for proof of guilt, the revolutionary masses dug tunnels under their floorboards, until the tunnels connected, and ripped their ceiling into pieces. If Mr. Chang didn't answer a question posed by one faction, he was beaten. If he answered, the other faction beat him. New wounds were added to old. Not a tooth remained in Mr. Chang's mouth. This was the most difficult period; later, when more and more "enemies" were flushed out, his beatings gradually became less frequent.

The day Mr. Chang's eye was wounded so severely, I was afraid he'd been blinded, so in the middle of the night I crept into his room. After I had a look, I felt better, but I couldn't sleep when I got back to my own room. I thought of a few words and, after covering my lamp for safety, wrote them down. I sent a poem in free form over to Mr. Chang and his wife the following night:

TO MR. CHANG SHUHONG

This place was desolate in past years, a mournful camel
    bell clanged in the cold
Mountains sank into desert sand, sand heaped up around
    an ancient temple and dais
Foxes and rabbits ran among steep crags, wall paintings
    gathered moss and mold

You toasted the dream of prosperity farewell, arrived
    through miles of hardship
Wild plants tasted sweet to you, at night a weathervane
    clinked like a woman's bracelet
You perservered and white hairs grew, many days flew
    away like dust
The master's attention was at the tip of a brush, unaware
    disaster came from above
Disasters caused by the Party ensnared the naive, crowds
    swam into the net
Your disciples ransacked your rooms, books flew like
    moths, scrolls like ribbons
Absurdities never seen before, no one knows how this
    drama will end
Fame is decided over many years, who determines failure
    by a single night
Smiling, you point to the changed scenery, carved railings,
    stone steps lead high
Scholarship is immortal, one volume is stored for another
    age
China's true voice enters the painting, paper like gold is
    stored in the world
I send you this, urge you to eat more, don't lose hope in
    your artistic purpose
Forge your vision in cold weather, hide within your work
    until it's spring.

Li Chengxian said that after Mr. Chang read it, he cried. When his eyes cleared, he replied in a letter: "At the beginning I didn't think things would turn out this way. All my life I sought after truth and had absolute faith in Marx and Lenin. Even though I was falsely accused, I have no regrets. The name 'Ox Demon' isn't bad. An ox is a kindhearted animal.

'If the masses are well fed, what matter if at evening I lie starving.'[4] That's precisely the virtue a Communist Party member should have."

I wrote back: "The masses aren't well fed; everyone can see that. And who caused that, everyone can see, too. Making a nation of enemies out of ordinary people is this regime's nature. Things have come to this pass as the result of their extreme policies. This can be seen by everyone also. Kindly think this over."

He replied, "Young people have no understanding of recent Chinese history and no experience of the dark times of the old society. It's easy to simplify. Conditions aren't that simple."

Even during the most oppressive times at Mogao Caves, secret communications weren't difficult. It was, after all, an isolated island in the middle of the desert. There were only forty-nine people in the Institute, and if you added family members, the entire count was less than a hundred. Most times it was deserted. During the Cultural Revolution, all episodes of shouting and yelling took place in the Middle Temple's court, while outside it was desolate. When the Red Guard were mobilized and scattered over the country, they left only a few behind to keep watch, and it became even quieter. Talking wasn't easy, but it was easy to set aside a place in which to leave a letter, and by these letters we reported our circumstances, talked over our ideas. Whatever we wanted to say, we said. It was a joy. Some of the letters were lengthy polemics, others brief notes. Some remain today. Events have passed and conditions changed, and when I read them now they sadden me.

At that time wages were frozen. Every month a person received thirty yuan as "living expense," usually not enough to purchase meat. At the beginning of 1968, on the eve of the lunar New Year, Mr. Chang and Li Chengxian invited me to their small room in the quiet of the night. They lifted the cover of a clay pot on an iron-lidded stove, and to my surprise: a chicken. Piping hot, its strong aroma permeated everywhere. After a bit of euphoria, I panicked. The aroma couldn't be contained; it was floating all over the place. If it was noticed, it would provoke an inspection. I didn't want to think what would happen. We quickly talked it over. If those in charge came, where could I hide? There wasn't anywhere. The only thing to do was grab a chicken leg and quickly get out of there. I left behind something I had written to cheer them up. It was only for two readers. The original remains today:

NEXT YEAR'S NEWS—A DEVISED PREDICTION.

January Zero:
Chairman Mao ordered martial law over the Soviet Union. The military command center is stationed in Cheta on the Soviet/China border. Subsequently the revolutionary center of the Soviet Union has been moved from Moscow to Cheta, etc.

January First:
The name of the Soviet newspaper *The Literary Journal* has been changed to *Protect the East* and has resumed publication. An article exposed Tolstoy's exploitation of peasants at Yasna Polyana through extortion of rent and imposition of heavy interest. Several photos of unfair leases were published. After reading them, the people cried out in rage! An attached editorial pointed out that Lenin wrote a commemoration for this great landlord. This is a serious mistake in the Party line.

June Sixtieth:
The Xiangtan Middle School Peerless Fighting Team discovered an abundance of letters wedged into a wall of the St. Peter and Paul Fortress, which proved that Marx and Engels, along with a bad egg named Myshkin, traveled to Siberia to hook up with Chernyshevsky,

who continuously begged favor from the Tsar. This is extremely despicable. [5]

September Twenty-fifth:
In order to celebrate China's National Day, the Japanese Revolutionary Committee and the Cuban Revolutionary Committee in succession held conventions to send Chairman Mao congratulatory telegrams calling him the most, most, most, most, most beloved paragon of a leader. The *People's Daily* successively published *The Red Sun Shines on Mt. Fuji* and *Spring Waves on the Carribean.* Associated editorials offered congratulations.

December Twentieth:
The New York Red Guard, after ransacking homes and looting piles of gold, have decided to erect a golden statue of Mao on the original site of the smashed Statue of Liberty in New York City Harbor.

Second December of Next Year, the third:
Oxford, Cambridge, and Harvard have united to celebrate the triumph of re-education. They introduced their experience by saying their basic teaching materials are the Four Volumes of Mao plus laboring in a farm.

The Hundreth December of Next Year, the fifth:
The International Society of Scientists convened a ceremony to bestow awards on those who best followed the Mao model. Awards were conferred on Copernicus, Darwin, Edison, and Einstein, among others, because all inventions and creations are the great achievements

of Maoist thought. Someone suggested giving Marx
an award. It was shelved and left under consideration.
Someone else suggested giving an award to the winning
horse of the Hong Kong Derby. He was arrested for the
crime of having an ulterior motive.

Anyone reading this, unless they were mainland Chinese who had lived through the Cultural Revolution, would be baffled, but for the three of us it provided some laughter at that time.[6]

In 1968, Criticism and Denunciation Sessions aimed at Mr. Chang lessened. Except for times when the Red Guard was mobilized from outside and "On-the-Spot Criticism and Denunciation Sessions" were set up, he remained mostly under supervised labor. His spine had been injured in the beatings, though, and he couldn't stand. During labor he could only wrap two pieces of old sheepskin around his knees, prop himself up on two hands, and, while kneeling, crawl along. He was responsible for feeding a pig, a Yorkshire, which was being raised in the yard behind the kitchen. Every day he'd crawl to the backyard, kneel, chop pig feed until it was smooth, boil it until it was well done, pour it into a bucket, lift the bucket down from the stove, lift the bucket again and place it one step in front of him, crawl to the bucket, lift the bucket, place it, crawl to it, and so on, lift, crawl, lift, crawl, until he reached the pig, poured out the feed, and crawled back for a second bucket.

When hungry, the pig squealed in Mr. Chang's face. To meet the pig's demands, Mr. Chang crawled nonstop, back and forth, morning till night. The back lot's soot pile stained his body an ashen black, and before long he, a filthy silhouette, became part of the landscape.[7]

The day the pig was slaughtered, Mr. Chang was left with nothing to do. He was ordered to accompany me on a job for Dou Zhanbiao constructing tablets of Mao slogans along the Gobi's highway. Our duty was to prepare the materials. We loaded the still-wet brick, clay, cement, limestone, and so on, onto a horse cart and delivered it to the work site.

Mr. Chang wasn't able, so I did the work, but baking beneath the Gobi's sizzling, toxic sun while riding in a cart was hardship enough.

Seeming not to care and to be above it all, he said, "Last night, when I fed the pig, I thought of a line from Li Bai: 'Kneeling, I offer a simple meal, moonlight bright upon the plate.'"[8] We laughed. But he continued, "Our two sons came to visit from Lanzhou, but the Revolutionary Guard kept them from seeing us. My wife and I were heartbroken."

After the cart left the front gate, he was silent for a long time. Looking into the vast desert through his broken glasses patched with plastic tape, he said, "When we arrived, this road didn't exist. We came from Laojun Temple by camelback and descended in front of cave number three. We couldn't get anything we needed. It was very difficult. But once we saw the murals, the painted clay figurines and scrolls, we were elated."

Later he spoke about Zhang Daqian. "Zhang didn't understand the conservation of murals." Mr. Chang was angry. "But this man was really intelligent. He learned fast and adapted fast and whatever he learned became his own. Picasso imitated primitive tribal art, while Matisse imitated children's drawings and Arab motifs. Both had that ability. They weren't limited and their talent evolved even into old age. That's rare."

"Some of Zhang's splashed-ink landscapes are very good," I said, "but his portraits are vulgar, especially those decorative ones of upper-class women; they smell of cosmetics."

"Vulgarity and decorativeness aren't the same," Mr. Chang said. "There's decorative art that's vulgar and decorative art that isn't. We just need to select the best."

We had never had a chance to talk like that before. Those days, when I drove myself back and forth on that long and tedious road through the Gobi Desert, nodding off in a cart, I had my fill of loneliness. I was happy when Mr. Chang came along. And he, who crawled and twisted behind the kitchen through that cluttered and dirty back lot between piles of soot and waste containers, was suffocated enough. To be able to inhale fresh air and speak loudly in this naked and vast wilderness was more than we could wish for.

Unexpectedly for that night, the kind-hearted Dou Zhanbiao gave a suggestion to the production manager, Kong Jin: "Chang's old. If he's left out in that blazing sun and dies of a stroke, who's going to take the blame?"

The next day Mr. Chang didn't come. He was in the canteen sorting vegetables.

In 1969, the case against us was finalized: Mr. Chang was named a counter-revolutionary, was stripped of Party membership, was proscribed from public service, and was remanded to supervised labor.[9] Li Chengxian was stripped of Party membership and her salary reduced six grades. My salary was reduced three grades. Soon after, the Jiuquan District Revolutionary Committee delegated several people from Dunhuang to conduct the Agricultural Exhibition. I was among them. While I was in Jiuquan, my wife, Li Cilin, died at the Dunhuang Labor Camp, to which she had been transferred, leaving behind our three-year-old daughter, Gao Lin. I went back, took care of the funeral arrangements, and brought the child to Jiuquan. I didn't want to ever return.

At Jiuquan I heard that a foreign woman named Han Suyin was in China and had asked Zhou Enlai for permission to meet with Chang Shuhong.[10] Because of this, Chang and Li were liberated, reinstated in the Party, reinstated in work, restored in reputation, issued back pay, and hospitalized for rehabilitation. Orders came from high up to appropriate funds for the immediate restoration and refurbishment of their wrecked, devastated rooms in order to make the rooms suitable to "receive foreign guests." After this, Mr. Chang was installed in Lanzhou and became a public figure. I heard that because Mr. Chang now had influence outside the country, as well as the patronage of Zhou Enlai, many Party, bureaucratic, and army bigwigs sought his company; even the highest leader of the Northwest, the Party secretary, Xian Hunghan of Lanzhou Military District, was a frequent guest.[11] I knew hearsay can't be trusted, but I couldn't help thinking that I might improve my situation by my connection with Mr. Chang and his wife. In balance, their crimes were more serious than mine, and if they were no longer in trouble, why should I be? I thought that if they could only mention me to an official, my problems would be over. Besides, I wanted to have a heart-to-heart talk with them and alleviate the sorrow and pain I felt. I asked the cadre school for leave, took Gao Lin with me on a train to Lanzhou, and searched them out.

Li Chengxian opened the door smiling, but was taken aback as soon as she saw us. An awkwardness and a look of calculation flashed in her eyes. Quickly she smiled broadly again, invited us into the room, and asked us to sit on a long sofa. She brought out candy and tea, offered Gao Lin some candy, and said, "The Director's making a phone call. He'll be here shortly."

I saw the large round table spread with a white cloth and set with goblets, a platter, and wine bottles, while a caretaker went back and forth.

I asked, "Are you expecting someone?"

"No matter, have some tea first."

She sat closer and lowered her voice. "Those letters, poems, and things, do they still exist?"

I said, "Yes."

"Where?"

"At Jiuquan."

Just then Mr. Chang walked briskly in wearing new eyeglasses, false teeth, and a metallic back brace, looking years younger. He smiled intimately and sat directly in front of me.

Li Chengxian asked again, "Where in Jiuquan?"

"Locked in a box."

"That's too dangerous. You must quickly burn them."

Mr. Chang said, "If you keep them, there'll be no end of trouble. Better burn them."

"Sure, sure." Actually they were in my inner pocket, but I remembered that look in her eye, felt uneasy, and didn't produce them.

Li brought out several albums containing recent group photographs of them with well-known international and national personages, with Party bureaucratic and military leaders, at banquets, on outings, or in intimate conversations. Among them was a scrapbook pasted full with newspaper clippings. They looked on with me, explaining who this was, who that was.

I flipped through a few pages, then stood up, picked up Gao Lin, and said, "We're leaving."

With one voice they said, "Leaving? Can't you stay a little longer?"

Li, as she was speaking, reached for a bag of milk candy, thrust it at Gao Lin, and said, "Today is not a convenient day—we're expecting guests. Otherwise, you could have dinner before you go."

"Next time," Mr. Chang said. "Come next time and have dinner with us."

I told Gao Lin to put down the candy, but the child was unwilling and clutched it to her chest. I grabbed it, threw it on the table. With a few steps I was outside and slammed the door with a bang that startled me.

As I walked down the street, the more I thought, the angrier I became. They didn't ask me how I was doing, why I had come to Lanzhou, when I had arrived, where I was staying, or why Cilin didn't accompany me. During the Cultural Revolution, when Cilin visited me at Mogao Caves, she brought them medicines and mimeographed reports, and gave them food. They liked her and always greeted her with affection. I thought this time they would at least ask after her. I would have talked to them about her, about her kindness and sincerity, her misfortunes, her death. I really, really wanted someone to listen to me, but they didn't ask and there was no way I could have brought her up. Bad habits are hard to change, so on the train I wrote four lines. As soon as I reached Jiuquan, I sent them to them.

ONCE AGAIN TO—

Your paintings well known in former times
Your name lingers in Dunhuang after thirty years

How can you neglect the painter's hand
And flatter the powerful in old age

A few months later I met a man called Wu Jian in a Jiuquan district hostel, who before the Cultural Revolution was propaganda director for Gansu Province. After he was denounced, he was never reinstated. When Mr. Chang was the Art Institute director, Wu was the Institute's Party committee secretary; there was nothing the two didn't talk about. From him I learned that Mr. Chang's situation wasn't good.

Wu said, "Once over the threshold and there are many ways to go.[12] He's a scholar and can only follow the road of a scholar. How could he manage the twists and turns? Nowadays the faction within the Party that opposes Zhou Enlai is very powerful. It's all clandestine. Playing the Zhou card could work against him. He's too old to understand."

Wu went on, "Did you know, the time you visited him you frightened him? Think about it. If Xian Hunghan arrived and came face-to-face with a sullen, insolent fellow in rags, how could Old Mr. Chang maneuver? You've been in trouble, and not only during the Cultural Revolution but also back in '57. How could Old Mr. Chang maneuver?"

After Wu Jian left, I thought about that time. I thought how those two elderly people were very accommodating to receive me while I was in such an agitated state, and to allow me to stay for so long. I thought if I had acted like a sensible, reasonable person, they would certainly have informed me of the real situation and asked me to leave for the time being. But they were considerate and didn't do that. Suddenly appearing at the door, startling them, frightening them while I was really angry, wasn't just callousness and crudeness but acting beyond all reason.[13] Mr. Chang showed me great favor and esteem. Why did I answer with resentment? And why did I have to go on and use such abusive words? I'm a real bastard, I thought. I thought even if Mr. Chang broke off relations with me, I couldn't get rid of this shame.

At the end of the '70s, the rightists were rehabilitated and I was "returned to the team." At the Institute of Philosophy in the Chinese Academy of Social Science, I received a telephone call from Mr. Chang. He invited me to his living quarters at the Foreign Ministry's hostel at Taijichang to meet and talk. In the intervening years he and Li had aged. Their baggy eyes and loose skin gave them an appearance of weariness. I inquired about their health. They both said they were fine but tired easily. All along they thought about Dunhuang but couldn't return. It wasn't because higher authority prevented them but because of those who denounced them. Gansu Province had appointed as director of the Dunhuang Institute Duan Wenjie, who bore them enmity. This person was clever and had a way with words. It wasn't a contest. Mr. Chang could stay only as a guest in Lanzhou or Beijing and couldn't return to Dunhuang.

I advised him to let it be. I said, "Don't return to Dunhuang. Life's like a journey from inn to inn: where you find safety, you find your home. You're over seventy. It's better to let go and relax. Why insist on going into a hostile environment, where you would need to continuously struggle for survival?"

Mr. Chang disagreed. "As long as I live, I will struggle."

He dedicated his whole life and energy to Dunhuang and was driven out, and no matter how much he tried, he could never find peace. Over the past years he repeatedly wrote to the Central Party requesting a return to Dunhuang, but they never replied. When Hu Yaobang ascended the stage, he gave orders for an investigation, which dragged on. The other side gave a different story, so the investigation spun, entangled itself, and became more and more confused. The final report was a thick volume, which concluded that both sides were half-wrong, and so the matter ended in a stalemate.

This grievance, this heartbreak, we can only imagine. More than a decade passed in the blink of an eye. Mr. Chang died in Beijing. When I learned of his death I was in Los Angeles at the Xilai Temple, painting portraits for the Buddhist master Xing Yun. Since I didn't have Li's address, I couldn't send her my condolences. In the main hall of the Buddhist temple

I lit a stick of incense, joined my hands, and made an offering. I wished that the gentle smoke, curling and drifting upward, would convey to Mr. Chang's spirit my respect and gratitude as well as my shame and regret.

On the bank of eternity everything disperses, as this cloud of smoke dispersed and left no trace. I wished him rest.

THIRTY-TWO

Jiuquan Revisited (Extracts)

The mere mention of "Jiuquan" once made grown men pale. Jiabiangou State Farm, the terrible concentration camp of death, was located within its confines. Countless men entered the farm's gates and vanished, not even their bones ever to be found. The Lanzhou-Xinjiang railway line passed a long way off, but the passengers got whiffs of the farm's foul smell without knowing that its source was rotting corpses.

I was shut up in that camp from winter 1957 to spring 1959, and was lucky to come out alive. My mother prayed for me every day, and said that I survived thanks to the Bodhisattva's protection.

The camp itself vanished after all the men died, but it remained forever in my mother's mind. Some ten years later, she got a shock when she received a letter from me posted in Jiuquan. Her hand shook so much, she could not open the envelope: How in the world could he have ended up there again?

1.

I was sent to Jiuquan the second time in 1969. The Revolutionary Committee of the Dunhuang Research Institute had announced the verdict on me, handed down by a higher revolutionary committee: namely a demotion of three grades in salary, which in fact confirmed the original verdict of the 1966 Task Force. My "rightist" category was not renewed, meaning I was finally being given my freedom. I was told to move out of the Cowshed and to go to Jiuquan City to paint for an exhibition of "Agriculture Learning from Dazhai," organized by the Regional Revolutionary Committee. Going with me were two colleagues from the former fine arts section: one was He Shan, who was head of the Revolutionary Committee at the Institute; the other was Sun Jiyuan, who was in charge of the case investigation team. Because our Research Institute came under a national ministry, He Shan should have been on a par with the military men who held the top offices in the Jiuquan Regional Revolutionary Committee, and Sun Jiyuan should have ranked not far below. This trip to assist in the exhibition was assumed to be in the nature of mutual support between fraternal units.

However, when we got to Jiuquan we were shown no special consideration. We were not known to the regional leadership, which consisted of a few veteran cadres and army representatives who had stayed on. The people involved in the exhibition were mostly on temporary transfer from various counties and units, and they did not know us either. We were all lumped together, doing the same overtime, lining up for the same food, sleeping in the same dormitories. He Shan and Sun Jiyuan felt this affront to their dignity extremely keenly and did not put their backs into their work. All our coworkers were fed up to the teeth with them. I, in contrast to them, was not given the cold shoulder, which was a pleasant surprise. Having the extra incentive of getting my wife and daughter out of the village they had been sent down to, I pulled out all the stops in my work. Since I also excelled somewhat over my colleagues in professional ability, I was generally made very welcome.

A space-time reversal in personal relations thus seemed to have occurred. These two colleagues warned me, "Don't forget about your thought remolding. Don't take advantage of people in a new place not knowing your background to put on a false show of zeal." They indicated that the pictures I was painting were not art, that I was simply catering to the taste of laymen, which was a form of dishonesty. If I did not cast off my old self, I would become another cropper, and if I did come another cropper, neither my descendants nor I would ever raise our heads again. They added, "You're one of us—otherwise we wouldn't be so concerned to help you. Think it over."

2.

There was a hunchback at the exhibition named Liu Guangshen. He was only about four feet tall, had short limbs, and was exceptionally ugly. For that reason I was especially respectful to him. Only after becoming friends did I discover that he was much more than he seemed. He was phenomenally quick-witted. When he served as secretary to the Revolutionary Committee, he had the reputation of being a genius, being able to produce a thousand-word script at the drop of a hat. The Party Secretary always read his big speeches from drafts that Liu had written. After Liu Guangshen was targeted in the Cultural Revolution, he was made gatekeeper at the guesthouse of the Revolutionary Committee. He often invited me to his home, that is to say the gate lodge, where he would give me the lowdown on the staff and operations of the region's offices and institutions. News, trends, factions, networking, and ways to get things done—all very practical knowledge. There was nothing he didn't know. For me, an innocent abroad, he was a beacon in this bureaucratic maze. I consulted him on my predicament.

"This is just a beginning," he said. "The sticky business will come later. Nowadays carrying on the revolution is all about pontificating: the important thing is not what the facts of a matter really are—it's what they are made out to be. When something is made an issue, the situation gets tricky, so you'll have to watch your step. But don't worry, I think the political pressures are easing, things are calming down, the tide is turning in your favor. You are in the right place, here in Jiuquan, and everybody says you do your work well. That stands you in good stead. Just keep your mouth buttoned, whatever happens, get on with your painting, and you'll be all right."

One day Liu Guangshen found a jeep and accompanied me on a trip to see the forsaken ruins of Jiabiangou Farm. He warned me in advance, "The driver doesn't know who you are or what you're about. Don't refer to the past. Don't take any pictures on the way. If you see any bones or such, don't take on; and when we get back, don't mention our going. That should do it." He spent our journey explaining Jiuquan to me, telling me of its produce, geography, and history—and a lot of interesting stories, too.

All the canals and ditches we had dug ten years earlier had been filled in by drifting sand. Apart from broken lines of low walls, shored up by yellow sand and looking like dunes, the mud huts we had lived in were gone. Nature had reclaimed the landscape. Here and there white bones broke the surface, frequently snagging rolling balls of grass. Our driver said, "There used to be a farm here, but it closed up shop after the men died off."

"Is that so?" I said. "You couldn't tell." That you couldn't tell was the truth. There is no fact unless there is a memory of it. Who can say how many civilizations, how many stars, have come and gone in ages past?

It was already dark when we got back to the city. The lights were blazing in the exhibition hall; everyone was working a night shift. He Shan and Sun Jiyuan were very concerned about my absence. They were just asking me where I'd been when Liu Guangshen suddenly appeared between us, as if he had popped up from under ground. He said to me, "How come you left? We haven't finished work yet." He turned to them and explained, "We were temporarily short-handed, and asked him to lend us a hand."

I should mention that Liu was head of the reference materials section. My two colleagues took him to one side to remind him that I was a rightist, a criminal released from reform through labor under a liberal dispensation, and to warn him that I had not been performing honestly and must have no access to important material, particularly data concerning war preparations.[1]

Liu told me: "Their tone implied that I, Liu Guangshen, was at fault, and that they were prepared to make things awkward for me. It's no use bandying words with these revolutionary intellectuals. I couldn't offend them, but I could get them off my back. I took them to see the man with overall responsibility for the exhibition, Wang Ren, head of the Propaganda Department. Wang did not dare to take responsibility, so he went with us to see Commander Wu, head of the Regional Revolutionary Committee. Wu in turn referred us to Political Commissar Zhang Zhefeng. Zhang heard He and Sun out, then made two points: The purpose of the exhibition was to publicize and promote; material coming into the exhibition was intended to be widely known, so there was no question of confidentiality. Second, the Party's policy was solidarity. The man's case had been thoroughly investigated, and been dealt with under the heading of 'contradictions within the people,' so he should no longer be treated as an enemy.[2] He should be given room to prove himself. That was the way negative factors were turned into positive factors. Zhang asked if there were any objections. There were none."

3.

He Shan and Sun Jiyuan knew their way around, and in particular had established relations with the Lanzhou military area command during the Big Linkup.[3] So when they were disregarded, they felt strong enough to take on the Jiuquan authorities. The upshot was that the Dunhuang Research Institute lodged a complaint with the Lanzhou Military Command, saying that the Jiuquan Regional Revolutionary Committee had departed from the correct class stand, had given priority to professional skills, sidelined revolutionary intellectuals, and placed trust in dissident elements. The Research Institute backed its complaint with a big parcel of material, which included a diary I'd been keeping. The head of the Political Department of the Lanzhou Military Command, Li Lei (a woman) read this diary and said I was an extreme die-hard reactionary and should not have been given any license. She said politics must remain in command; on no account could professionalism be put in command.

The news spread like wildfire that the Regional Revolutionary Committee had been criticized by its superior body. The word was that those who wielded the pen were more fearsome than those who wielded the sword, and the old adage was stood on its head: Now it was "When the soldier meets the scholar, he can't make him see reason." I was very worried and asked what I should do. Liu Guangshen said: "You can keep right out of it. Just look after your work. Actually, it had nothing to do with you in the first place; it was a contradiction between the Dunhuang gang and our local Revolutionary Committee. Now it's a contradiction between the Lanzhou Military Command and the Jiuquan military sub-area, so it's even less to do with you. When they dump on you, it's a way of dumping on Jiuquan. Jiuquan for its part has to stick up for you to prove it is in the right. As long as you're in Jiuquan, you have nothing to fear."

"In the armed services," I said, "orders have to be obeyed without question. How can a puny little sub-area set itself up against a big military command?"

"I wouldn't expect you to understand," Liu said. "In the services you've got political departments and operational commands, field armies and stationary armies, different branches and different factions, and the relations between them are extremely complex. On top of that you've got the relations between military and civil authorities, which complicates things even further. Even I find it bewildering. To sum things up in a sentence, who is right and who is wrong is unimportant. The dealings between one party and another are based on strength, not correctness. If you remember that, it will be to your good."

"Didn't you say that what really counts is what you make things out to be?"

"I was talking about the business of revolution. This is something else again. An argument you can't make convincingly, you can leave unsaid; if you have strength, you needn't explain yourself. If you needn't explain yourself, naturally you have a good argument. There is more than one truth, and you can even get by without any truth on your side. However menacing your maneuver against me might be, I don't redeploy in response: you fight on your front, I fight on mine. That way you can't hurt me, do you see?"

Listening to him, I thought, It's not you who are the dwarf; it's me.

4.

By the summer, preparations for the exhibition were coming along well, and the opening ceremony was looming. The people who had been transferred in were all due to return to their own units, apart from those who were to be exhibition guides and one painter. The regional authority hadn't announced who that painter was to be. All three of us hoped to be chosen (life being more comfortable in the city than in the desert). He Shan was my immediate superior and had control over personnel on his own ground, but he was now in Jiuquan and couldn't call the tune. I had taken this opportunity to put in an application to have my wife, who had been sent down to the countryside, released from registration as "agriculturally domiciled." If I went back to Dunhuang, not only would my application be denied, I would be under He Shan's thumb and he could take his spite out on me. That prospect was not to be borne!

Before long the order came that He Shan and I were each to do a big oil painting. We were given a month. Wang Ren, the man in charge of the exhibition, said it was to be a contest: the better painter stayed. Liu Guangshen guessed that the idea came from Commander Wu. It was an absurd arrangement, but absurdity passed for normal in the Cultural Revolution. He Shan asked who would be the judge of which painting was the better. Wang Ren replied, the masses—workers, peasants, and soldiers. We each took up our position, He in the revolutionary committee's assembly hall, I in the meeting room of the guesthouse. Gongs banged and the battle commenced. At first I was bemused, feeling like the circus monkey being dressed in armor to go to war. My bemusement gave way to anxiety. He Shan, given first choice, had chosen "The Grand Union of All the Nationalities" as his subject. My subject, "Panorama of Tanjiawan," was actually a flat-plane birds-eye view, not suitable for oil painting. The size was to be thirteen by thirteen feet, too big to fit through a door. I would have to divide the painting into four pieces and join the sections together afterward. There would be a cross in the middle, which was bound to be ugly.

Tanjiawan was a production brigade in a Jiuquan village that was promoted as the model for the Northwest in the national drive to "Learn from Dazhai." I stayed with the brigade for a few days, and came back with a multitude of sketches to fill my stage with incident. For example: mending a cart and chopping fodder in a stable; shoveling up manure and spreading fresh earth in a piggery; rinsing greens and watering a donkey beside a well; miniature men and animals; houses like matchboxes. An old carter catches his horse's droppings; a little kid chases chickens away from the threshing floor; wives make good use of their midday break to stitch shoe soles. Festive couplets are pasted on doors, paper cutouts stuck on windows. There are preserved fruits, strips of melon, thick beans drying on roofs; chili peppers, garlic, and corncobs hanging from eaves. There are cart ruts on grass verges, with water in some of the ruts and reflections in the water. All in all I strove for vividness and interest, trying to make the work exactly detailed and lifelike. It was a depiction of minutiae that almost called for the use of a magnifying glass.

Regardless of whether it was art or not, on its success hung my safety and my marriage. I worked round the clock, at first out of desperation to win, then because I found the painting absorbing. The weather was sweltering. I stripped down to a pair of shorts but still sweated like a pig. A steady stream of people came in to watch me paint; I had no idea who they were. Northwesterners are not in the habit of stripping to the waist and did not take kindly to seeing me like that. People talked about me behind my back, calling me uncivilized, a madcap. I took no notice when those views were passed on to me. I had started out to appeal to popular tastes and now, paradoxically, went on to bow to no one. I seemed to put self-preservation behind me, really became "madcap."

The painting was not finished until a couple of days after the deadline had passed. The day before it was taken away to be displayed, Liu Guangshen turned up, all on edge. He said: "Those two gentlemen are going round saying you have painted what is supposed to be a model for "Learning from Dazhai" as a small-peasant economy, and turned the nature-transforming revolutionary spirit into nostalgia for the placid, backward old village. The worst thing is, this line of theirs can't be faulted politically!"

I got into a panic and worked through the night. I stuck red flags in workplaces, slogans on walls. I put placards on the roadside bearing quotations from the Red Book and pictures of our Supreme Commander and his deputy Lin Biao standing shoulder to shoulder. I added numerous delegations come to listen and learn, reporters with cameras slung over their shoulders, school kids clutching their Red Books, cadres in a circle listening to a lecture, buses of every description lined up at the village gate. All this gave the painting a lot more bustle and excitement. Looking at it in the light of morning, I saw that the colors were not harmonized, the scene garish. But there was no time for revision; the thing was carted away.

The opening of the exhibition happened to coincide with the opening of the Joint Assembly of cadres at province, county, and district level, so visitors flooded in. To general surprise, my "Panorama of Tanjiawan" turned out to be the most popular exhibit. The spectators followed the story serially along the rutted main road through to its end with keen interest, as if they were reading a picture book. The fact that it was small yet lifelike, and that it showed life as people knew it, such as they had never before seen in a painting, gave it extra novelty. People crowded around, airing their views and eager to point out new discoveries to each other. The hubbub attracted even more people to join the throng. Though there were some who objected that sticking on revolutionary labels had not changed the "olde worlde" character of the village, that opinion was not well received. The Branch Secretary of the Tanjiawan production brigade and delegate to the Ninth Party Congress, Yang Guigui, was taking part in the Joint Assembly. He said the picture was quite first-rate. That more or less settled the matter: no argument, however strong, could prevail against his verdict.

Zhang Zhefeng, commissar for the PLA Jiuquan sub-area, was very pleased. When he referred to the exhibition in his speech to the Joint Assembly, he went out of his way to tell the story from the *Book of Zhuangzi* about a scribe who sat naked and cross-legged while waiting to join a painting competition. Zhuangzi's comment, Zhang said, was that this chap who stripped was the only true painter.

He Shan's painting was very well done, but "The Grand Union of All the Nationalities" paintings were all over the place: You could see them in train and bus stations, and prints were even more widespread. They were all the same, portraying representatives of assorted minority nationalities gathered round one Mao Zedong. The subject seemed trite no matter how it was painted, and no spectators vouchsafed it a second glance. Liu Guangshen said: "The truth is, He Shan is on a losing streak. When fortune runs in your favor, everything goes without a hitch; even bad things can turn into good things. When fortune runs against you, even good things can turn into bad things. At present public opinion is on your side; it's your turn to be lucky."

5.

Not long after the Joint Assembly, Liu Guangshen was appointed head of civil administration for the region, and the granting of permission for my wife's change of domicile fell within his remit. I rejoiced. For a long time I had effaced myself to get into people's good books and had worked like a dog, with the sole object of seeing my family safely reunited. If this hope could be realized, it would have been worth any price.

But my wife was not able to hold out in her exile until this last moment. I had just received permission for her to rejoin me when news came that she was at death's door. Despite my desperate hurry to get to her, I arrived only to see her remains. I left that bleak hamlet on the edge of the desert with only my three-year-old daughter to accompany me.

Soon after the exhibition closed, Zhang Zhefeng, Wu Zhenxiang, and other military representatives withdrew from the local administration and returned to their bases. Taking my daughter with me, I went to the May 7 Cadre School for the Jiuquan area and stayed there until 1978. In 1979, while I was in Beijing, I got a letter from Zhang Zhefeng inviting me to his home in Xi'an to meet some well-known authors, painters, and calligraphers—"all very interesting people." I wasn't able to go because of my work, but I sent him a matching scroll:

> *The sea accepts a hundred rivers, grows big by accepting*
> *The cliff stands a thousand feet, is strong by not desiring.*[4]

Liu Guangshen was still in Jiuquan, still in the same post. When I was at Lanzhou University in 1983, he asked a student of mine, whose home was in Jiuquan, to bring me a jade brush holder, inky-green in color with a cloud pattern, sleek and with classically simple lines. Regrettably, I had no desk of matching quality on which to place it. I lost contact with him after I left the Northwest. My first news of him after that was that he had been lonely after he retired and had taken to drink. The later news was that he passed away without warning, leaving no worldly goods.

At the Dunhuang Research Institute, bitter internal warfare proceeded as before. In time the "Cultural Revolution politicos" were weeded out, and both He Shan and Sun Jiyuan left Dunhuang. Sun went to the conservation center attached to the Maijishan Caves in East Gansu. As for He Shan, he eventually made his way to America and was taken on at the Tianlong Gallery in Los Angeles.[5] In '93, I was in LA, and he visited me with his wife and son. He was in fine fettle. When he asked me how I came to the U.S., I said as a political refugee. He said, "I entered under the Distinguished Personage category."

On
Beauty

❀

On Beauty

A esthetics, or the study of beauty, is the most perplexing branch of philosophy. It can be approached from an ontological, epistemo-logical, or historical-materialistic point of view. If an ontological or epistemological approach is used, we need to ask whether beauty is subjective or objective, but if a historical-materialistic point of view is used, we need only to ask how beauty is determined. However, there can be no completely satisfactory answers. I will formulate my ideas from an epistemological standpoint. These ideas may not be fully formed, but if I do not bring them to light now, I fear they may be put off indefinitely and would never mature on their own. In the spirit of seeking truth, I'm willing to consider all opinions.

1.

I s there such a thing as objective beauty? If by objective we mean a thing in itself entirely independent of subjective human thought and motiva-tion, then the answer must be no.

We understand life as matter in motion and human life as the most complex and developed. Human life, having attained an advanced stage, could not be reduced to mere biological phenomena, such as eating and sleeping. Natural evolution changed into sociohistorical evolution as humankind, in the process of reconstructing the world, created, first spontaneously, unconsciously, and then with resolution and intent, an interior psychological structure as a counterpart to exterior material reality. Psychology on one hand refers to the activity of an individual's inner thoughts and emotions, but on the other hand to the externalization of those thoughts and emotions over time into a shared human realm. Civilization is the creation, unified yet filled with contradictions, of those interior and exterior human realms, and as humankind further evolves, civilization continues to expand and replenish itself.

The psychological realm that emerged from a material foundation is the summation of human thought, including all signs and symbols that make up mental phenomena; this summation should not be understood as a generalization wrapped in a specific and static concept called the mind. The mind, in fact, is not an inert container but the totality of thought, emotion, desire, and will, expressed through activity. This totality, therefore, may best be understood as a class of equations, independent and unified under its own logic, with beauty as one of its solutions expressed through an individual. We cannot define beauty with any accuracy if we discount the vital connection it has with the mind.

Humankind establishes—without necessarily being aware—standards for beauty, and when objective phenomena correspond to these standards, the phenomena are said to be beautiful. Conversely, these standards for beauty correspond to objective phenomena. This is how beauty is ascribed to Nature. These standards are abstract, subjective, a product of human thought and sentiment, while only the correspondence itself is objective and can be studied and empirically tested. An objective phenomenon may possess the qualities that may correspond to a human standard for beauty, but it is an error to suppose an objective phenomenon in itself possesses beauty.

Beauty cannot be created ex nihilio. If either a human being or an objective phenomenon is absent, beauty cannot exist; beauty must be actualized in an objective phenomenon, which needs definitive preexisting qualities in order for beauty to be perceived; however, these qualities in themselves are not beautiful. Indignation rises from injustice, but indignation is not injustice; likewise sympathy rises from misfortune, but sympathy isn't misfortune. Confounding beauty with these preexisting qualities is a common error.

If there is no one to perceive them, these qualities remain qualities, and beauty cannot be predicated of the objective phenomenon that contains them, but the qualities become conditions-for-beauty when they correspond to a human standard.

If a certain quality of an objective phenomenon gives rise to an aesthetic perception, this quality is called a condition-for-beauty. If there is no one to perceive this quality, how can we say this quality by itself gives rise to an aesthetic perception?

These qualities preexist indifferently, objectively, primordially, and only become conditions-for-beauty insofar as they affect a human being. It is precisely because these qualities preexist that they cannot be in themselves conditions for beauty. Matter persists independently of human beings, and only when a certain quality inherent in matter corresponds to a human standard can it be considered a condition-for-beauty.

For example, clay possesses certain prerequisite qualities, such as softness, plasticity etc., that make it material for pottery. However, these prerequisite qualities became conditions for pottery only after human beings found a need for pottery. Likewise, an aesthetic object may possess certain prerequisite qualities that cannot by themselves become conditions-for-beauty. Without a mind, there is no perception of beauty and therefore no beauty.

Beauty in an objective phenomenon and beauty in a mind appear almost simultaneously, meld into each other, expand, enrich each other, and cannot be separated. But beauty ceases when it ceases to be perceived. There is no such thing as beauty without the perception of beauty.

Beauty can only temporarily be predicated of an objective phenomenon, while beauty is being perceived. It may be said that if a farmer doesn't appreciate a play's beauty, the play still is beautiful. But, insofar as the farmer is concerned, the play is not beautiful. There is no right or wrong, only the presence or absence of the perception of beauty and whether there is an active appreciation. This is the only basis for critical judgment.

To an unappreciative ear (by "ear" I mean a cultural organ or capacity to perceive music that has developed historically) there is no distinction between a Beethoven symphony and a chromatic scale. To an appreciative ear the symphony is beautiful. The appreciation of music is a psychological structure, and the history of music is the history of these structures. External objects and phenomena are merely the medium through which these psychological structures are expressed.

A human percipient determines whether a quality present in an objective phenomenon becomes a condition-for-beauty. The quality in itself remains only a potential. The cultural capacity to realize this potential is attained by human activity through a long history. This realization also depends upon certain circumstances, such as the percipient's experience, knowledge, and mental state. But whether the potential is realized or not depends entirely on the human percipient.

2.

If we attribute our subjective perception of beauty to an objective phenomenon, we have made a mistake, which obscures aesthetics just as dust obscures a painting.

Attributing beauty to a morning glory is an expression of our emotion; it does not make beauty an objective property of the morning glory. No botanist can do a chemical analysis on the morning glory to isolate its beauty.

We perceive qualities of light, such as color, as beautiful, but color itself is a function of the absorption and reflection of photons within physical objects. We assign the term "red" to light waves perceived between

670 and 580 nanometers in length. Any other term will not change the wavelength. Wavelength is an objective property of light.

Some consider beauty, like wavelength, to be an objective property of phenomena, but this gives rise to dualism because it implies beauty is separate, absolute, and enduring.

Many living creatures evolved an eye and an ear to detect environmental light and sound. If beauty, like light and sound, were a constituent of the environment, beauty would have objective properties, but no special organ has evolved to detect beauty. If a special organ had evolved, what is beautiful for one person would be beautiful for everyone, and there would be no gradations of beauty; concepts of beauty wouldn't change over time.

Some argue: If the majority regards a phenomenon to be beautiful, wouldn't it be, in this sense, objectively beautiful? The answer still involves the individual: individuals react divergently—but within a range determined by the historical stage of human psychological development in which they live in common. Human psychological structure is a total, organic structure, combining both common and individual components. Therefore, the reaction of the majority cannot be separated from the reaction of the individual.

Nature endows a toad as much as it endows an oriole or a butterfly, yet humans do not consider the toad to be as beautiful as the oriole or butterfly. However, toads are attracted to other toads, and to a rooster, a wheat grain is more precious than a pearl. Likewise, human standards of beauty and value are contingent on being human.

One theory states that beauty resides in the relationship between an individual and an objective phenomenon, but this is ambiguous, since the mind links the individual and the phenomenon.

Certainly, perception has objective and subjective aspects. However, reflective perception by the senses isn't the same as creative perception by the mind. The content of perception by the senses is objective phenomena, while the content of perception by the mind is an expression regarding objective phenomena. If the perception of objective phenomena ceases, the objective phenomena still exist, but if the perception of beauty ceases, beauty vanishes.

The perception of beauty is born through the mind's activity and cannot be permanently transferred to an object. The perception of beauty is profound and complicated, intimately linked with reason and sensibility, which is why it differs from the sensual perceptions of smell and touch.

Everyone feels the sun's light and heat. To the poet the summer sun is a symbol of passion and vitality, but to the dust-covered, sweat-drenched peddler on the road the sun is a searing reality. The sun's light and heat give rise to the perception of both beauty and hardship.

The sun itself is independent of human response: its light and heat are produced by chemical reactions constrained by unalterable and unchanging physical laws to which the poet's passion and the peddler's bitterness cannot add or subtract anything. On the other hand, the poet's and peddler's responses may change with circumstance and time.

The perception of beauty is a human determination, which couldn't occur without subjectivity. Furthermore, this perception of beauty is a determination of value, and there can be no sovereign concepts of value independent of humans. The standards of value are human standards.

Human consciousness, intentionally or not, strives to comprehend reality and transform it into a surrounding presence. When consciousness comprehends reality with human expression, subjectivity is in full play.

Subjectivity strives after the objective, seeks to transform it, and is most itself when it most succeeds. On the one hand, humans comprehend and transform objective phenomena; and on the other, they determine the value of the phenomenon. The concept of beauty is such a value determination.

The basis of beauty is the humanization of Nature, which is an active process of human sentiment. A humanized object becomes a beautiful object.

We gaze at clear, indifferent, voiceless stars moving by their own natural laws and feel they are beautiful because they're pure, reticent, and inaccessible. A hawk circles the sky hunting for prey and we feel it is proud, free: the sky upon its back, it soars a thousand miles. In fact purity, reticence, indifference, haughtiness, freedom, etc. are human concepts and have nothing to do with stars or hawks.

To those far from home, who know the lines from a Tang poem ("A cuckoo calls; I am saddened. I listen; tears fall"), the cuckoo call is humanized with a sad, deep resonance. But to the farmer, ignorant of this poem about the Shu emperor's tragedy, the cuckoo seems to urge *bu gu, bu gu*—sow seed, sow seed! Even today, when I hear the cuckoo during a dry, scorching desert summer, I recall the endless stretches of rice paddies brimming with water around my home and the humid, sweet-smelling breezes of early spring.

In a moonlit evening, listening to the chorus of crickets as if they were just wetted by dew, I recall childhood, and those chirrups seem to be cries, laments, or entreaties. Actually it was the lower evening temperature that brought the crickets to life, while they, sheltered in the shadows of leaves and grass, rubbed their legs together, unaware that they were creating a melancholic mood.

The Tang poet, Bai Juyi, said of the pipa, "A tiny string whispers secrets." A pipa string and a secret are two different things. But a vibrating string produces a tone (a natural, independent, and objective phenomenon), and the tone and the secret are similarly produced (i.e., by a vibrating string and by vibrating vocal cords). So sentiment links the two: the tone is humanized and felt to be beautiful. Similar to "a pipa string whispers" are "the wind howls" and "the Yellow River roars."

All these examples have a subjective basis.

These humanizing psychological processes require both subjective and objective conditions. Subjectivity is tied to the objective physical world through the categories of benevolence and love.

Beauty is forever linked to the human ideals of benevolence and love. We perceive stars, lamps, fireflies, as beautiful because we love light when it adorns the darkness with warmth and tenderness—but not if we discover the light is in the eyes of a wolf. Both cases, in which a faint light glows in the darkness, would be identical, except that feelings of love and hatred create or destroy aesthetic experience.

It would be difficult to think that humans could find anything beautiful for which they felt a strong hatred. We love Nature because we find Nature beautiful; we love a person because we find their appearance or mind beautiful. Conversely, if we love an individual, we find their appearance and/or mind beautiful. These simple examples have a profound inner logic.

Humans are social beings attached through sentiment, not only to Nature but also to society. When the object of an aesthetic experience is a social phenomenon, the aesthetic experience will have an ethical characteristic because social phenomena are necessarily ethical. And so beauty is linked to benevolence, as evil is linked to repugnance.

Anything, as long as it is not contrary to benevolence and love, can be beautiful. Only through their representation in art do evil things from real life gain aesthetic stature. Beautiful things embody a human ideal, and benevolence and love represent the ideals every human seeks. Therefore, if beauty is parted from benevolence and love, beauty loses significance.

Many limit their investigation to objects because they consider beauty objective. Some regard an object beautiful if it typifies a universal. Others suppose an object beautiful if it substantiates the natural laws that activate it. These theories do not bear analysis. For the first, one need only point out that an ugly object can typify a universal. For the second, one need only point out that there cannot be any object that at the same time exists and does not substantiate natural law. Otherwise, this would mean that anything that exists is beautiful. But class oppression and exploitation also exist and substantiate social laws just as wolves and snakes exist and substantiate natural laws.

Confusing standards for drawing have come from such theories, such as "symmetry and balance," "variety and unity," "harmony and distinctness." There's a golden rule: every form proportioned in a 1 to 1.618 ratio is beautiful. But some markings on poisonous snakes are proportioned according to the rule and are harmonious, distinct, symmetrical, balanced, exhibiting variety within unity. Humans, however, do not perceive snakes as beautiful because snakes can kill and are in conflict with benevolence and love.

The Western theory of types regards art as a reflection and imitation of the physical world. In China, a similar theory states that beauty lies in balanced elements. The most frequent example cited is from Song Yu's poem: "A bit more rouge, the complexion's too red; a bit more powder, too white." But why is a wildflower that opens at dawn and closes at dusk bestowed with the same aesthetic value as a majestic, ancient, and snow-appareled mountain? The objective theory of types has no answer.

Since beauty is subjective, aesthetic laws can be sought only within the subjective, within the process of the continuously remodeling and re-concerting human ideas, feelings, and free associations that are grounded in benevolence and love. Beauty unifies truth and benevolence but is more allied to benevolence than truth.

Are those artists who are lost in inspiration, who forget themselves, forget even their lives, who are at the most intense point of their aesthetic experience (not easily attained), also inclined toward benevolence and love? In reality, no one completely forgets themselves. If they did, the apprehension of beauty couldn't exist, because what we really mean by being intoxicated by beauty is that our apprehension of beauty suppresses all other psychological activities. At those times we are in an amazed, wordless admiration, but this wordless praise, this wordless language, is suffused with love.

Praise of this kind has always been human praise, because with it humans attain the greatest ideal—freedom. And the greatest ideal is the greatest good.

3.

The concept of sublimity lies within the concept of beauty.

I bring this up, because some, like Chernyshevsky,[1] have erroneously tried to separate the two.

Sublimity is one of beauty's expressions; take it away from beauty and sublimity is lost. The sun, a thundering rain, a storm-raging sea, a lion, the pyramids, the Himalaya Mountains, a wind-tossed pennant, the sphynx, a tragic play, and righteous anger are all beautiful, just as autumnal stars, an evening rain, and falling leaves are beautiful. The former spur us to passion; the latter waken us to emotion: the former elevate us above the mundane; the latter bring us to our world. But both are measured by the same standard: the former rises above that standard, and the latter barely ascends to meet it. The difference is in quantity, not quality.

Since the concept of the sublime lies within aesthetics, the sublime also embodies benevolence and love.

It's said that legendary demons were more fierce and savage than giants. These demons couldn't be sublime, however, because humans have a dread of demons, and dread casts out the sublime. The terrifying may be overwhelming but cannot impress us as sublime. The sublime is created only if it embodies benevolence and love.

Chernyshevsky's aesthetics is permeated with insight, but his concept of the sublime needs to be reconsidered. We must understand the unity of the sublime and the beautiful if we are to avoid philosophical confusion.

4.

Beauty that isn't felt isn't beauty. Art uses human emotion to bring to light, organize the unrevealed conditions-for-beauty in the world, and vitalize them.

Therefore art doesn't create beauty but energizes the conditions-for-beauty. Beauty isn't produced during the process of artistic labor but when the percipient is moved. Art is not artwork; artwork is the material of art.

Who gazing from a mountain peak at the haze-covered Earth beneath fails to be moved? Some, standing atop Mt. Tai, feel insignificant; some as if they were tigers about to leap miles; others, overwhelmed by grandeur and the totality of life, feel melancholic; some, before the vast Earth, feel negligible; others, moved before their ancient and beautiful land, choke back tears; while some, when water vapors float lazily at the mountain-foot, barley and wheat play in the spring wind, wish to resign their official position and return to a simple life. All these are beautiful. But the fields, roads, forests, ponds, ridges, villages, graveyards, make up a vast and naked surface—on that surface live people, animals, in wetland and woods; and the lives of both the people and the animals are dull, difficult (even cruel), with short, fleeting moments of happiness. Everything is caught in the machinery of natural law; truth is submerged in necessity. There's nothing more. But when a mist suddenly rises and the Earth is imbued with the ash blue of silk cloth, and everything is cloaked with a dim, ambiguous haze, the poet on the mountaintop will be moved. Perhaps inspiration, like a small bird, will startle him. Who knows if that inspiration wasn't alive in the wilderness before it flew into his net?

A work of art may be an assemblage of oil pigments, canvas, and wooden frames or a compilation of words and symbols. These assemblages and compilations can only be animated, made organic, through the creative activity of a sensitive and appreciative percipient. It follows that the beauty created is different for different percipients. A Chinese saying states, "There are no limits to poetry." And there are as many Hamlets as there are readers of Shakespeare. There is an essential difference between a natural phenomenon and a work of art: a natural phenomenon is formed through natural processes, but a work of art is formed through the process of an artist's labor and is the crystallization of the artist's internal constitution. There is, however, a parallel between the creation of inspiration in the artist and the creation of beauty in the percipient. The artist fosters inspiration, uses words, colors, sounds, or clay; forms them into concrete works of art. Art therefore is the embodiment of inspiration, while a work of art is the medium of that embodiment. The content of inspiration is beauty; the principle of benevolence and love is the principle of beauty and also the principle of art.

Art teaches us to love, to look at Nature from beauty's perspective, to look at what binds us to our environment. And so art is the engine of humanism, allowing us effectively to strive after benevolence. It teaches us to actively and bravely create our own lives.

The representations in art are always self-refuting. The Tchichikov in art refutes any real-life Tchichikov; the Tartuffe in art refutes any real-life Tartuffe. These art representations attain aesthetic significance only by this refutation and could not exist in real life. That is why situations and characters in art have a beauty not found in life.

A real-life Rudin can only make speeches, but the fictive Rudin in Turgenev can call men to real action. We admire the book *Rudin* as a call to real action, not as a realistic portrayal of a brilliant orator.[2]

Therefore art is not a pallid reproduction of life but a revelation of passion and inspiration; it creates beautiful things that are absent in real life. We cannot appreciate a real-life Tchichikov, but we can appreciate the created one in art, because the Tchichikov in art refutes any real-life Tchichikov to actualize Gogol's story of benevolence, and thereby to embody the beautiful.

The real-life Tchichikov is objective, while the fictive Tchichikov is made subjective through the poet's refutation of real life. And when, by the artist's labor, this subjectivity is again made objective as a work of art and is perceived, this secondary objectiveness is beautiful. For the poet to externalize his or her inspiration into a perceivable, concrete representation, he or she must undergo an arduous struggle.

If art is the concrete reproduction of inspiration, isn't the work of an artist merely a translation? No. The artist's labor (including conception and nourishment of a central theme) is to assiduously, fully express that which inspired creation. Inspiration isn't formed during the creative process, but comes first, evokes creative desire, and the creative desire in turn evokes new inspiration and passion. The artist doesn't begin with an abstract desire that produces work. However, this simple series doesn't hold in all cases.

The complexity of the relationship between reality and art reflects the complexity between reality and the mind's capacity to transform: to say art is a pale reproduction of reality denies this complexity. Chernyshevsky carried this misapprehension one step further when he said the beauty of life is greater than the beauty of art, thereby putting life and art in opposition. Life and art have different qualities: one cannot be placed higher than the other.

Beauty in art is identical to beauty in life, although realized differently: the psychological process always takes the same distinct form. The perception of beauty originates in experience to which this psychological process is added. No matter if an object is natural or one of art—if it is perceived emotively and with this psychological process, it is beautiful. Beauty that is not perceived with emotion is not true beauty, and beauty, when it is perceived with emotion, is always true. Walking by the river verge at dusk, I am exhilarated by Nature; reading a poem, I am inspired by words. Both experiences are moving, even intoxicating; it's meaningless to judge which is superior.

5.

Philosophy speaks with the language of ideas, art with the language of images. The profundity of a work of art is dependent upon the profundity of its imagery. Benevolence and love are implicit in imagery when imagery is material for beauty.

Only images that embody benevolence and love are images of beauty; when we evaluate the effect of a work of art, we not only determine if the work urges us to strive for benevolence and whether this desire is fully expressed, but we must further determine whether the work urges us to love: love Nature, love humanity—and also whether the work incites us to those passions.

Benevolence and love are the definitive principles of art criticism. Since these principles are derived from the laws of the production of beauty, they are not man-made; since they spring from the human need for progress, they are not arbitrary.

In the past, there was no agreement about this. Thinkers squabbled over the validity of what other thinkers felt, thereby compounding questions with more questions.

Tolstoy said Chekhov's short story "The Darling" had the opposite effect of what Chekhov intended. However, I felt the effect the story had was the same as Chekhov intended. Who is right? We can say with good reasons that Tolstoy allowed his religious beliefs to overcome his human feelings or that Tolstoy was looking through the eyes of the peasantry, and each explanation would be valid. But the only objective fact is that Tolstoy felt the story had an opposite effect than Chekhov intended. There is no right or wrong. We can only be wrong if we try to contradict the fact of Tolstoy's interpretation. We cannot alter empiric, historic facts no matter how much we will it. Feelings that lead to an interpretation are facts in themselves that cannot be denied.

Don Juan and Don Quixote were objects of castigation and satire respectively. But under the pen of some critics, they acquired a more positive significance. These conflicts cannot be resolved if we depart from the principle of benevolence and love.

In fact, Olenka, Don Juan, and Don Quixote are all examples of beauty, because no matter how we interpret them, they move and encourage us. No matter if it's Chekhov, Tolstoy, or Cervantes, no matter if it's myself or another reader, and no matter if Olenka or Don Quixote affects us either directly or indirectly, we are always inspired.

The intelligent reader may ask: If a monk and a revolutionary are ordered forward and the direction isn't clearly delineated, wouldn't they set out in different ways and wouldn't one of them be wrong? Isn't my aesthetic theory a bit like that? No, because there is only one direction that leads to benevolence and love, although the roads are many. Love is life, happiness, truth, and beauty rolled into one. The road to love is for the individual to decide. The forms art takes are rich and diverse; so it is with beauty.

Is this principle of benevolence and love too abstract? No, it is appropriate for the study of beauty and art. Just as a clock, unlike an abacus or a ruler, is derived from the laws of time, the principle of benevolence and love is derived from the laws of beauty.

Art reflects inner human complexity, richness, and versatility, and simplifies, incorporates, and regulates them. Otherwise we wouldn't be able to comprehend art's full implication, but would distort and debase art. Although the true and gifted artist cannot be corrupted by distortion and debasement, just as an abacus or a ruler cannot be affected by time, these depravations are damaging to human cultural development.

6.

Poetry is preeminent in aesthetics. Both beauty and poetry are created through sentiment; however, poetry is more profound, more intricate and comprehensive, than beauty: poetry is beauty intensified.

Poetry, like beauty, has no fixed material form. Just as knowledge exists in the mind by means of concepts, poetry exists in sentiment by means of forms. Poetry is a very subtle psychological phenomenon, founded on sentiment. Inasmuch as the philosophic incorporates sentiment, it is tied to the poetic and is expressed through a poetic work.

However, many thinkers identify poetry with poetic genre, and occasionally even with one specific poetic genre. When they encounter the word "poetry," these thinkers gradually conflate a genre and poetry into one concept, thereby blurring understanding. Philosophic poetry emerged in literary history, and many poets employed it to express manifold and resplendent ideas: the immortal pieces of Tagore are just one example. The majority of so-called philosophical poems, however, weren't produced through sentiment but were merely ideas in poetic wrappings, and even though poetry is a more rational concept than beauty, poetry is still fundamentally different from dressed-up ideas. If ideas in themselves can be termed poetry and art, we must revise what we mean by both poetry and art.

The relationship of poetry to its external form is the same as human thought to the mind. But those poems that aren't created through sentiment, even though they employ normative poetic expressions, aren't genuine poems, just as wax mannequins aren't living people. If one is engaged solely with the question of form, neglecting sentiment, the essence of poetry cannot be revealed. Formalism of this sort was so prominent in our country at one time that beauty in a poem was equated solely with the poem's architecture. This theory is unacceptable even on the technical level.

When the perception of beauty developed into its highest phase, it became poetry. Beauty is the foundation of poetry, and like beauty, poetry always embodies the benevolent and the good. If it does not, it ceases to be poetry.

Gogol's story "The Story of How Ivan Ivanovich Quarreled with Ivan Nikiforovich" has a gray surface, but from within that grayness, vibrant, living desires leap forth, which grant this short piece density, vividness, and verisimilitude.

The simplest language is the most beautiful because it is closer to the true and the benevolent and therefore closer to poetry. True sentiment isn't necessarily poetic sentiment, but poetic sentiment is always true sentiment. Lyric poetry's most precious asset is its sincerity, without which nothing could be achieved. This is why ballads are so valuable. If the diction and structure aren't indispensable to the thought and emotions conveyed, they are irrelevant. It isn't essential to evaluate the elaborateness of diction, cadence of prosody and tone, or the craftsmanship of parallelism; one must above all determine how much poetry a work contains.

This treatise is finished. The theory, especially as it concerns poetry, seems abstract, but when dealing with a subject that is abstract in its nature, abstractions must be used; otherwise the conclusions would be impeded. Whether this theory is correct or not, time will judge.

Foreword

1. The War of Resistance was from 1937 to 1945.

FRAGMENTS IN THE SAND

Chapter 2: Wild Goose Tracks in Mud and Snow

1. From a poem by the Song dynasty poet Su Dongbo (1037–1101). The title suggests human transience.
2. A li is about one third of a mile.
3. The Foreign Affairs Movement was a modernization movement during the Qing Dynasty in the late nineteenth century.
4. The German philosopher and essayist Ludwig Feuerbach (1804–1872). He wrote *On Philosophy and Christianity,* among other books, and was an important influence on Marx. Many people trying to gain favor would claim to be convinced by Feuerbach; therefore Gao's remark is ironic.
5. The Party branch secretary was responsible for answering all ideological questions.

Chapter 3: The Failure of "On Beauty"

1. This is an ironic reference is to Adam Smith. The "invisible hand" here belongs to the regime.
2. Romain Rolland (1866–1944), French novelist and essayist, wrote biographies of Beethoven, Gandhi, Michelangelo, and Tolstoy.

3. The name Ping Ming, or "Coming Dawn," could not be accepted by the Communists because for them, the dawn had already arrived.

4. The Theory of Reflection holds that mental states are reflections of physical states.

5. Literally translated, the name means "a man in coarse clothing," that is, a humble man.

6. A Czech physicist and philosopher, Ernst Mach (1838–1916) held that physical laws were predetermined by mental structures. Lenin argued against this theory.

7. 8,000 characters: 4,000 to 5,000 English words

8. In 1956 Mao initiated a new policy called "The Double Hundred Policy." The slogan for literature was "Let a hundred flowers bloom" while for science it was "Let a hundred schools contend." Intellectuals were exhorted to speak out, but when the response exceeded what the Party would tolerate, Mao initiated a counter movement called "The Anti-Rightist Struggle," with the slogan "Entice the snakes from their holes." The Cultural Revolution was not far behind.

9. At the age of nineteen, Gao received the attention of the nation's preeminent theorists.

10. "Long" is another name for Gansu.

11. Hu Feng was a dissident of the generation before Gao.

Chapter 4: Gongs and Drums in a Movie

1. These are set phrases used in political condemnations.

2. The directives are decided on the highest level. They are given in printed form to high officials and in turn "passed down" verbally at meetings to the less powerful. Xiao wants to emphasize the importance of the directive, but Gao cannot leave with the printed version.

3. A sedan was used for important people or matters.

4. Lei Xuhua replaced Xiao Ying after Xiao was removed during another crackdown.

5. "Mister" is an address of respect but also of exclusion. If Gao was a Party member, he would have been called "comrade."

6. This was under Deng Xiaoping. "Reverse verdict," the literal translation of *ping fan,* meant his "rightist hat" had been removed.

7. Gao quotes from the Tang poet Liu Yuxi (722–842).

Chapter 6: The Gate of Hell

1. Nicolai Chernyshevsky, born in 1828, was a Russian intellectual. He advocated for populism and wrote *What Is to be Done?* He was exiled to Siberia in 1872, and died there in 1883 at the age of sixty-one. He influenced Lenin and many other revolutionaries.

Chapter 10: An Zhaojun

1. From the Song Dynasty poet Zhu Dunru (1081–?).

Chapter 11: By Pale Moonlight

1. Kalidasa was a fourth-century Indian epic poet and dramatist; Rabindranath Tagore (1861–1941), Indian poet and philosopher, won Nobel Prize for Literature in 1913.
2. The antibiotics were probably an effective treatment in this case because the raw wheat was likely contaminated by fecal material.

Chapter 13: Deaths of Soldiers

1. Zhuangzi, also known as Chuang Tsu, was an influential Chinese philosopher of the fourth century BCE. His name is also spelled Chuang Tzu, Zhuang Tze, Chouang-Dsi, or Chuang Tse. He is generally thought to be a Daoist, but there's some debate. He's best known for the book titled *Zhuangzi*.

Chapter 17: Toward Life

1. In 1957 Mao decided the time was right to fully implement Communism. Money was abolished. The entire country set up local village furnaces to refine steel, in which peasants threw woks, hoes, etc. However, the steel produced was unusable. The years 1959–1962 mark the time of the "three-year natural disaster," which was actually man-made, when tens of millions starved. This chapter starts at the crucial time of 1962, when free markets were beginning to be reestablished.
2. A jin is about 1 1/3 pounds.

Chapter 20: Quiet at the Sanqing Temple

1. Mao Dun (1896–1981) was a novelist.
2. *Lao Da* could be translated as "the eminent one."
3. The Cangjing Cave contained the Buddhist scriptures; Zhang Daqian (1899–1983) was a famous painter and art critic; Zheng Banqiao (1693–1765) was a Qing Dynasty painter. He was one of the Eight Eccentrics of Yangzhou.
4. Yu Youran (1878–1964) was an artist and calligrapher. He opposed Mao. Gao makes the point that the best writers have been erased by the regime.
5. Guo Moruo (1892–1978) was a prominent poet and essayist. He was supported by Mao.
6. The *biao hua* is the important artisan who binds the paintings into scrolls and thereby ensures their preservation.
7. Mizong is a sect of Buddhism. It is considered by outsiders to emphasize the grotesque.
8. The wooden eaves over the caves held dangling iron horses. Their function may have been aesthetic or merely to frighten birds away from the eaves.
9. This phenomenon gives the name *Mingsha*, or "Singing Sand," to the mountain.

Chapter 21: How Many Flowers Have Fallen

1. A line from the Tang poet Meng Haoran. The image is one of lament for a loss that can't be changed or rectified, as if for fallen flowers. Also, no one can determine how much was lost.
2. These are the names of archaeologists who brought Dunhuang art back to their native countries: England, France, and the United States respectively.
3. In this sect of Buddhism, the depictions of Hell have been described as stark and strange.
4. Gao would have had no knowledge of Akhmatova, Tsvetaeva, or Mandelstam.
5. "Tone" is used in the same sense as a musical tone. It is a Daoist concept and can mean the "essential quality."
6. Gao argues that there is a natural decline in art and compares the decline in Dunhuang art to that in Central China. Dunhuang art, Gao argues, has declined at the same rate as that in Central China, even though it is isolated and its economics have declined at a faster rate. This is comparable to the

Western idea of the Golden Age, which in the case of China is the High Tang. Whatever readers think of this, they should bear in mind that the Communists considered their culture to be the pinnacle and therefore this whole essay could be interpreted as subversive. The Jian'an is the last period of the Han. Its "air and bone" style was heroic, lofty, and harsh. The idea of "purity and the void," or more literally "cleanse and empty out," was to extirpate the clutter of tradition. It is a Song idea, and the art associated with it is considered to be blander and less vigorous. Cheng and Zhu were Neo-Confucian scholars of the Song period.

7. Ma Bufang was a warlord of the period prior to the establishment of the People's Republic.

8. The title Research Academy has more prestige than Institute.

Chapter 22: Initiation

1. Daqing was an oilfield in northeastern China that was promoted as the model for industry on account of its rapid development; Dazhai was a mountain village in Shanxi province that was promoted as the model for agriculture on account of the huge increases in crop yield brought about by collectivity.

2. Lei Feng was a common PLA soldier who died in 1962 at the age of twenty-two while in charge of a transport group. In 1963 Mao Zedong chose Lei Feng to be a symbol of self-sacrifice for the common good. "Emulate Lei Feng" movements were launched repeatedly. The Lei Feng myth persists in today's China.

3. *World Reports* is a paper published by the Xinhau News Agency; it specializes in reports from outside China, incuding Taiwan and Hong Kong. The paper received a boost when Mao praised it in 1957.

4. Gong Zizhen (1792–1841) was a progressive poet and thinker, an advocate of social and political reform. Very highly regarded in modern China, hence safely quotable.

Chapter 23: Red and Black

1. Deng Tuo (1912–1966), a historian and essayist, was at one time editor of *The People's Daily*. His newspaper columns in the early 1960s largely ignored dogma and expressed independent views, for which he was eventually hounded to death.

Chapter 24: Andante Cantabile

1. Lu Xun (1881–1936) was the most famous Chinese writer of the twentieth century. Highly praised by Mao Zedong, his works were regarded as holy writ in Communist China.
2. Eighty-three yuan was a respectable amount at the time, enough for Gao to live on with some left over to send to his mother.
3. The Four Cleanups were to purify politics, the economy, ideology, and organization. Originally a socialist education program for rural areas in the early '60s, the Four Cleanups developed into a political purge.

Chapter 25: Alien Tears

1. Liu Shaoqi was a Chinese Communist leader and president of the People's Republic of China from 1959 to 1968. He came to oppose some of Mao's policies during the famine of 1960. During the Cultural Revolution, he was denounced as a "capitalist roader" and expelled from the Communist Party. Deng Xiaoping was head of the Communist Party, but like Liu came to oppose some of Mao's policies, and thus during the Cultural Revolution was forced to resign all of his posts.
2. He Shizhe had been head of the entire Institute. He was stripped of his post and, with many others, sent to the country for reform through labor. About a year later, he was then returned to the Institute and to his post. Thus he "came back" to both the Institute and his position.

Chapter 26: Curious Tales from the Cowshed

1. The terms "cow demon" and "snake spirit" were used during the Cultural Revolution to refer particularly to deviant intellectuals.
2. "Hat" was the common expression for a label as an anti-Communist element of some kind.
3. "Black line" designated the literature that continued the relatively free values and practices of pre-Liberation literature, as opposed to red-hot Communist ideology.
4. "Link up" originally referred to Red Guards traveling free to Beijing from all over China to meet Chairman Mao and exchange revolutionary experiences. The term later expanded to include cadres traveling at public expense to various centers for the same purpose of exchanging experiences.
5. Saduona is an incarnation of the Buddha.

Chapter 27: Facing Walls

1. "Long life," or *wan sui*, was frequently chanted to the "Great Man," Mao.
2. The quoted lines are by the poet Zhu Yizun (1629–1709).
3. *Worldly Stories Retold* is an ancient text about the history of the Three Dynasties Period (220–260 CE). *Famous Paintings of Different Dynasties* is a seminal text on painting written in 847 CE by Zhang Yanyuan.
4. The *Chu* Songs were written by Qu Yuan (340–278 BCE) during the Warring States Period.
5. These two periods demarcate the High Tang.

Chapter 28: Sunset on Barren Mountain

1. So called because the name of the school derives from the directive that Mao Zedong issued on May 7, 1966. The directive led to the setting up of rural camps where intellectuals did manual work, political study, and learned from peasants.

Chapter 29: Dou Zhanbiao

1. "Old" is a term of respect, not of age.
2. Lohans are mythical beings frequently depicted in Buddhist sculpture and paintings. Because of their supernatural powers, they serve as temple guardians.
3. Xiaoyu is Gao's present wife, Maya.

Chapter 30: Companion

1. *Shifu* means "master," in the sense of a master craftsman.

Chapter 31: Chang Shuhong

1. This means he cannot be employed. There is no private sector.
2. Public Security is an enforcement agency; its agents are responsible for the arrest of dissidents as well as other police duties. Gao's problem is with the Ministry of Culture, which implies that he has transgressed on cultural affairs. Here, Xu is at the national level, while the two in Public Security are on the provincial level.

3. Chang is removed from the human world and is identified with the animal world. He will soon be placed below the animal world.

4. The quote is from Li Gang (1083–1140), a poet and patriot who helped prevent a northern invasion of barbarian tribes.

5. Xiangtan is the hometown of Liu Shaoqi, who was the leader of the People's Republic when Mao was Party chairman; therefore he was a direct rival of Mao. The rest of the title is a parody of Maoist organizational names. Chernyshevsky was the radical Russian essayist imprisoned by the Tsar.

6. As the months of the prediction build up, December upon December, they never break through into a new year and renewal. Both Gao and time are prisoners.

7. Chang was placed below the animal world as a servant to a pig. This final identification with the passive and objective mineral world marks his final degradation before his resurrection as a showpiece and parody of what he formerly had been.

8. When Han Xin was poor and traveled in beggar's clothes, a peasant woman kneeled before him and served him a simple meal. After he became a famous general, he returned the favor. The joke is that Chang was forced to kneel before a pig.

9. This is the year the prediction was to come true.

10. Gao was in Jiuquan at a May 7 Cadre School from 1972 to 1978. Han Suyin was a novelist whose mother was Belgian and whose father was Chinese.

11. The Northwest is an important economic region and has a large army associated with it. This is a very powerful person.

12. This is a classical reference. Once a courtier enters a court in service of a nobleman, there's no end to politics; so, by extension, the regime may seem quiet to the outside observer, but inside, it's seething with power struggles. As is characteristic of Gao's style, we know Wu by his use of language and not by description. He is literate but pedantic as befits a propaganda minister. Gao's extended Polonius-like pun depends upon the word *dao*, which can mean "road," "way," "manner of resoning," etc.

13. This is an allusion to a line by Confucius: If a parent is close to a child, the child acts inappropriately; if the parent is distant, the child complains.

Chapter 32: Jiuquan Revisited (Extracts)

1. At this time air-raid shelters were being dug in northern and northwestern China in the event of war with the Soviet Union.
2. The "man" here is Gao. Liu is quoting Wang Ren.
3. "Link up" originally referred to Red Guards traveling free to Beijing from all over China to meet Chairman Mao and exchange revolutionary experiences; later expanded to include cadres traveling at public expense to various centers for the same purpose of exchanging experiences.
4. Such presentational scrolls are assumed to be the work of the donor, in this case Gao, unless otherwise indicated.
5. *Tianlong* translates as "Heavenly Dragon."

ON BEAUTY

1. Nikolay Gavrilovich Chernyshevsky (July 12, 1828–October 17, 1889) was a Russian revolutionary democrat, materialist philosopher, critic, and socialist (seen by some as a utopian socialist). He was the leader of the revolutionary democratic movement of the 1860s, and was an influence on Vladimir Lenin and Emma Goldman.
2. Tchichikov is the anti-hero of *Dead Souls* by Gogol (1809–1852). *Tartuffe* is the comedy written by Moliere (1622–1673). *Rudin* is the novel witten by Turgenev (1818–1883).